ALICE COOPER, GOLF MONSTER

ALICE COOPER, GOLF MONSTER

A ROCK 'N' ROLLER'S 12 STEPS TO BECOMING A GOLF ADDICT

ALICE COOPER

WITH KEITH AND KENT ZIMMERMAN

CROWN PUBLISHERS · NEW YORK

Library of Congress Cataloging-in-Publication Data

Cooper, Alice
Alice Cooper, golf monster : a rock 'n' roller's 12 steps to becoming a golf
addict / Alice Cooper.—1st ed.
p.   cm.
1. Cooper, Alice, 1948–   2. Rock musicians–United States–Biography.
3. Alice Cooper (Musical group)   I. Title.
ML420.C67A3 2007
782.42166092–dc22
[B]   2007004677

ISBN 978-0-307-38265-8

Printed in the United States of America

Design by Lenny Henderson

10 9 8 7 6 5 4 3 2 1

First Edition

My liver would like to dedicate this book to me
for giving up drinking and taking up golf.

Contents

Introduction
Alice Cooper Plays Pine Valley:
Welcome to MY Nightmare • 1

Chapter 1
The Fabulous Furniers • 9

Chapter 2
Black Slacks and a Tight Windsor Knot • 17

THE FIRST STEP OF GOLF ADDICTION

Be a Good Imitator • 23

Chapter 3
James Bond, the Beatles, and Cortez High • 29

Chapter 4
Earwigs and Spiders • 33

Chapter 5
L.A. Dreams and the Draft • 39

THE SECOND STEP OF GOLF ADDICTION

It Don't Mean a Thing if You Ain't Got That Swing or
On Being an Amateur vs. Becoming a Pro • 45

Chapter 6

The Birth of Alice • 53

Chapter 7

Frank Zappa, Syd Barrett, and the GTOs • 57

Chapter 8

Managers and Record Deals • 63

THE THIRD STEP OF GOLF ADDICTION

Play for the Right Reasons • 69

Chapter 9

Motor City Migration • 75

Chapter 10

"Eighteen," the Chicken, and the Snake • 79

THE FOURTH STEP OF GOLF ADDICTION

Let the Adrenaline Flow • 87

Chapter 11

School's Out Forever • 93

Chapter 12

Alice as Macumba! • 99

THE FIFTH STEP OF GOLF ADDICTION

Play on the Road! Play All Over the World! • 105

Chapter 13

The New Millionaires • 111

Chapter 14

Sold-Out Arenas • 115

Chapter 15
Welcome to My Nightmare • 119

THE SIXTH STEP OF GOLF ADDICTION
Confront Your Demons and Defeat Them • 127

Chapter 16
The Lair of the Vampires • 131

Chapter 17
Rocky, the King, Clouseau, the Dalí, and Groucho • 139

THE SEVENTH STEP OF GOLF ADDICTION
Play with Those Who Inspire You • 151

Chapter 18
Hanging with the Legends in Hollywood • 161

Chapter 19
From the Inside • 171

Chapter 20
More Fog! More Blood! • 181

THE EIGHTH STEP OF GOLF ADDICTION
Replace the Bad Addiction with the Good Addiction • 187

Chapter 21
I Am Not Worthy • 193

THE NINTH STEP OF GOLF ADDICTION
Construct a Spiritual Support System
That Works for You • 201

Chapter 22
The Importance of Being Alice • 205

THE TENTH STEP OF GOLF ADDICTION
Learn How to Play Through • 211

Chapter 23
Ely and Alice • 217

THE ELEVENTH STEP OF GOLF ADDICTION
Pay Attention to Innovation and Technology • 225

Chapter 24
Prodigal Son • 231

Chapter 25
Snakes, Stars, and Swords • 235

THE TWELFTH STEP OF GOLF ADDICTION
Keep on Rockin'! • 239

Appendix
*Alice's Golf Clinic: 15 Tips for
Achieving Your Best Game* • 247

Acknowledgments • 253

Index • 254

ALICE COOPER, GOLF MONSTER

A hole-in-one or headed for the rough?
Alice in 1974 before he developed his straight, sweet swing.

Introduction

Alice Cooper Plays Pine Valley

Welcome to MY Nightmare

ONE DAY I GOT A CALL from Ely Callaway, the famous golf-equipment maker. "Alice," he said, "do you want to play Pine Valley?"

Now, the Top 100 golf courses in the world are rated by experts, organizations, and hopeless golf addicts . . . and at the top of my list is Pine Valley in New Jersey. It's an impossible course to get onto, especially if you're an outsider. Some say it's the number-one course in the world. You have to be born onto that course to get in—or be blue-blood royalty, a Fortune 500 CEO, or the great-grandson of a member of the club. A rock 'n' roller? No way. I would never make the cut.

So this was as if Ely had called and asked if I wanted to go to paradise for a day. *Pine Valley?* Sure thing! Ha! Alice Cooper plays Pine Valley. Who would have thought?

On the day of my tee time, I got into a limousine for the two-hour trek from New York City to the hallowed grounds of Pine Valley. Sitting in the back of the limo, I thought about recently running into Lou Reed, whom I remember from our days at the Chelsea Hotel in New York in 1972. Back then, the hallways were filled with dope addicts, druggies, transvestites, and boozers. People passed out in the hallways, too high to put the keys in their doors. Thirty-five years later, Lou is asking me how he should adapt his swing to gain greater distance and accuracy. I gave him advice on where to place his hands on the club. Who would have imagined the two of us, three decades removed from that drug-filled, hazy lifestyle, discussing golf swings?

1

I wondered, *Is Lou like me? Is he a golf junkie now, too, outrageously addicted to this alluring sport?*

It actually took me three hours to get to Pine Valley, because the driver got hopelessly lost. The course, it turns out, is almost impossible to find if you've never been there. It's situated rather anonymously in the middle of a wooded neighborhood. Suddenly, it appears. When I arrived, I jumped out of the backseat and walked into the clubhouse.

I was playing the greatest golf course in the world!

I didn't quite know how everything would work, especially since I didn't have anyone to play with, but I shortly found out that everything was already in motion. When you arrive for the first time, the tradition is that rookies first sit and have coffee with a member. No other course I'd ever played had that rule. It sounded a little strange, but I had come this far. What did I have to lose? So I was introduced to a couple of guys, and we all sat down and looked at one another.

All right, I get it now. Alice Cooper, the crazy rock star, sits down with a couple of members to give them a chance to look me over and say, "No, thanks, we don't want to play with this guy." Had I come in drunk or loud or stupid, this was their opportunity to give me the shaft and show me the door. I had passed the first hurdle; next it was time to prove myself on the green.

After the coffee test, it was decided I would play with the caddy master and two other fellows who served as his assistants. The caddy master was from Scotland and spoke in a thick brogue. He looked about sixty-five years old; he had been there for forty years and knew every blade of grass on the course. He immediately asked,

"Eh, laddie, what's your handicap?"

"Seven." Actually, I was closer to a five.

"Well, the running bet around here is $20 that you can't break 85 on this course."

"Okay." I nodded.

I pulled out a twenty-dollar bill. I wanted to be in on this one; it was money well spent. Of course, at that point, I didn't care what I shot. I was on Pine Valley! Some of the greatest golfers in the world have shot 82, 83, or 85 at Pine Valley.

So we got to the first hole. The first thing that an amateur does (and I am an amateur) is look at a golf hole and take his driver out. But the caddy master stopped me: "Sonny, use a five-wood here. You only want to hit it 220 yards. Any further than that, it's going to go downhill into a spot where you can't hit out of."

Okay: a five-wood. I used it, and the ball went exactly where it needed to be. Dead straight. Right down the middle.

"Well done, laddie! Now that you've got 170 yards in, hit the wee six-iron."

I hit it with that six-iron: dead on the green. From that point on, everything the caddy master told me to do, I did. I hardly missed a fairway or a green all day—I made two minor mistakes, and those were the only blemishes on that round all day.

I was in the zone.

It was a beautiful day. The course looked like it might have been the course in the Garden of Eden. If God designed a golf course for himself, this would be it. The greens were perfect. It was like putting on velvet. The sand traps didn't seem man-made (even though they were—it was natural sand with no rakes), which made the course especially unique. At every hole, the caddy master recited a poem. Then he'd give me a round of seasoned, sound advice.

After our eighteen holes, the caddy master marched me into the pro shop, where all the members were assembled. "Attention! Attention! I just played with this young rock fellow here. He shot 73! Never before has an amateur come here and shot a 73."

The pro shop members broke into applause. I had made my mark at Pine Valley. The members knew that their caddy master wasn't giving me putts. He was too hard-core, way too Scottish, and he played by the rules. He did give me some interesting tips on how to make my way around the course, but the members knew that if I shot 73 with him, it was an honest-to-God 73. As the caddy master patted me on the back, he whispered to me, "Seventy-three at Pine Valley, laddie. That's something you must always be proud of."

I never played Pine Valley again. I've had to battle with myself to stay away, but that was a perfect day. The next time, I might overthink my game and shoot a 93 or something. Had I shot for four days there, I might have averaged about 85. But on that day, I avoided the Golf Monster.

I shot one over par at Pine Valley.

So I am obviously a golf addict. I am the first to admit it. But it didn't used to be that way . . . my addictions used to be much more destructive, and the road to redemption was a long, painful one.

Even though golf and rock 'n' roll are two very different animals, both remain very strong forces in my life. If rock 'n' rock *made* my life, then golf *saved* my life. Included in this tale of my life in rock are the twelve golf steps I created that enabled me to trade in those harmful addictions for healthier ones.

♀   ♀   ♀

October 1977, on the Nightmare tour. After five months of grueling rehearsals that began in the spring of 1975, I had spent two solid years on the road and in the studio making records without much of a break. We played more than 200 sold-out dates all over the world before I finally took some time off. Then, after a short break, Shep Gordon, my manager, set up more dates to resume the tour. But I couldn't go through with it. I was worn out; there was no way I was ready to go back out on the road again.

But being the obedient rock star I am, I reluctantly said yes. Okay, let's do it. Let's go out there again. So I went back out on the road. I was working so hard, doing shows every night. And I was my usual jovial self, always willing to do anything for the cause—you could call me up in the middle of the night and say, "Alice, you've got an interview in five minutes," and I'd do it. Then, all of a sudden, I couldn't do it anymore. I was drinking nonstop. I was shaking. I was depressed. I was throwing up blood every morning in my hotel room.

I knew I was dying, but with another leg of the tour already booked, I was caught. I couldn't give up alcohol. I was so exhausted that my whiskey and Coca-Cola was the only thing that made me *feel* and got me through each day. I don't know how I got through the last of the tour, being a trapped alcoholic with so many musicians, roadies, dancers, and crew depending on me. But somehow I made it through, even in the fog of depression and drink. Alice did it. Alice came through. There was never a time when I gave up.

When I was a long-distance runner in high school, I *never* stopped in the middle of a four-mile run. No matter how winded and achy I felt, I always finished the race. But this time I had pushed myself way too far to get to the end. I crawled inside the bottle and refused to come out.

That's when my manager, Shep, and my wife, Sheryl, grabbed me and sat me down. Today, they call it an intervention. Back then, they were just trying to save my life.

"Alice, you need to be in a hospital."

I didn't know how to react. I was still too full of pride to admit I had a problem, but at the same time I was kind of hoping somebody, anybody, would just knock me over the head and I'd wake up in a hospital—that way I wouldn't have to actually give myself up. I just couldn't do that.

"I'm not going."

"Alice, the limousine will be here at six o'clock."

"I hope you guys have a good time, because I'm not gonna go."

By six o'clock, I was sitting between Shep and Sheryl in the back of the limousine, drinking as much as I could. We were on our way to a sanitarium in Westchester, near Cornell University, a place that Shep had found. He had a house nearby so he wouldn't be that far away. Everything had been arranged. They checked me in. I had a hard time signing my name, because my hand was shaking so badly I could barely hold the pen. It was embarrassing. But I managed to sign.

Then I looked around. Sheryl and Shep were gone.

"That's it. I'm leaving," I announced.

"No, sir, you're not," the admitting nurse calmly informed me.

"I can leave anytime I want."

"Not exactly. You've signed this paper, which means that for seventy-two hours, we have you."

"You mean I can't walk out of here right now?"

"The law states that according to the paper you just signed, you might be a danger to yourself. You're now officially under observation for seventy-two hours."

I was trapped in this place for three days! Oh God. No alcohol. No VO and Coke. Not even a can of beer. I panicked. I tried to call Sheryl, but she wasn't answering. She and Shep were under strict orders not to talk to me.

I had been conned, and I was boiling mad. I considered trying to escape, but I had no money. Not a nickel. But surely somebody on the outside would buy Alice Cooper a drink!

I stayed. When I woke up the next morning, my first impulse was to grab the whiskey bottle, and it was a terrible shock to remember that I couldn't. For seventy-two hours, I was steamed and shaky. It was as if my nerve endings had been placed on the outside of my body. I felt brittle and exposed, like every fiber of my being was made of glass. If anybody so much as clanked a plate or a dish, I wanted to jump out of my skin.

Once again, sitting in the sanitarium, Alice Cooper was ahead of his time. This was pre–Betty Ford Clinic, and the concept of the celebrity designer rehab center was still years away. This wasn't your standard country club rehab retreat. From the looks of the patients muttering to themselves all around me, I was trapped in an insane asylum surrounded by nutcases. This was the booby hatch! The straitjacket was for real.

I'm fragile. I'm weak. I'm lonely. I'm ready to crack into little pieces. Am I slowly going insane?

Welcome to MY nightmare.

Alice chasing demons on stage during the Madhouse Rock tour in 1979.
(Ken Ballard)

Vincent Damon Furnier at age six.

Chapter 1

The Fabulous Furniers

I WAS BORN VINCENT DAMON FURNIER, named after one of my uncles and Damon Runyon. From the age of ten, I grew up in a religious home; my grandfather was an evangelist and my parents joined his church too. Before then, though, we lived in East Detroit and worshiped baseball. I was the happiest kid in the world.

The Furniers were Huguenots, part French-Canadian people who came over to the New World with the French Protestants in the seventeenth century. They eventually married into some Sioux Indians and a lot of Irish. As a result, two out of three parts of my ethnic background are very alcohol prone. My seventh cousin was the Marquis de Lafayette, the same Lafayette who secured the support of the French during the American Revolution and fought alongside George Washington at Valley Forge. Look at a portrait of Lafayette and you'll notice the same high cheekbones and long black hair as me. Some say I look just like him, especially when I'm on stage with my sword. I can feel my bloodlines, since swashbuckling comes naturally to me—that's the French part of me, I guess.

My grandfather, Thurman Sylvester Furnier, was the president of what was called the Church of Jesus Christ. It wasn't the Church of Latter-day Saints—it wasn't a Mormon church. In fact, their biggest religious rivals were the Mormons. If you called one of his church members a Mormon, that was like stabbing them in the heart.

My mother was born Ella McCartt in Glenmary, Tennessee. You can't find Glenmary on a map. It was a whistle-stop. Her mother died when she was very young. She has childhood memories of putting clear liquid into Ball jars for her dad, who was a moonshiner in Glenmary. She had six brothers and sisters, and all of them helped out with the "family business"—and meanwhile the old man kept about forty or fifty thousand dollars in cash buried in the yard. This was in 1946, and at that time, fifty grand was equivalent to about half a million dollars. My grandfather didn't trust banks.

At age sixteen, around the end of World War II, my mother ran away from home and found her way up to Detroit to work in the factories. That's where she met my dad, whom people called Mick, though his real name was Ether Maroni Furnier (another Mormon-sounding name). He had just been discharged from the Navy. They were soon married.

♀   ♀   ♀

I was born in Detroit on February 4, 1948. My first memory of growing up in working-class East Detroit is sitting in a smoke-filled living room with my dad and his brothers, watching Friday-night boxing. There was lots of Carling's Black Label beer and Lucky Strike cigarettes; I would drink Vernor's ginger ale. There was always so much smoke in the room, I'm surprised I didn't contract lung cancer. All the girls stayed in the other room while I sat with the men, my uncles and their buddies, watching the fights on a tiny black-and-white TV set.

Growing up in Detroit was great. I loved my life because my dad and my uncles were so cool. I was the only boy in our family. There was me (Vince) and my sister Nickie, then thirteen cousins, mostly girls. I was the only male left to carry on the Furnier name. So, of course, I ended up legally changing my name to Alice Cooper.

My uncles were Damon Runyon–type characters—tough guys with colorful speech and fascinating stories. Uncle Jocko ran a crooked pool hall in East Detroit. He was my dad's oldest brother, a spry lightweight prizefighter with a broken nose and not an ounce of fat on him. We all called him Jocko, but his real name was Vincent Collier Furnier. I was named after him. If you wanted to buy anything hot, you went to Jocko's pool hall. Or if Fast Eddie Felson came in to play Minnesota Fats, that happened at Jocko's too. It was a famous Detroit dump. During a hot game, the doors would close and lock for hours, sometimes days. My uncle would bring in food and drinks and host the game in exchange for a small cut of the winnings.

Jocko was a swell guy. He used to come over and poke me in the ribs, saying, "Watch that right hook!"

My uncle Lefty, whose real name was Lonson Thurman Furnier, was a whole different deal. He was what you would refer to as a playboy. I never saw Uncle Lefty without a tuxedo, his shirt half-buttoned. He had left Detroit and moved west to Los Angeles, and he worked for Jet Propulsion Labs there. He was the guy who wined and dined the company's biggest accounts, which is why he was always dressed to the nines. He was part James Bond, part wheeler-dealer—a total Rat Pack–type guy. He would have fit in well with Sinatra and Martin. In fact, he actually hung out with Lana Turner and Ava Gardner, some of the same girls the Rat Pack dated (without my aunt knowing about it, of course).

♀ ♀ ♀

The great industrial car town of Detroit has always been your classic sports city. The Red Wings were unbeatable. The Pistons were great. Even the Detroit Lions were a really good team at one time. But the Tigers were a religion in our household. They had Ty Cobb, the greatest player of all time, on their team, plus Al Kaline, Mickey Cochrane, Hank Greenberg, and Denny McLain. These were legendary players playing on mythical teams. It was all my dad and I talked about: "What did the Tigers do last night?" I was transfixed with Ernie Harwell's colorful play-by-play commentary on the radio.

I lived for baseball. When the sun came up, I grabbed my glove and I was ready to play until the sun went down, when you couldn't see the ball anymore and it was time to rush home for dinner.

East Detroit was a real American melting pot. Each street had their crew—not so much gangs, but characters who banded together as teams. One street over might be all-Italian, while the street after that could be all-black. And next to the blacks were the Irish. Lincoln Street, where I grew up, was principally Polish. People's names ended in "ski." Kowalski, Jankowski, Adamski . . . Furnier. We were practically the only non-Polish family on Lincoln. So we were the Polish team. Mornings during baseball season, someone would invariably ask, "Who are we playing today?"

"We're playing the Irish."

So we'd walk over to Corktown, the old Irish district. The Irish were cool enough guys. The next day, we'd play the Italians. Hopefully, Bruno wasn't pitching, because that guy threw hard. We all knew each other, and there weren't any ethnic or racial problems. Every day a different team, every day a different ethnic nationality. Sandlot rules. No grass. A brand-new baseball was just unheard of. Our baseball had a great big flap coming out of it until it was eventually taped up. Then we batted around a ball wrapped tight in black electrician's tape. We did whatever we could do, just to play.

I went on to become a pretty good baseball player. One of my best skills was hand-to-eye coordination. I could put the bat on the ball inside or outside the strike zone. If somebody threw a pitch two feet out of the strike zone, low and outside, I could put my bat out and hit it. And I had good rhythm.

My room was a shrine to the Detroit Tigers. No posters, just pictures. A dozen shoe boxes stuffed with baseball cards, cards from packages bought for a nickel apiece, that came with flat squares of bubble gum that congealed into one giant gum brick. I'm sure I had a Mickey Mantle rookie card stashed in there somewhere, along with other cards that could have been worth hundreds or thousands of dollars today if my mother hadn't thrown them out after I left home. That's where my allowance went. We traded our cards and flipped doubles. Played tops. When I wasn't playing baseball or trading cards, I was lying on my bed in my room memorizing batting averages and ERAs. Music wasn't such a big deal to me. Elvis was out there, and yeah he was cool, but I was addicted to baseball.

On my seventh birthday, my dad got us tickets to a Tigers game at Briggs Stadium. It would be the first time I had seen my heroes play in person. With the game still two months away, I couldn't sleep. I was a basket case. I was going to see Al Kaline, Harvey Kuenn, Charlie Maxwell, Rocky Colavito, and Jim Bunning.

I remember it distinctly. It was the Tigers vs. the Cleveland Indians, a doubleheader. I remember walking up the ramp of Briggs Stadium and the smell of freshly mowed grass and hot dogs. I remember hearing the cracking sound of batting practice, the sock of a baseball soaring into the outfield. I sat there dumbfounded throughout both games, not moving. I didn't want a Coke. I didn't want a hot dog. I didn't ask for anything. I was afraid if I moved, it was all going to be over. Jim Bunning vs. Herb Score. Charlie Maxwell hit four home runs in two games. We won 7–0 and 8–2 and swept the doubleheader. I went home that night exhausted but in heaven. It was the best day I could ever have imagined. If someone had offered me a choice, Disneyland or a Tigers doubleheader, it would have been a no-brainer: Tigers all the way. To this day, when ESPN flashes MLB scores, I still check to see whether the Tigers won or lost. The Tigers run deep in my psyche.

♀   ♀   ♀

In our family, there were three basic rules:

1. You had to be a Democrat.
2. You had to pull for the Tigers and the Michigan Wolverines.
3. You had to be American League.

The All-American Detroit family. If you strayed outside any of those rules, it was "What's wrong with that kid of yours?" While Catholicism was very common and a lot of my friends were Catholic, we didn't fuss over who was Catholic or who was Protestant. Nobody cared. The black and white thing didn't exist in my home, nor did we see any difference between the Italians and the Irish. Honestly, if a black guy played baseball, especially if he was a shortstop (a rare commodity), or if he could hit, we simply didn't see color. The only question was, Is he a power hitter, a singles hitter, or a strike-out pitcher? Was he a good basketball player? Sports was the measuring stick of a person's worth during my childhood.

Music and sports never mixed back in the neighborhood. Only later did we find out that Rod Stewart could have been a pro soccer player, or that Elton John was a great tennis player. Just recently, in Britain, they listed the top rock-star athletes. For instance, Bruce Dickinson, the lead singer of Iron Maiden, is a highly ranked fencing champion. (I was the only American in their top ten, and rated number two as the golfer on the list.)

And nobody played a game like golf when I was a kid in Detroit.

Nobody played tennis, either. A sport in Detroit was considered any activity where you hit somebody or knocked them down. Only five sports existed in our world: baseball, football, hockey, basketball . . . and grand-theft auto. Golf and tennis weren't even considered sports. They ranked right down there with badminton or girls' field hockey. Bowling was big, but it wasn't considered a sport as much as just an excuse to drink on a Saturday night.

♀   ♀   ♀

Over the years, my dad did many things for a living, things like driving a cab and selling used cars. At the car lot, he worked for a couple of nefarious characters, and unfortunately my dad couldn't sell a used car to save his life! He wasn't corrupt enough. My dad would be almost through a sale, and just as the poor sucker would be driving away, he would run out across the lot and yell out, "Stop! We turned the odometer back and the whole left side of the car is Bondo!" His bosses would warn him that he had to get out of the business. He was just too honest.

My dad worked strictly on commission, so if he sold a car for $300, he only got about thirty bucks, maximum. I remember going to work with my dad. He would put all his spare change in a cup on top of the icebox, and whatever was in the change cup was our lunch money. If there wasn't much, then lunch might be just a candy bar. It was cool with me. I was in hog heaven, working alongside my dad and eating a candy bar for lunch.

♀   ♀   ♀

Although I was a fairly normal, fun-loving kid, I had one nagging health problem. I had constant bouts with asthma. Every time the leaves fell in Michigan, my asthma would kick up and I had real problems trying to breathe. I spent hours leaning over a pail of Vicks VapoRub and hot water gasping for breath. I hated being cooped up inside when that happened. I couldn't go out and throw snowballs or play hockey, all the stuff my friends were doing. The doctor took one look at me and told my parents that I needed a change of scenery.

"You've got to get this kid out of here," he said, "to a hotter climate, maybe California."

As much as Detroit was an integral part of my childhood and while as a family we were very close to our relatives in Michigan, my father and mother had to make a move to greener and sunnier pastures. My parents would look to my Uncle Lefty to help us make the smooth transition. Just like him we decided to make the move to the West Coast and resettle in Southern California.

Vince at age twelve, one year before moving to Arizona.

Chapter 2

Black Slacks and a Tight Windsor Knot

MOVING FROM MICHIGAN TO CALIFORNIA was a gradual process. Between 1948 and 1958, my family bounced back and forth between Los Angeles and Detroit. One of our first trips across the country was in a Ford Fairlane. After that we drove a Ford Anglia, a British Ford that was about the size of a couch on wheels and had maybe seventy-five horses under the hood. My sister and I were squished in the backseat, our knees to our chins, for those entire long journeys. No AC. Windows wide open. But as long as we had a coloring book or if the radio was on, we were fine. It was hot, but we were tougher back then. My dad sang his Sinatra songs until he drove my mom nuts. We would find a cheap motel, and if it had a pool, then great—although we were usually so road weary, we rarely went swimming. We'd get to our room and conk out. Then my dad made sure we were back on the road before sunrise. We must have made that Detroit-to-California trip four times before 1958. And then, when I was ten years old, we moved to L.A. for good.

My dad counted on the fact that his brother Lefty could score him a job. Back then, defense was the number-one industry in Southern California, not Hollywood and the film biz. My father was an able draftsman (he had taken up drafting in the Navy) and a very respectable electronics engineer, as well as a really good designer. So Uncle Lefty got my dad a job at Jet Propulsion Lab. Mom was a waitress at Van de Kamp's. Our needs were simple. All my dad wanted was enough to support his family.

He always earned a decent living, but we didn't live extravagantly. I remember my dad came home one night and said, "You're not going to believe this. I went to lunch today with Uncle Lefty and a couple of clients. The bill was $30!"

At the time, we were paying $60 a month rent. Our jaws dropped in shock. Thirty dollars for lunch? That was ridiculous! How much was the tip? Uncle Lefty left a six- or seven-dollar tip? Get outta here! How crazy! That much money for just one lunch?

California was a like a whole new world for us. There were no girls in Detroit named Stephanie or Jennifer, nor were there any Jews. Now all of a sudden, half of my friends in L.A. were Jewish. Of course, Jews or non-Jews, it didn't matter to me. Did they like Dion and the Belmonts? At this point, in addition to sports, my father and I listened to the rock 'n' roll hits on the car radio, and to me, that's what mattered.

♀   ♀   ♀

One of our favorite pastimes was looking in the paper for rentals in Los Angeles. My mom and dad *loved* to move, and we were always jumping around. One rule: Rent couldn't be over $70. We had so much fun combing the newspaper ads for new and exciting places to live. One night my dad came home and announced that he had just rented us another place. When we got there, lo and behold, a swimming pool! To a couple of kids from Detroit, there was no such thing as a pool at home. Only in motels on cross-country trips. We were ecstatic.

My mom looked at us, appalled, and then she asked my dad the big question: "How much is this place?"

"Ninety bucks a month." Our jaws dropped again.

"What were you thinking?" my mom asked.

"I got a raise," my dad admitted proudly. "Five dollars an hour!"

Suddenly, we were millionaires. My allowance went up to fifty cents a week.

♀   ♀   ♀

When we first got to California, my dad still liked his beer and cigarettes. He smoked three packs a day, nonfiltered cigarettes ("coffin nails"). Lucky Strikes. I know because I used to run down to the corner store and buy them for him, or pick up some from a vending machine. Nobody thought anything about selling cigarettes to kids, because smoking was so ingrained in our society. It was very "in" to smoke, and everyone did. Nobody thought about cancer. There were no such things as warnings on the pack.

But then my parents converted to Protestantism and started attending the church that my grandfather headed up, the Church of Jesus Christ. Once my dad became a Christian in my granddad's church, our whole world was transformed. No more drinking in the house. My dad quit smoking. There was no swearing. But Mick Furnier stayed cool; he was still the hippest guy I'd ever met, next to Uncle Lefty. Although we didn't have a lot of money, my dad knew how to dress sharp. He would get dressed up in the morning, looking like the cover of *GQ* magazine just to go to work. A very dapper guy, but one of the most humble of men. I think his sense of style rubbed off on me.

The church was very Bible-oriented, Protestant but nondenominational, filled with a lot of old Italians and all-American middle-class white folks. I spent Sundays in church . . . Wednesday nights in church . . . Fridays in church. Saturdays cleaning the church. Pretty soon all of our friends were this new group of church kids. I was okay with that. I liked being around friends in church who were my own age. I was content. It seemed normal to me.

♀   ♀   ♀

On weekends, we drove down to Arizona, out to the San Carlos Indian reservation. It was a site of abject poverty. I'd never seen anything like it. People lived out of old cars kept together with mud and cardboard; they called them wickiups. There'd be eight people living in one wickiup. In the summertime, it could get up to 120 degrees; in the winter, 10 below in the snow. They were the most vicious living conditions I'd ever seen. Back in L.A., our little $6,000 rented house was a palace compared to where these people lived.

When I was eleven, in 1961, my father felt the itch to move on. He wanted to possibly become a missionary and work with the American Indians. I think he felt drawn toward the Southwest to help out the Native Americans. So he announced the inevitable: We were moving to Phoenix, Arizona. As a family, we went along with his dream. My sister Nickie and I were used to being nomads. One of the reasons I get along well with people today is that I went to so many schools and was always the new kid in class.

First, I'd get everybody laughing. I was Vince the smart aleck, the funny guy. I had to be. I was a little skinny kid, but I was a good enough athlete, and that plus being the class clown meant that I was a pretty cool guy. That's how I survived, since I couldn't fight.

When we moved to Phoenix, my dad went to work at Goodyear Aerospace. I used to watch him get dressed up for work, and he still looked like a million bucks. His hair was snow white, but perfectly coiffed and swept back. He wore a tailored gray suit and a matching gray shirt with a maroon tie tied in a perfect Windsor knot with the gold stickpin underneath. He taught me how to tie that same perfect Windsor knot so that when I went to my elementary school—and this was before the Beatles and the British Invasion—I dressed up in smart dark slacks and a white shirt with a skinny tie.

We lived modestly in Phoenix. My dad had a job drafting and a steady paycheck, but nothing extravagant. We got one present for Christmas, which was sufficient. We lived in a trailer. My dad drove a Dodge. My mom continued as a waitress, helping out the household with her tips. No class consciousness loomed over us; we never went hungry and there was never a time when we were destitute.

♀   ♀   ♀

While we lived in the trailer park in Phoenix, we went out to the Indian reservation each weekend. One Sunday night when I was eleven years old, I came home and threw up a bunch of times. We thought I had the flu. When it got worse, we thought perhaps I was bitten by something, a black widow, or whatever was around when the Indian kids and I played around a dead cow or something. There were tarantulas and scorpions on the reservation—we were used to being bitten. But my stomachache got worse and I was throwing up this green stuff, so finally my mom decided to take me to the doctor.

The doctor took a blood test and freaked out. "Get this kid to the hospital right now!" My appendix had burst two days before. Stuff was oozing out into my innards, but it didn't hurt that much because it had already sealed over. That's why I was so sick. My body was filled with peritonitis.

When they cut me open, they realized that every organ was poisoned. I had checked in weighing only ninety pounds. I wasn't a strong kid to begin with. My white cell count was poor. The doctor shook his head sadly as he explained everything to my parents: "This kid doesn't have a chance. I'd give him ten percent odds of pulling through." My mom and dad were literally on the floor weeping and praying.

Eventually, though, I woke up. I had tubes coming out of both arms. I stayed in the hospital for another three months. I went down to sixty-eight pounds; my cheeks were sunken and hollow—I must have looked like a Biafran baby. I had a curvature of the spine and shoulders that left me slightly hunchbacked. At first, all I could digest was ice chips. But one day I picked up a comic book and began reading. When the doctor came around, he asked me how I was feeling. I felt fine. The doctor turned to the nurse.

"This is a miracle."

Eventually, I would return for a couple more surgeries, but I came through it, though I still have the scars to remind me. My parents looked at that episode as a trial of endurance, testing us as a family to see if we could handle adversity.

♀   ♀   ♀

There were other family tests. I remember one night when I was twelve years old and my mom had calculated our debts down to the penny. We needed $146 by Friday to stay in Phoenix; otherwise, we were moving back to California where Uncle Lefty could help us.

The Thursday night before we had to leave, my mother opened up the mailbox and found a blank envelope containing $146. Nobody else knew we needed that exact amount of money except my father. We were all convinced it was another miracle. We never figured out who sent it; I still don't know.

It looked like the family was destined to stay in Phoenix. Then, suddenly, my dad got a better job. We were doing well. I had survived my illness and was growing stronger by the day. Arizona was now our permanent home.

Not a bad stance: Alice whacking the ball in 1976, wearing his Budweiser cap.

The First Step of Golf Addiction

Be a Good Imitator

Learn to watch and mimic. Listen to good advice.
Hit a million balls. Use your imagination.

When I was a little kid and Elvis Presley starred on the TV, I would stand in front of a mirror and imitate him. The lip. The sneer. The swivel hips. I was a great mimic.

When I was a little older, I would play baseball with my dad. He would try to get me to stand in front of a ground ball and, in one continuous motion, bend down, field the ball, and throw it. I couldn't get the hang of what he was talking about then, but after watching baseball on television and seeing them field and throw in one fluid motion, I was able to do the same thing.

"Where did that come from, Vince?" my father asked. I told him that's how they do it in the major leagues: catch, pivot, throw. I watched on the television and learned it.

I imitated. You have to, to make it in sports or rock 'n' roll.

I was the guy who watched sports on television, partially to pick up on moves. I studied Al Kaline's perfect level swing on TV or in a picture in a magazine whenever he smashed a home run. I didn't want to be a golfer in high school—if you were a letterman athlete, the last thing you wanted on your jacket was a golf club or tennis racquet, so I stuck to track—but once I got interested in golf, I paid close attention to the PGA tournaments on TV. I watched and calculated every player, noticing their subtle nuances and

23

their different swings. Johnny Miller was the first guy who prompted me to seriously pursue golf; after watching him, I said to myself, "I'd really like to be able to play like that."

I studied Johnny's moves. I noted where he placed his hands on the club. How his left hand was swinging right through, whereas my left hand was doing something different. So I mimicked him, and I developed this really good swing.

My buddies on the green sometimes ask me, "Hey, Alice, where the heck did you get that swing?"

"Oh," I shrug like I did with my father, "that's how they do it on TV." Really, it's not something you're born with. Find someone whose swing you like and watch it, imitate it.

Behind every great rock star—especially lead singers—is a mimic. Everybody in rock 'n' roll cops somebody else's moves when they're first starting. I never really made the grade as a lead singer in the amateur bands I joined—until I was sixteen years old, after I watched the Rolling Stones play.

When I saw Mick Jagger for the first time, he opened up a whole new world for me. He was the first guy to break away from the band and move around the stage to become the focal point. He was charismatic. When lead singers saw him, we all took his cue and invented our own versions of Mick Jagger—he was the prototype, and we all were derived in some ways from him. I sometimes still catch myself doing a Jagger rooster step. (Whoops!) Jagger was the cock of the walk, and he had the confident stride of a pro golfer. The whole thing about Jagger is his stance—chin out, shoulders back. The ego. The man. A long time ago, I learned an important rule from Jagger by watching him sing: You never look down. *Always* up and out.

So after seeing Mick, I realized that I didn't have to just stand there in front of the microphone like a lump and just sing! I could walk around on stage. I could dance. I could point at the pretty girls in the audience. I could move around the stage like I own the place. *Hey,* I thought, *I can do this music thing after all.* From there I crafted my own style.

Now that I'm a desperate golf junkie, just like with Mick Jagger in those early days, I improve my game by observing better players and mimicking some of their moves. The better golfer you are, the better you'll be at evaluating what great players are doing and emulating them. Some people just don't get imitation. I've seen swings where I'll say to myself, "Man, where did he learn that? There's nothing good about that swing at all. Nobody swings like that." I can look at a guy's swing and figure out right away if he knows what he's doing, or if he has no idea how to evaluate and ape a good swing.

Luckily, I just happen to be one of those people who can learn quickly by mimicking. But anyone can improve at it. At first, I just wanted to be good enough to play celebrity Pro-Am tournaments alongside guys like Lee Trevino and Arnold Palmer and not embarrass myself. Now, the more great players I watch, the loftier my goals to become a great player.

In golf, there's so much to adapt to. The ball can spin this way or that. How well are your hands placed? Is your head positioned so you can hit the ball square-on and make it go dead straight down the middle without over- or underswinging, all with a smooth rhythm? I can't imagine there being any more variables in a sport than with golf. Luckily, though, you are most likely surrounded with experienced people who might be willing to give advice.

I once asked Vijay Singh after a bad practice shot, "How did I hook it like that?"

Before he answered, he said, "Hit five balls for me."

I hit them. They all looked okay to me.

"Alice, it's your shoulder," he told me, "it's not tucked under."

That was a $10,000 lesson! Since I'm on the Pro-Am celebrity circuit a lot, the pros will occasionally help me out. Maybe it's because they like my music. Maybe they feel sorry for me. One time, after I missed a couple of chips, John Daly came up to me and said, "After this round, meet me over at the driving range and I'll show you how to never ever miss that chip again."

John dropped a hundred balls and showed me what to do. I listened and took it all to heart. Since that day, I have rarely missed that chip shot again.

One of the best pieces of advice I ever got came from Johnny Miller and Davis Love. They both told me to relax my right hand and turn it a little. "That's the correct position," they assured me.

I went out and hit the ball. It felt horrible, but I trusted their advice. Since golf is constantly about relearning what you think you know in the first place, I had to hit a thousand more balls before it felt natural! Yet once I achieved the improved stroke, it brought me that much closer to the Perfect Swing.

Since the majority of us are right-handed, we want our right hand to do everything. We shake hands, we write, and we eat with our right hands. Now they're telling me I can't use my right hand to control the club? Well, the golf game involves the left hand. Your right hand is only there to stabilize the club. You don't need to apply any pressure with your right hand, because when you do, you're going to throw the ball everywhere.

Once I fixed my swing (after hitting a zillion balls), if you told me to go back and guide the club with my right hand again, I couldn't do it. It would feel awful. I now *have* to let my right hand relax, because I want to hit with my left. I can now hit the way the pros instructed me, and I understand why it's correct. It was a matter of taking good advice and being an imitator.

Just like in rock 'n' roll, it's scary to do something new and outrageous. The temptation in golf is to enjoy your comfort level instead of changing or tweaking your grip or swing in order to improve. But you're not the only one who has had to rebuild their games. When Tiger Woods started playing on the PGA scene, the best players in the world had to go back to the driving range and relearn a lot of things simply because Tiger took the game to another level. Tiger was so good that established players had to go back and imitate his strategies and game.

Why is Tiger so good? Because like any great rock star, *nobody* is hungrier to win or more willing to work. He practices eight hours a day, just like Rod Stewart and the Faces used to. If he wants to sink a hundred two-foot putts in a row, and he gets to eighty-nine and misses one, he'll start all over. In a tough-down-the-stretch tournament, most golfers will hit that putt nine out of ten times, but Tiger, he won't miss it *ever*. That's the difference between winning or losing a Masters. One lousy stroke.

If I'm playing with really good musicians and we're rehearsing hard for eight hours a day, we can become a pretty tight and kicking band. Still, there comes a time when you have to rely on your imagination and your ability to write a really good song.

In golf, the player with a little bit more technical ability, better hand-to-eye coordination, and more imagination will win holes. I always visualize my shots. If I get behind a tree, I use my imagination. I'll know how to make the shot, or at least get back on the fairway again. Someone with more technical ability and less innovation might not. Use your imagination. Create your own *unique* shots. That's the difference between being good and great.

And sometimes, in golf as in music, sometimes it's beyond learning, beyond imitating, beyond imagination. Sometimes you need something that can't be taught—passion, talent, an intrinsic understanding of the feel of the game. Take putting, for example—it's almost something you can't teach. It's an acquired feel. It's like throwing darts. Certain guys have great natural aim and motion, and other guys don't find the rhythm. You can't just putt it *at* the hole. I like to hold the putter like I'm holding on to a bird—light and loose. Once the ball gets there, it needs to lose speed and simply fall into the cup with grace. It's like a pianist with a magic touch. It's all about feel. And feel is something that's difficult, or impossible, to teach. Either you have it or you don't.

But being a good imitator is the key in developing a solid golf swing—it sharpens up those hand-to-eye skills you were born with but you might not be utilizing to the fullest. In music, if I didn't have the Beatles or the Stones to mimic as an adolescent, my music career would have never happened. Now, in golf, I listen, I watch, and I learn new things every time.

Cortez High School track team photo. Alice is third from the left on the top row.

Chapter 3

James Bond, the Beatles, and Cortez High

I N 1961, THREE YEARS BEFORE the Fab Four and the British Invasion, I started school again in the seventh grade after my near-fatal bout with peritonitis. Just out of the hospital, I looked emaciated and pale. My hair had fallen out in bunches from the antibiotics. Though I wasn't bald, my hair, like my body, was thin and brittle. I started at Squaw Peak Junior High. Unlike Detroit and Los Angeles, Arizona and the great Southwestern desert communities were like a new frontier, the Wild West. Once I started classes, I discovered another interest.

Girls! Girls! Girls!

The Arizona girls were built like *women*. The Lil' Abner–type seventh- and eighth-grade girls at school dressed in cutoff shorts and skimpy tops. We even found out that two of them had gotten "in trouble" with a teacher who got fired. One night I went home and thanked my father.

"Why?"

"Just thank you, Dad. Thank you. Thank you. I love this school so much. I *really* love this school."

"Great." My father shook his head, puzzled. "Glad to hear it."

He may not have understood then, but a few weeks later he visited my school.

"How old are these girls?" he asked in amazement.

"Fourteen," I answered, shaking my head knowingly.

He turned to me and whispered, "You're welcome, son."

♀   ♀   ♀

Just like my dad, I stayed a step ahead of everybody in school in terms of fashion style and coolness. I made friends fast. One kid named Jerry Brandon let me read all of his Ian Fleming James Bond novels. There was a lot of sex in those books! One day we heard that *Dr. No* was coming out as a movie. We were excited—James Bond was our hero! The other kids had no idea who James Bond was. That's how cool Jerry and I were.

Even at age twelve, I was gunning to be the suave guy, looking more like a beatnik than your average schoolkid. I listened to Henry Mancini. I studied *Peter Gunn* because I dug the way Craig Stevens, the guy who played Peter Gunn, dressed. I watched *Mr. Lucky* and his floating casino. I was mainly into art at school, and I dug Salvador Dalí. I'd watch *The Twilight Zone* and read O. Henry and Alfred Hitchcock mystery short stories. I would write catchy stories for my creative writing assignments with trick endings that would impress my teachers. One of my stories was titled "Dr. Lived," so that when you looked at his name in the mirror, it spelled "devil." It was a pretty slick story hook for a twelve-year-old kid.

To most folks at the time, Phoenix was a stopover city on the way to L.A., full of mostly cowboys and electronics companies like Motorola and Honeywell. My dad found a job in Litchfield Park, an hour-and-twenty-minute ride back and forth to work.

Around this time, we moved to the west side of town into an honest-to-goodness $10,000 tract house. By the time I started Cortez High School as a freshman, I'd recovered to the point where I was able to play sports again. I tried out for the baseball team. I was a great hitter and a good fielder, but I had no arm at all. Cortez was the state baseball champion, so their guys had to both hit and throw with power—I didn't make the team. I was crushed, but hardly surprised. The other ballplayers were bigger and stronger.

I met a sophomore in my art class named Dennis Dunaway. He was a year older than me, but we really got along. I'd go over to his house, or he'd come over to mine, and we would do art and writing projects together. My artwork reflected my interests in surrealism and comic book art. Dada. Dalí. Cubism. Heady stuff for a high school kid. Dennis and I became friends and scored a few bucks apiece when we were hired to paint a mural during summer break. Now we both considered ourselves working artists.

Dennis became a long-distance runner at Cortez. He asked me, "Vince, since you're so skinny, have you ever considered running?"

"Running? From what?" Was running even a sport? I had no clue about the world of track and field, and I hadn't even considered that it was something I would be able to do. But then another guy at school, John Speer, also urged me to try out for track and cross-country, so I went out on a three-mile trial run. It turned out I was a natural long-distance runner—I finished fourth, beating out three of the varsity runners. Running felt great!

I made the varsity cross-country team as a freshman, which was almost unheard of. I first lettered in track in September 1962. Now I could hang out with and compete against the seniors, juniors, and sophomores. Starting so early, I was cruising toward becoming a four-year letterman at Cortez High! By my senior year, I would earn the fourth stripe on my sweater, which meant a lot. The toughest senior guys in school usually had only *two* stripes, because they generally only lettered in sports during their last two years. My rare four stripes became my ticket to ride at Cortez. Nobody messed with me. Those stripes on my sweater made the world my oyster.

♀   ♀   ♀

During this time, the Beatles were becoming huge in England. By my sophomore year in 1964, the Beatles hit America hard. It was like a cultural tidal wave. I came to school the day after they played on *The Ed Sullivan Show,* and it was as if a weird revolution had struck the students. Some kids dug John, Paul, George, and Ringo; some hated them. Dennis and I fell squarely in the "I dig the Beatles" camp. We liked them. A lot. My parents were very apprehensive about the Beatles . . . until they saw the Rolling Stones. Then suddenly the Beatles, those nice boys in the suits, weren't so bad.

The Beatles had a major effect on high school kids. Suddenly, the music thing was no longer just about vocal groups like Dion and the Belmonts, the Beach Boys, or the Four Seasons, whom we all dug. It was all Beatles all the time! Nothing against the Four Seasons—they were one of the greatest recording bands of all time—but there I was, experiencing a true cultural revolution almost without realizing it. The Beatles were the ultimate catalyst for me to move beyond art and painting and to try my own hand at music.

Vince on graduation day with his first car in Phoenix.
If you look closely, there's a sticker in the window for his band, The Spiders.

Chapter 4

Earwigs and Spiders

IT WAS MARCH 1964, MY JUNIOR YEAR. At this point Dennis Dunaway, John Speer, and I were among the BMOCs (big men on campus) at Cortez. I wasn't exactly a brainiac. I was skinny, but athletic and stylish. I didn't do well in class, except for English literature, art, and physical education. I was worthless with anything that had to do with science or math. So I had this deal: I'd entertain the class and help the teacher keep the kids under control. I'd make the class fun and supply jokes and funny answers. I wouldn't be a jerk—if a teacher gave me the look, I'd shut up. But for the most part it made classes fun and easier for them, and besides being a letterman, that's how I squeaked through math and science.

My sister used to get pissed off that I got away with so much because of my personality. I could talk my way out of a sunburn. That's how I got through high school. I didn't pass one algebra test all year, but my teacher told me that if I managed a D– on my final, he'd pass me. So I made a deal with the girl who sat in front of me. In exchange for me taking her to the Christmas dance, she helped me up my grade from a 60 to a 64.

The Annual Lettermen's Club Variety Show was coming up, and somehow I got roped into recruiting talent for the show. I put up signs all over the school. No response.

We used to sing Beatles songs as we ran our laps, changing the lyrics to be about track. So Dennis Dunaway had the idea for us to perform at the show ourselves—we would put on Beatles wigs and wear our black track outfits. The plan was for us to play phony guitars and lip-synch Beatles songs. We would hire a couple of girls to scream in the audience.

Actually, we did have a guitar player, who really played while we mimicked. This kid, named Glen Buxton, dressed like the biggest juvenile delinquent in the school. We worked together on the school newspaper, the *Cortez Tip Sheet*. Glen was the photographer and I had my own column, called "Get Out of My Hair," which I wrote under the pen name Muscles McNasal. So I knew that Glen and another kid named John Tatum were in surf bands. These two guys were not athletes—they smoked cigarettes and fought. But they also played guitar. We talked them into playing in the background at the Variety Show.

We called ourselves the Earwigs, after those little bugs that crawl into your ear. It was a total joke. We learned two Beatles songs. Everybody laughed at the screaming girls, but something out of the ordinary happened the next day. People came up to me and told me they admired my guts for getting up onto that cafeteria stage. Girls who never noticed the skinny guy with the big nose from the track team suddenly noticed me now.

I figured, "Hey, what if we rehearsed a little more? What if we found a guy who could play drums?" Then John Speers volunteered to learn to play drums. Dennis decided to switch over from guitar and learn to play bass. During summer vacation, he went away and came back able to play bass. All of a sudden, everybody could play a little bit. Next, we learned four songs with a plan to play parties.

We became the Earwigs, and we were awful. Simply awful.

But we rehearsed regularly and we were determined. After we finished track and cross-country practice, we'd go over to Dennis's house and practice Beatles songs. It was so hard. Eventually, we'd play a song enough times to where it was semirecognizable. Four whole chords! Pretty soon we had more than a dozen songs crudely worked out. In October of 1964, the Earwigs played during a few lunch hours at Cortez. We were also the house band for the Halloween "Pit and the Pendulum Dance" on October 23.

♀ ♀ ♀

We graduated to playing school dances and became one of the most accomplished garage bands around. It took our junior and senior years to do it, but by 1965 we were a full-fledged rock 'n' roll band. So we changed our name to the Spiders. We were still just playing Beatles tunes, so we added some Rolling Stones songs to our set.

There weren't a lot of working rock bands in Phoenix. One of our earliest gigs was playing the Pizza Pub for all the pizza we could eat. But soon we got a regular gig at the VIP Club, run by a guy named Jack Curtis, playing multiple sets every weekend. Word about the Spiders spread quickly. Soon a thousand or twelve hundred kids might show up on Friday and Saturday nights at the VIP. I was making $200 a week playing with the Spiders, which was serious cash—more than my dad made. But I was headed for family conflict.

I was in a rock 'n' roll band, but I was still a church kid. My father had become an unpaid pastor and found that he was a skilled preacher. He'd come home from work and study theology at night. He went from being a Bible teacher to an apprentice pastor to a fully ordained minister to an elder in the church. He preached every third Sunday, and with his sharp suits and swept-back silver-fox hair, he more than looked the part of a flashy reverend.

On the other hand, I was gigging with the Spiders and had grown to become an independent, self-sufficient musician. My father didn't make a fuss about it, but my lifestyle became a conflict. He was getting more and more flak from the church members about my music and appearance. My hair was getting longer and longer—church members would bug me to go get a haircut. I was dressing more outlandishly. Then I was suspended from school for my hair. But people were also hearing my name on the radio as the Spiders became the biggest local band in Phoenix.

The ironic part was that my dad loved the British Invasion music! Even though he dug Sinatra and Tony Bennett, he was very aware of the newer sounds.

In the mornings, my father would shave while I'd help him study his theology lessons. I'd open the Bible and throw out a book and verse. "Ezekiel 7:13. Thus sayeth the Lord, you shall come into my presence . . ." He would finish the verse verbatim.

Then I'd ask, "Who plays bass for the Animals?"

"Chas Chandler."

My dad was genuinely interested in my music. He showed up on a few Friday and Saturday nights to watch the Spiders play. He dug our music and respected our progress.

Despite our success, we were still pretty innocent. We didn't play bars because we were underage. But we did win a huge battle of the bands. First prize: a trip to Los Angeles. Now my parents were saying, "Uh-oh. This is getting serious."

So not only was I a high school kid who was getting paid to play rock 'n' roll, but on the sports front, I was on a running team that hadn't been defeated in four years. I bought myself a car and I was still the funny and popular guy.

In those days, though, it didn't take much to stone me. Once, in my senior year, I went to a party with a girl I knew and she handed me a Coors beer. Not wanting to be a jerk, I drank it down. It felt pretty darn good, so I drank another one. It was my first beer buzz. It was an amazing feeling. After only two beers, they had to carry my skinny frame out the door. Meanwhile, my other buddies were all messed up and counting on good ol' Vince to come back and drive them home. I was usually the straight one. But I was at home completely drunk.

$$\Upsilon \quad \Upsilon \quad \Upsilon$$

I had life whipped. The Spiders were the pride of Phoenix, performing cover songs by the Yardbirds and the Who. Eventually, John Tatum left the band. We placed an ad in the paper for a guitarist, and a guy named Michael Bruce was the only one to respond. He was in a group called the Wildflowers and he drove a van. Hired!

By our senior year, we were also opening for headliners at the VIP Club, including the Yardbirds, Them, the Hollies, the Lovin' Spoonful, the Animals, Peter and Gordon, and the Byrds. Topflight bands like the Kinks routinely played the VIP Club in front of two thousand people, and we opened for a lot of them. Otherwise, we hung out at the club a lot. We met the Jimi Hendrix Experience, who opened for the Young Rascals. Jimi was one cool hipster. And a nice guy—he let us buddy around with him.

In the summer of 1966, we cut a little record called "Don't Blow Your Mind," which made it to number one on a local Top Forty radio station. We found ourselves then needing to make the big decision: Should we make a commitment to go to Los Angeles to become a *real* band, or should we hoof it to college? We had already made several road trips back and forth to L.A. trying to break into their scene, which was plenty rough. I submitted to parental pressure and signed up for Glendale Community College, where I would study fine arts. However, the band agreed we still needed to take our shot in Los Angeles.

We saw how bands like the Yardbirds and the Animals made it look easy but had a pretty basic performance setup. Our goal was to take *our* show up a notch on the entertainment level. Who knew what that would entail? We brainstormed. Our live show needed to be more visual, so we wore all black, with a huge web backdrop behind us. I roamed all over the stage, pacing back and forth, and Dennis played bass more aggressively. All the members adopted a different look. We were becoming exciting to watch. We knew we had something. We just needed to improve musically. We'd already conquered Phoenix, but the best bands from all over the world were converging on Los Angeles. How would we rank against that kind of competition? We rehearsed every day, realizing that we had to be as proficient as the bands we opened for.

In spite of our parents freaking out, the Spiders decided to drop out of college and relocate to Los Angeles. I was eighteen years old. Who was going to stop us? We needed to audition for clubs like Gazzarri's, Whiskey a Go Go, and the Cheetah. This was during the heart of the hippie movement. Bands like Love, the Doors, Buffalo Springfield, and Jefferson Airplane from San Francisco were on the scene and established, but we wanted to ride the next wave. We rolled into L.A. as green as green could be and took on every audition. At the time, we had just about enough money to last us a couple weeks.

But our plans were cut short. It was 1967, the year of the Summer of Love and the height of the Vietnam War. We were summoned back to Phoenix to address a major problem facing all high school grads—the dreaded military draft.

The earliest traces of theater rock. Alice on stage in Los Angeles circa 1969.

Chapter 5

L.A. Dreams and the Draft

BY 1967, I HAD GOT MY HAIR permed out into a huge Afro, just like Eric Clapton of Cream wore it on the cover of *Disraeli Gears*. Dennis's hair was now halfway down his back. Everybody in the Spiders had long, long hair.

We all received our draft notices around the same time—I remember it was the same time I had broken up with my girlfriend from high school, who left me for a guy who drove a Corvette. When we opened the notices, we found we were all classified 1-A, available for unrestricted military service! As far as the draft board knew, we were all still in college, so I thought we were deferred—but apparently not. We all got called to show up at the draft board at roughly the same time to determine our future draft status.

Dennis, Glen, and I went down to the draft board determined to get deferred. We figured we'd be so freaky, so outrageous that surely they'd have to throw us out. I marched down to Selective Service dressed as a rock 'n' roller. I wore a pair of gold lamé pants. While I didn't normally drink, that day I sure did. I drank Southern Comfort all night. It was six in the morning and we were whacked out of our heads, sitting in the induction room. Then a uniformed guy walked in and looked around the room. He took one look at Dennis Dunaway and yelled, "You, out!"

The guy, Sergeant Somebody—boy, did he look familiar. I couldn't quite figure it out. I was there all day while I went through my preregistration physical exam. A couple of the other band members who came down with me that morning were let go. Then I was the last Spider standing. Suddenly, I realized that Sergeant Somebody was the guy my girlfriend had

39

ditched me for–the guy who drove the Corvette. My goose was cooked. Now he was calling the shots at the induction center and seemed eager to get me out of the picture.

"You're 1-A," he told me.

"But I weigh ninety pounds! I'm no soldier."

"We'll put weight on you."

I gritted my teeth as I left to go back home.

Dennis was officially deferred. So was Glen Buxton. Meanwhile, Neal Smith, our drummer, guitarist Mike Bruce, and I were still 1-A. We had reservations to board the bus when we turned nineteen. Next stop, Vietnam! How would we get out of this mess?

♀ ♀ ♀

At that time, the Spiders hung out with an all-girl band called the Weeds of Idleness. We partied together and we'd take .22 rifles out into the desert at night and shoot rabbits. With some of the guys perched on the hood, we'd chase rabbits and shoot them by the light of our headlights. In 1967, you could do stupid things like that in the middle of the desert and nobody cared.

One night, while we were chasing this huge jackrabbit, I fired my rifle just as Neal got in my range. He fell off the car hood, took off his boot, and there was a bullet hole through his ankle. I was aghast! I had just shot our drummer! We got our story together for when the police showed up: We had all got our draft notices and Neal tried to commit suicide.

By shooting himself in the foot.

We were all so stupid and high, I guess it made sense at the time.

"Lemme get this straight, Mr. Smith." The cop scratched his head. "You took a rifle and shot yourself in the ankle. Is that what happened?"

"Yes, Officer," I answered for him. The cop immediately knew that I had shot Neal.

"Next time, son," he said to Neal, "put it to your forehead and pull the trigger."

♀ ♀ ♀

Looking back, it was a funny thing. I probably would have enlisted in the Army eventually. I wasn't antiwar at all. I wasn't into the peace-and-love movement of the day. I wasn't a protester. I wasn't a conscientious objector. I had no bones about going into the Army and fighting for my country. It's just that I looked so freaky at the time and I didn't want to go into the Army right then because I was in a rock 'n' roll group. I wanted to go to L.A. and become a star!

The rest of my band members escaped the draft. Neal Smith was deferred because he had a bad foot (apparently, one of his friends had shot him!). Mike Bruce was actually on the bus, on his way to boot camp, when he freaked out and was ultimately deferred. I was the only one left hanging.

Finally, just after my nineteenth birthday but before I got on the bus, the government instituted the draft lottery in an effort to be fair. Fortunately, my number came in near the bottom, which put me at the back of the line. So I went back to being 1-H with the rest of the guys in the band. We were now all deferred, and were ready to take on the L.A. music scene.

Meanwhile, our nearly seven-foot-tall drummer, Neal Smith, still had a cast on his foot from the .22 bullet wound, but he continued playing double bass drums. To this day, Neal still has that fragment lodged in his ankle.

♀   ♀   ♀

With our draft problems behind us, we could come to L.A. and stay for a few weeks at a time. We met a guy named Doke Huntington, a kind gentleman who offered the band a room to crash in his house on Weatherly Lane, right off Santa Monica Boulevard. Doke was this ridiculously handsome guy who was Tony Curtis's private secretary. The entire band slept at Doke's house in sleeping bags. Pretty soon, we noticed that Doke's friends really took a shine to Mike Bruce, our pretty boy, when they came over to Doke's. We got the picture. But we didn't feel threatened, and nobody ever came on to any of the band.

By this time, the L.A. rock lifestyle had gotten its claws into us. We were quickly getting street smarter. I had arrived in L.A. a total virgin. Nineteen and still a church kid. Even though I'd messed around a bit, I hadn't really "done it" yet. Well, the L.A. girls saw to it that we were sexually initiated. They whipped through us like hot knives through butter. The rock 'n' roll gals of L.A. pretty much taught us everything about sex. Free love and all. Soon we'd wake up with a different girl most every morning—it was kid-in-a-candy-store time. Still, I didn't want my parents to know I was sleeping around with girls. After all, I was still under twenty-one.

One night at Doke's house after our third trip to L.A., the other guys in the band began to experiment with acid. Personally, I was never much of a druggie. I barely even touched alcohol at the time. Still, everything changed after that. We were no longer virgins—on any level.

Hundreds of bands were doing exactly what we were doing—trying to achieve rock stardom by struggling and starving and tripping. We had no permanent home base in L.A., and unlike the VIP Club days, we were always broke. We stumbled from place to place.

Back in the day, we were a band of gypsies and we slept and ate wherever and whenever we could. The original idea was that we would stay with buddies and friends, and that we would manage somehow on a wing and a prayer. Before, we were staying with Doke and we had various crash pads where we lived communally as a band. One time we met a guy in Griffith Park, and for $160 he lined up a place where we were able to move in our stuff, rehearse, and barely exist. After one club audition, the girl who was going to book us kindly offered a place to stay, a small and dingy two-room apartment near the Hollywood Freeway. Hey, it was free. Except all night long we could hear the sounds of a steady stream of L.A. traffic. Unfortunately that opportunity lasted a grand total of three days before the LAPD came knocking on the door and threw our sorry tails back out on the street. Apparently the rent hadn't been paid in two months, and we were a group of unwitting squatters.

This was still the hippie era. People would take us in and let us crash on their floors. Otherwise, we'd have to drive back to Phoenix whenever we ran out of money. We figured that with all this struggling and poverty, the Spiders would soon fall apart. But it didn't happen. We persisted and rehearsed. We wouldn't give up the dream. We were making the key transition from amateur to pro. The band was tight and swinging. Plus, L.A. was a swinging city in a league of its own.

Alice practices his putting in black leather pants and snakeskin boots on the *Mike Douglas Show* in 1974 with Mike (center) and Peter Falk (left).

The Second Step of Golf Addiction

It Don't Mean a Thing if You Ain't Got That Swing or On Being an Amateur vs. Becoming a Pro

Cindy-Crawford and the one-piece swing. Thinking too much. Head games. Timeless swings. Goin' PGA pro.

Golf is the hardest game in the world to play. You can take the best athletes in the world, put a golf club in their hands, and they'll admit to it: Golf is tough! You've got to put a tiny ball into a tiny hole, four hundred yards away . . . in four strokes! How hard is that?

I never get bored with the game. I can play twenty-eight days in a row, and someone will ask me, "Wanna play golf tomorrow?"

And my response is always "What time should I be there?"

Why? Because I'm sure the next round I play just might be the round when I shoot my best score. Hope springs eternal. Your next record might be your biggest hit.

Your ability to swing—in both music and golf—is something you should be working on for the rest of your life. It's a lifelong quest. Some golfers find their swings early, and those are the guys who turn pro. Some golfers search all their lives. All the stuff they do with their hands, shifting their weight, moving their bodies, adjusting their stance. There are so many variables that go into developing your swing. Some guys try them all. A lot of the time, when I write a song, I work hard to include all the various nuances. But what are my biggest hits? The most basic songs I write in ten minutes.

I subscribe to the philosophy that the best swing is the simplest swing. The one-piece—a golfer's nirvana. Some guys doubt its existence, proclaiming it as myth. A one-piece swing is a swing executed in one simple motion. It looks so simple, but it's soooo hard to achieve.

"One-two. One-two."

Or as Johnny Miller once explained it to me, "Cindy-Crawford. Cindy-Crawford."

No need to force the ball. Just like the baseball shortstop I emulated as a kid, it should be one smooth motion. Throwing a baseball or a football, hitting a tennis ball, swinging a golf club: It's all about the seamless one-piece. If you can perfect that swing, you can hit the ball as far as any three-hundred-pound guy, probably farther. He may have muscles and mass on you, but that doesn't mean his ball is going any farther. People are always surprised at how far a welterweight like me can swing the ball.

"How much do you weigh?"

"A hundred and forty-six pounds."

"How far can you hit the ball?"

"Two hundred and seventy yards."

"But I'm 250 pounds and I can't hit it over 200 yards."

"That's because you have bigger muscles but I have better rhythm."

My swing is a combination of about fifty great swings that I've seen and collected over the years. I might see a guy's hand position and try it. If it works for me, I'll remember it. Another guy might finish with his right foot straight up. Maybe he does it every time he makes a great shot. I might try that.

As far as my swing, I figure I'm 80 percent there. If I really wanted to get any better, I would practice more. But I figure I have a good enough swing—I don't really need to get much better than I am now in order to love the game. I'm way past the dues-paying stage. I've reached the point where I can tee up on the first hole, take it back, and hit the ball down the middle nearly every time. When anyone asks how I do it, I say,

"It's simple. Take all the distractions out of your head, rear back, and let it go."

Thinking too much is the worst thing you can do in golf. My best round of golf was a 67 at Camelback Country Club. Five under par, and it happened when I didn't have a single thought in my head all day. No bats fluttering about in the belfry. I barely kept score that whole day. I didn't keep track. I knew I had a bunch of birdies and no bogeys. But I was a million miles away, hitting the ball so good. I was fluid, and nobody or nothing was getting inside my head.

Now I'll go out of my way to psych people out of their swings if they're out to beat me. That's a big part of my game. If an opponent has something consistent going, I'll try to crawl inside his head. If you ever want to mess somebody up, if your opponents are beating your tail, you can psych them out by saying something like "Do you always take a breath on the back swing like that?"

Or, "Did you know that your hand clenches a little bit on your back swing?"

Or, "You've got a great, smooth swing. Every single shot is supersmooth. Except for that last shot. I could tell you were struggling on that one."

Or, "You were coming over the top a little bit. Do you always start your swing with your shoulder?"

Maybe he didn't, but I want to plant it in his head that he did. If he's a really good secure golfer, he'll shrug it off—but if not, there's a good chance he'll immediately start thinking too much. It's the little things that will screw your opponent up and get them thinking instead of swinging smooth. Pretty soon, it's congratulations time. You've just derailed their swing and their confidence. They might not hit a good shot for the rest of the day.

When someone tries to mess with me, I'll tell them straight

up, "Look, I may have been born at night, but not last night." Don't hustle a hustler.

If you could play a game now with the finest pro golfers— Palmer, Trevino, Daly, Tiger—all from different decades, they would all still be great because their swings are timeless. Bobby Jones's swing didn't change in fifty years. If the Jack Nicklaus of old was competing now, with all the latest equipment and all the great balls and all the changes and strides made in golf today, he would still be winning Masters and PGA Championships. They all would.

Sports, like rock 'n' roll, revolves around its heroes (and anti-heroes) who come in and change the game. Basketball had heroes like Wilt Chamberlain, Bill Russell, and Larry Bird. Then Michael Jordan came along and played two steps above that, and everyone had to hustle to catch up. Golf had heroes with the magic swing, but then Tiger Woods came along, and now *he's* two steps above everybody. Today, whoever is in second place is way below Tiger in terms of tenacity and discipline. The Beatles were like that in music. They set a standard that stands to this day. In my opinion, nobody has ever been more swingin' than the Beatles.

Plus, there are exciting things happening on the LPGA front. I like the idea of women players like Michelle Wie and Annika Sorenstam competing against the men. It makes the game more interesting. Most golfers seem pretty low key, because most pros are so into their game, they might not emit a lot of personality. It's fortunate when you find personalities, truly funny guys like Fuzzy Zoeller, Craig Stadler, Gary McCord, John Daly, or Peter Jacobsen, or a flamboyant golfer like Jesper Parnevik, on the tour. Following a guy like Jim Furyk, who is so good and consistent, is often akin to watching paint dry.

And then along comes Michelle Wie, sweet sixteen *and* she hits the ball every bit as far as Jim Furyk. Plus, she's as pretty as her swing. There's a certain amount of sex appeal to players like Natalie Gulbis that makes the game of golf more interesting.

Annika Sorenstam could play alongside anybody. I believe that without all the pressure, she could play one-on-one in a Skins Game with the guys and she would definitely hold her own.

But heroes and dynamos aside, the bottom line applies to everyone. At the end of the day, like a great drummer, it's gotta swing. You still have to swing the club. It doesn't matter what equipment you have, either. If you took Tiger Woods or Vijay Singh or Phil Mickelson and gave them hundred-dollar sets of pawnshop clubs, they'd probably still shoot 69s. Just like if you saw Eric Clapton, who usually plays a $12,000 Fender guitar, and you handed him a pawnshop special, he'd tune it up and probably play just as well. It's down to this: If you can't swing the club, or if you don't have a solid enough simple swing, the ball's going nowhere.

Ⴘ   Ⴘ   Ⴘ

People who don't know much about golf frequently ask me if I ever thought about going pro. Let me put being a PGA pro golfer into proper prospective.

The first time I shot under par was a major milestone for me. That's because something like .0001 percent of amateur golfers do it. Hell, 90 percent of amateur golfers rarely break 100. So every once in a while I'll shoot a 68 or 69.

That's what Mickelson shoots every day.

Which means that every once in a while, I'll have a round where I could actually compete with Mickelson. But the trick is, Phil does it five days in a row. If I shot a 68 one day, the next day I might shoot 78, followed by an 81. A PGA pro shoots my best score several days in a row. That's why they win the millions.

A lot of people don't realize how great a PGA pro really is, just like some classical musicians don't understand how hard it can be to play great rock 'n' roll.

They are the best of the best. They are the guys and gals who don't miss shots. They do this for a living. They're the difference between a quick-draw trick shooter and a professional killer. The guys on the tour are the two hundred best and baddest players on the planet. Just to get on the PGA Tour, they've gotten by thirty or forty thousand players to make cut after cut after cut, just to get a touring card. To do that, you have to know every shot and perfect every weapon in your bag and inside your head.

Competition in golf, especially now, is fierce, even on the college level. There were kids in my son's high school team whom I couldn't beat—these kids shot three under par frequently! The best kids in college golf can't get on the Gateway Tour, the minor league pro tour, because there are five hundred players better than them. Then, of the people who make Gateway, twenty guys might get their cards, and once they do get their cards, half of them might lose their cards because they're not as good as the two hundred PGA pros. Those two hundred PGA pros are the cream of the cream of the cream.

And then there's Tiger.

What I'm saying is that I know my game, and I'm a long way from being as good as a PGA pro. If I wanted to become a PGA pro, here's what it might take: two years on hiatus from performing, golfing at the level I'm playing at now, and then taking on a teacher like Butch Harmon (the guy who taught Tiger) or David Leadbetter. Then practice eight hours a day to even qualify. Two years out of my life dedicated to the Golf Monster.

I can go out and I might hit the ball as far as a pro. But after eighteen holes, the quality of his play, if you look at the scorecard, will show consistency—he can go up and down at any time, but if he gets into trouble, he knows how to get right back into the game.

Also, a PGA pro doesn't miss four-foot putts. There are things that pros can do that even the best amateurs don't do. They have to know every shot, every angle, the seven basic shots according to Johnny Miller, or they wouldn't be on the PGA Tour. Plus, the one hundred best PGA players have something that we amateurs don't have. What is it?

It's a mystery.

Nobody knows what makes a PGA pro golfer excel with his swing. They just do. Outside of the years of practice and dedication, nothing takes the place of natural talent. If you ask Sergio Garcia to hit a ball twelve yards and make it stop dead, he can do it with his eyes closed. PGA pro golfers, like rock stars, are in another world from the rest of us. While we play the same game, we don't play the same game.

A little advice. Play a pro and expect to get your butt kicked. When amateurs play pros, we want to talk about golf. Get the vital information. The inside scoop. Why do you use a steel-shafted driver? When I play a pro, they want to talk about music, ask me if I ever met Jim Morrison. Usually, I'll steer it back to golf— anything to get the inside information. Any shred of an inside scoop to improve my game and get my swing truly swingin'.

But when you're playing alongside a touring pro, you *really* understand how limited your game is compared to them. It's like when an amateur band plays on a bill with a veteran band. They might play a great set, but once the headliner climbs on stage, that's what separates the men from the boys. That's exactly what happened when we opened for the Yardbirds when I was sixteen.

I'll play with a pro, and often after I hit a good drive, he'll politely say, "Nice drive, Alice. Straight and right where it needs to be." Then he'll shoot an amazing shot, just to remind me, "Oh, and by the way, I'm a pro. You didn't really think you were going to beat me, did you?"

The *Pretties for You* days in Topanga Canyon.
Alice, gaunt and with blondish hair, holds a gas mask.

Chapter 6

The Birth of Alice

IN 1967, THE SPIDERS CHANGED their name to the Nazz. We also got new wheels. My dad bought us a yellow van to haul our equipment back and forth from Phoenix to L.A. In addition to amps and instruments, even though we were barely scraping by, we had our own roadie and lighting guy, the latter a high school art student who traveled with us and liked hanging out. Not a lot of small bands from Phoenix were messing around with lighting. We used different-colored floodlights and a light show, although it was nothing compared to the liquid light shows happening in San Francisco.

One Friday morning, while driving into Los Angeles, someone cut us off. We lost control of the yellow van and rolled over four times before hitting a dead stop. *Who turned out the lights?*

When I woke up, I was lying on the freeway. I was disoriented. Stunned. I barely knew where I was. I saw Glen and Dennis lying close by. The van was a demolished pancake, with amps and gear sprawled everywhere. We all slowly got up and wandered around. I had scratches on my face but no broken bones. Otherwise, we were all in a bit of a shock.

The traffic crew working the freeway that morning assumed that everyone riding inside the van was dead, but all eight of us walked away without a broken bone. When the paramedics arrived, they looked at the van, then looked over at us covered up with blankets, staring at us in disbelief. For a split second, I thought that maybe we *had* all died. Was this the afterlife?

In the days that followed, we asked ourselves over and over how come no one had gotten hurt. After I called my parents, my mom nearly had a nervous breakdown. When she saw a picture of the wrecked van, all she could do was shake her head.

First, I should have been dead from appendicitis . . . now this wreck that should have killed all eight passengers. Nobody in the band wanted to get into a car for days. We were paralyzed with fear. But we came out of it. And luckily we had insurance, so we bought another van and new equipment and soldiered on.

We pushed on and went back to rehearsals. We went for tons of audition gigs. We even landed one at a hot club in L.A. called the Cheetah, where the Doors played a lot. They really liked us. Audition gigs usually meant we didn't get on stage until two in the morning, and even then we were always up against tight, more established bands like Spirit, who I thought was the best band in L.A. (and they weren't even signed yet). We were gaining gradual notoriety as this weird group who had really long hair, were fun to watch, but musically really weren't that great.

We bummed around L.A. for months, taking any gig that would keep us alive. One of the guys might pick up a secretary and take her to his room while we went through her purse. We'd only take about $10, not a lot of cash but just enough to keep the band in cereal and milk. Then somebody else would meet a girl and we'd score another ten bucks. It was just enough to keep us alive. Stealing is not something I'm proud of, but we had to survive, and looking back, that's how desperate we were to stay in Los Angeles.

♀   ♀   ♀

At this point, we learned that there was another hot group in Philly, fronted by Todd Rundgren, who called themselves the Nazz. We needed to change our name again. We sat down and had a band meeting. Over the past months, we had become more theatrical, and admittedly, we had a strange look. So why not call ourselves something spooky? Or instead of being outright spooky, we could go completely in the other direction, which along with our appearance might be even more spooky.

Somebody threw out Husky Baby Sandwich. The first name out of my mouth was a girl's name. Alice Cooper. Alice. Cooper. By the end of the night, the name kind of stuck. There was something about it. I conjured up an image of a little girl with a lollipop in one hand and a butcher knife in the other. Lizzie Borden. Alice Cooper. They had a similar ring.

Next we had to figure out what exactly Alice Cooper would look like.

One of the band's all-time-favorite movies was *What Ever Happened to Baby Jane?*, starring Bette Davis. In the movie, Bette wears disgusting caked makeup smeared on her face and underneath her eyes, with deep, dark, black eyeliner. She looks horrific and creepy because she put on traditional makeup thickly and badly. Another movie we watched over and over was *Barbarella*. One character, the Great Tyrant, was played by the gorgeous European actress Anita Pallenberg. She dressed in black leather with a black eye patch and had switchblades coming out of her. Alice Cooper's look evolved from a composite of those female movie characters, with a little bit of Emma Peel from *The Avengers* added for good measure.

Not bad. The name is Alice Cooper. A guy, not a girl. A group, not a solo act. A villain, not a hero or an idol. A woman killer. Weird. Eerie. Twisted. Ambiguous. It all came together—and nobody was doing anything remotely similar.

On top of it all, everyone in the band was straight.

"Do you know how many girls we're going to get?" I asked the guys prophetically, anticipating the fruits of our new identities. We figured the guys were gonna hate us, but the girls would love us.

Alice Cooper, the anti-hippie freak, in 1972.

Chapter 7

Frank Zappa, Syd Barrett, and the GTOs

RIGHT AFTER DECIDING TO REINVENT ourselves as Alice Cooper, we made our next important connection, a group of girls called the GTOs, otherwise known as Girls Together Outrageously. They were truly . . . well, outrageous. They were a gypsy band of crazed groupies. Miss Pamela, Miss Sparky, Miss Lucy, Miss Christine, Miss Sandra, and Miss Mercy. I first met Miss Christine at Canter's Deli. I told her about our band and the concept. We became friends and the GTOs started dressing us, giving us their old clothes, hand-me-downs, old slips and lingerie.

So Alice Cooper's prototype look became a pair of black leather pants worn underneath a torn black lace slip with some GTO lingerie, smeared Bette Davis makeup, unusually long hair, and black lace gloves. It was shocking—even to the hippies.

We booked our very first live show that would be billed with our new name. The posters listed us as the Nazz, but we were introduced as Alice Cooper at the Earl Warren Fairgrounds in Santa Barbara on March 16, 1968. Also on the bill were Blue Cheer and the Nitty Gritty Dirt Band. Blue Cheer was an earsplitting power trio guided by acid guru Owsley Stanley, while the Nitty Gritty Dirt Band played washboards and acoustic instruments. It was a typical strange billing of the times.

Up to this point, few bands in America performed like the British did, with windmill chords, mad drums, brash in-your-face ego. The American hippie bands were mellow, rootsy, or trippy, groups like the Grateful Dead or Crosby, Stills, and Nash. Even the Doors and Love were slightly laid-back and psychedelized.

There we were, stylistically a cross between an out-of-control freight train and a horrible car crash. We were hard *not* to look at. And we played louder than anybody—and that's saying a lot, being on the bill with Blue Cheer. We turned it up to eleven, loud and in your face, which wasn't the L.A. style at all. No stoned-out shoe-gazers in this band. We looked right into the eyes of our audience with arrogance about who and what we were.

♀   ♀   ♀

After playing our audition gig at the Cheetah, the swinging hip hangout for L.A. hipsters and movie stars, they actually booked us in August of 1968 to play Lenny Bruce's birthday party that would be held there. I saw Steve McQueen there that night, and the Doors, Buffalo Springfield, and a lot of other L.A. bands. There were six thousand people in the audience, the biggest show we had yet to play. We were to go on after the Paul Butterfield Blues Band, a Chicago blues-rock group. When we hit the stage with our blaring amps and scary uplighting, everybody on acid headed straight for the exits. No peace and love or buckskin and beads. We came onstage looking more like *A Clockwork Orange*. We opened our set with the theme from *The Patty Duke Show*. Then it was as if somebody screamed, "There's a bomb in the building!" We literally scared everybody out. We cleared the Cheetah crowd in four songs flat. People couldn't get out of earshot fast enough. We were overbearing and overwhelming. At the end, I looked down and there were five people left: Miss Pamela DeBarres, Vito from Vito's Dancers, two other GTOs . . . and a girl with red hair.

Sherry Cottle booked the Cheetah club. She saw the show and the reaction, and still loved us. She made us one of the house bands, along with the Chambers Brothers.

But we were still homeless. Sherry had a house in Venice with her two kids, and she offered to let us move in with her. So we did—we lived with her and the children.

The next band to roll into L.A. and cause a stir was a group from England called Pink Floyd. We listened a lot to their album *Piper at the Gates of Dawn*. But no one else seemed to know about Pink Floyd—when they first played L.A., about a dozen people showed up to see them. Their light show consisted of lights pointed upward from the edge of the stage, sort of like ours. They also played a similar kind of eerie music, bathed in Echoplex, a crude echo-tape-loop effects device. They dressed very Carnaby Street, with flowered shirts and velvet pants. We became fast friends with this Pink Floyd group. They were bona fide recording artists, while we didn't even have a deal yet.

After Pink Floyd ran out of money in L.A., they moved into Sherry's house along with us. So now Alice Cooper and Pink Floyd were living in Sherry Cottle's three-bedroom house on Beethoven Street in Venice by the beach. All these rock 'n' roll freaks under one roof. Nobody had any money.

I remember we had an audition at Gazzarri's one afternoon, and we had to get the job so we'd have money to contribute toward food and expenses. We got that one, and pretty soon Pink Floyd scored their own gig, so they were able to kick in as well.

They made us these marijuana brownies the day of our audition. I'd never had a grass brownie before, so I ate two. An hour later, my head was buzzing. That night the whole band struggled just to get through the set, and I nearly fell off the stage. Pink Floyd was in the audience, laughing their asses off. To this day, whenever I see anyone from Pink Floyd, we laugh about how they dosed us with those pot brownies.

The legendary Syd Barrett was still in the band then, and I remember him vividly. He used to sit silently in the kitchen, wearing his pink crushed-velvet pants. I'd wake up and there would be a box of cornflakes sitting on the table, and Syd would be watching the box of cereal, transfixed, the same way most of us would watch television. He was that gone early on. I later found out from Roger Waters that Syd was diagnosed with psychosis, so the continual doses of acid only made him crazier. One night we watched as Syd walked out on stage, strummed a chord, got a shock from the mic and his guitar, and just stood there like a statue for an hour, not playing or singing another single note. The band simply played around him.

The Doors frequently played the Cheetah as well. They liked us, and we were certainly no threat to them. "Light My Fire" had already become a huge hit at this point. The Doors were the big shark in the musical pond, while we were the minnows. But they'd let us come into the studio to watch and listen to them record, and that's where we met their producer, Paul Rothchild. We'd sit quietly like church mice in the corner, not wanting to be in the way. Later on, we opened a few dates for them and hung out with Jim Morrison and Robbie Krieger.

♀ ♀ ♀

I had developed a little crush on Miss Christine from the GTOs, and I think she had a little crush on me, too. One night she asked me to come with her to babysit Frank Zappa's kids, Dweezil and Moon Unit, and I gladly came along. Frank lived in a log cabin in Laurel Canyon. He was a major player on the L.A. freak scene. I wanted very much to meet him. He was the legendary bandleader of the Mothers of Invention, as well as an amazing composer and guitar player. He was putting his own record company together and had signed the GTOs as his first group. Later, Christine spoke to Frank about us.

"You know, Frank, I know this band that *nobody* will sign." She was right. Every label had passed on us. "Five guys, and their name is Alice Cooper."

"Nobody likes them?" Frank asked.

"They hate 'em."

That immediately got Frank's attention. "What kind of music do they play?"

"It's the weirdest stuff you've ever heard."

By that time we were writing our own songs, most of which ended up on our first album, *Pretties for You*. One song, "B.B. on Mars," was a minute and a half long with forty-two changes in it. And there were a dozen more of those kinds of songs! Most of our early material didn't make much sense to anybody, including ourselves.

Maybe that's why Frank was intrigued.

"Tell you what," Frank told Miss Christine. "Have them come over to my house and set up at seven and I'll listen to them."

We got to Frank's the next day at seven . . . in the morning. We set up, at 7:00 A.M. at Frank Zappa's log cabin, for a full dress performance with chrome pants and some of the outfits the GTOs had dressed us in. As we started our show, Frank came scurrying downstairs. He clutched his coffee cup, wearing a robe.

"What are you doing?"

"Frank, you said be here at seven."

"I meant seven tonight."

We performed our entire set, including all our new crazy songs, like

"Ten Minutes Before the Worm" and "No Longer Umpire"—songs and lyrics that still don't make any sense whatsoever.

Finally, Frank deferred: "Okay, okay! I'm going to sign you, but only because I don't get it. I don't understand any of your music and how you guys could be this freaky." This coming from the guy whose seminal album was the legendary *Freak Out*!

"Are you on drugs?" Frank asked me.

"No, sir," I answered honestly.

"Where are you from?"

"Phoenix."

Frank shook his head in amazement, still in his bathrobe, holding his coffee cup. "I'd understand if you were from San Francisco or the Village or England, but Phoenix? Okay, I'll sign you."

♀   ♀   ♀

The other house band at the Cheetah, the Chambers Brothers, were our buddies. After we played for Frank, they kindly offered us space to crash in their big house down on Crenshaw Boulevard in Watts, the black ghetto in Los Angeles where, in 1965, there were five days of riots and destruction. They gave us their basement to live in and rehearse in. So we moved to our new place in Watts.

The day before we were supposed to sign our record contract with Frank Zappa, the Chambers Brothers got a visit from Jimi Hendrix, whom we'd met before at the VIP in Phoenix. Jimi remembered us. (We were pretty hard to forget.) We told him about our pending deal with Frank. Jimi asked us if we had a manager. We told him we didn't.

Jimi told us, "I want you to come over to the Landmark and meet someone."

The Landmark Motor Hotel was a wild place. The GTOs were living there, and that's not all—the place was filled with rock stars. Creedence Clearwater stayed there. Jim Morrison stayed there when he couldn't get home. Bob Dylan and Bobby Neuwirth hung out there. It was a real music motel. Anybody who was anybody hung out poolside or lived at the Landmark on 7047 Franklin Street. Janis Joplin eventually died there, in October 1970.

Alice meets the press in Japan in 1973. Manager Shep Gordon stands behind him.

Chapter 8

Managers and Record Deals

THE NIGHT SHEP GORDON FIRST CHECKED into the Landmark, it was about midnight on a night in 1968. Room 224, right in the corner. He'd just quit his job (after one day) as a probation officer at Los Padrinos Juvenile Hall, a half hour down Highway 101 in Downey. Shep had just driven into Los Angeles on a whim without ever even having been to L.A. before, and had been there for only a little while. He saw the "Vacancy" sign lit at the Landmark Motel and pulled in blind.

Around about midnight, Shep heard a girl screaming. Since he'd just come from a jail and was already on his guard, he ran downstairs and saw two bodies tussling outside by the swimming pool, a guy and a girl. Fearing the girl was being raped, Shep threw the guy off her. But instead of being grateful, the girl got up and punched him in the jaw, splitting his lip. She screamed, calling Shep every name in the book.

Turns out the two were making love. Shep went back to his room feeling like a complete idiot. The next morning, he was back down by the pool nursing a big fat lip when he heard a girl laughing hysterically in the corner.

"Are you the guy I hit last night?"

It was Janis Joplin. She was sitting with Jimi Hendrix and the Chambers Brothers. Shep was embarrassed, but the musicians around the pool decided to be kind.

Hendrix approached Shep by the Landmark pool. "What do you do for a living?"

"Nothing I'm happy with." Shep was selling the *L.A. Free Press* on his corner on Sunset Boulevard, in front of Greenblatt's deli.

"Aren't you Jewish?"

"Yeah."

"You should be a manager." Jimi turned to Lester Chambers of the Chambers Brothers. "Don't you have that kid from Phoenix living in your basement? Why don't you introduce him and his band to this guy? He's Jewish. He could be a manager. Maybe he could be *their* manager."

Of course, the kid in the basement was me, and that's how I met my longtime manager and friend, Shep Gordon.

♀   ♀   ♀

At Jimi's suggestion, we arranged a meeting. It seemed as if only a few days earlier, nobody would touch us. Now Frank Zappa and his manager, Herb Cohen, were going to sign us. Then we had someone interested in becoming *our* manager. We headed over to the Landmark Hotel, found room 224, and knocked on the door. When Shep opened it, it was so smoky inside I could barely see into the room.

We walked into Shep's room at the Landmark. I looked over on the couch and saw Jim Morrison and Janis Joplin sitting there puffing away. I knew Jim but had never met Janis before.

Then Shep opened a drawer and took out a handful of cleaned grass and rolled a fat joint. He immediately agreed to be our manager, which sounded like a sweet deal for us. He even offered to move us into the Landmark Hotel. We now had a home, and the next day we were set to sign a record contract with Straight Records with Frank Zappa and Herbie Cohen. We were in business!

♀   ♀   ♀

"Just sign the contract here," Frank and Herbie told us the next day.

"First we have to talk to our manager," I replied.

"What manager?" Frank asked me.

"This guy." I pointed over to Shep Gordon.

"Where did he come from?"

"We met him last night."

"Last night? And now he's your manager?" Frank and Herbie both seemed pissed off.

They placed the contract in front of us and told us they would give us $6,000 a year. Then they said something about publishing. I didn't know what publishing was. Sheet music?

But Shep responded instinctively, "We'll copublish the music." I looked over at Shep. He shrugged. Later he told me that his logic was, if this guy wants all the publishing, then it must be worth something. He said, "We're not going to let anybody buy us for cheap." Shep got the game immediately. He had found his niche—the perfect manager.

Since some of the members (including me) were still underage, we had to legally get our parents to cosign the record contracts with Straight Records that had been set up by our new manager. My parents were wary of us signing any contract. Meanwhile, the band was jumping up and down saying, "Sign the contracts!!!! Please!"

"How about this?" Shep proposed. "I don't get any part of this record deal and we won't have a management contract. You can get rid of me tomorrow if you want to. I have no holds on the band." To this day, Shep and I are still together, going on forty years, and we still don't have a signed contract with each other. From the start, Shep was straight up with me.

We signed the record contract and agreed with a handshake to give Shep his 15 percent. We had signed our first record deal with Frank Zappa!

♀   ♀   ♀

As far as Shep was concerned, 15 percent of nothing was still nothing. He knew he would be providing for us out-of-pocket, and certainly not the other way around. He immediately put us on an allowance until more money came in.

And after hearing his new band rehearse, Shep knew we had a long way to go. But at least we had a record contract and a manager and a stage show. We were on our way. Shep was learning the ropes the same way we were: by doing it and paving the road as we drove it. But he was also highly intuitive.

I was so excited. "When are we going to record our album, Shep?"

"The record is due in a month. So we start tomorrow. What I don't want to do," Shep said, "is to ruin what you've built up so far. I don't want to produce just any record, but I also don't want you to sound like the

Yardbirds or the Who. It's got to sound like you. So I want you guys to play live in the studio. We'll cut the songs numerous times and pick the best takes."

We cut the album in three days. The album had thirteen songs, some barely a minute long, and featured a deluxe double-gatefold album cover. The entire band shared songwriting credits. After we finished recording, we played three nights at the Whisky a Go Go with Frank Zappa and the Mothers.

And that's how we recorded the *Pretties for You* album, released on Frank Zappa's Straight Records in June of 1969. Frank had high hopes for it. There were incentives in our contract for bonus money if we sold more than 150,000 albums. Of course, none of the songs ever got played on the radio.

♀   ♀   ♀

But at least we were a signed band and we were playing more shows, and we got to do festivals with bands like Steppenwolf, the Guess Who, Ike and Tina Turner, John Lee Hooker, Led Zeppelin, Santana, Ten Years After, and some concerts with Frank Zappa. We flew to New York City to play Steve Paul's Scene and lived in the famed Chelsea Hotel for a few days. And there were more shows with other Bizarre/Straight artists, including Wild Man Fischer, Tim Buckley, Captain Beefheart, and the Mothers of Invention. We were usually at the very bottom of the bill, underneath the GTOs.

Right from the start, we were the classic epitome of bad taste. It was 1969, supposedly a very innocent time. On one level the 1960s weren't so innocent, with the counterculture and the antiwar movement. On another level, yes, everybody idealistically bought in to the peace-and-love thing. "If we could all just smoke grass and get along, the whole world would be a better place." Everybody was all about world peace and free love.

Then along came this band called Alice Cooper with a whole new chaotic attitude.

At that time, no one would ever say, "I'm in a rock 'n' roll band for the glamour, the outrage, the art, to write great hit songs, to buy Ferraris, to snag blondes, and wield switchblades." None of that was what bands from the 1960s stood for—or at least they didn't admit it publicly. We did. Even Frank admitted it: "We're only in it for the money." Still, a lot of bands were trying to change the world into a better place while singing in three-part harmony. Nothing about Alice Cooper was harmonious except for our loyalty to each other. As a band, we were close.

We liked living at the Landmark apartments. We scraped by on our record advance, gig money, and cash from Shep. The GTOs also lived there, occupying four rooms on money Frank Zappa gave them. On New Year's Day, 1969, the Ohio State football team checked into the Landmark to play the Rose Bowl. The night before the big game, the GTOs partied with the team—and the next day, Ohio State obliterated O. J. Simpson and USC, 27–16. One day the Ice Capades checked in. Girls on ice! There was a line of ladies' underwear draped over the upper tier. The rock stars were licking their chops.

Alice Cooper was living the life. Twenty bucks a week in our pockets. Our rent was paid. We had rehearsal space at a place called the Psychedelic Supermarket. Thanks to Shep and our association with Frank Zappa, we were playing plenty of dates, but we were still the band that everybody liked to walk out on, nothing more than a curiosity. Now, though, people would listen for three minutes, *then* leave.

Still, with all the touring and rehearsal we constantly put into the band, we *were* getting better. Little by little, we were improving. But, unfortunately, we had worn out our welcome in the Los Angeles area. There was no place left we could play where they could tolerate our freakiness.

What were we going to do?

If we were going to leave L.A., we had to leave for the right reasons. Shep's solution: tour, and move to the first city that gives the band a standing ovation. That sounded like a right enough reason to us.

Alice Cooper with actor Verne "Mini-Me" Troyer. (Getty Images)

The Third Step of Golf Addiction

Play for the Right Reasons

Repel Stress. Gambling and Hustling.
When to Walk Away. Tiger's Two a Side.

One of the "right reasons" I play golf is to achieve Zero Stress. I understand that the average working person has career and family distractions. You slave away in an office or a factory. Maybe you're a corporate road warrior working for the man, all stressed out with back trouble. Or you're worried about the car payment, or whether your daughter is going out with a biker, or if your spouse is spending too much money. Or if you're going to be able to keep your job the next week. No question about it, stress is the biggest killer. It breaks the human spirit and the human body.

You're probably saying, "Right, Alice. You sure got it rough. Look at you. You're a millionaire rock star living in Arizona, one of the prime golfing spots of the world. You got it easy. That's why you can hit the greens seven days a week."

But wait a minute! It's not as if I'm retired. I work as hard as (or harder than) the next guy. My schedule is packed nearly seven days a week. I hold down multiple jobs. Between touring and traveling six months a year, I have my daily radio show, my sports bar and restaurant called Cooperstown, press interviews, and charity events to finance my Solid Rock Foundation. Plus I'm writing a new album. I keep plenty busy.

Most golfers play about twice a month. As a hard-core golf

addict, I'm out on the course every day. And when I tee up on the golf course, even with fourteen things to do later that day, I still don't collect stress. I repel stress. I visualize shooting a 77 or 78 today. When something unforeseen looms over me that I can't control or do anything about—like if someone dies or if I'm in the middle of some tense business negotiations—as soon as I step on the golf course, I deal with it. I don't worry. It'll work out.

Another right reason I play is when I have stupid, insignificant things that worry me. Like, for instance, I may have to do a blood test that afternoon. I'm petrified of needles. So I'll go out and play rather than sit at home and stew about going to the doctor's office. A stupid blood test will drive me nuts, but after I play my eighteen holes, I can deal with almost anything! I've got three radio shows and two interviews to do? Easy! What's my tee time?

Another right reason is to play to reward yourself. If I have a hard day lined up, starting at 1 P.M. and ending at 9 P.M., I'll play eighteen holes from seven until noon. Then I'm ready for any hard day. While I'm hard at work, I can reflect on that day's game.

I'll usually play every day when I'm on tour, a different course every few days. It used to fascinate people that Alice Cooper would be golfing in their hometown, but now they're well aware of my ongoing golf addiction. During my 2006 tour, I showed up at a course in the Midwest and the pro was already there waiting for me—along with the assistant pro and two of their best-playing members. They wanted to take me on.

What about playing for money? Is that a right reason? Some guys want to go out there and play for hundreds or thousands of dollars. To me, golf should be fun. Don't ruin the game by gambling on it. It's enough fun as it is. But sometimes I'll make an exception. I still don't like playing for a thousand dollars a hole, though. That kind of money takes the fun out of the game. It's more tense, and if you're playing round robin, your partner gets angry when you miss a putt. So I'll restrict my wagering to pocket money or a gentleman's bet. If I win twenty bucks, fine. (By the way, I beat the pro and the assistant pro by two strokes at their club, which I had never been on. I won their twenty bucks.)

Some guys play purely for money and don't even like the game. We've all heard about rich athletes who play golf and wager to the tune of $100,000 a round or $20,000 a hole. A gambling addiction on top of a golf addiction—that's scary.

First off, just because you're a brilliant professional athlete doesn't ensure you'll be a great golfer. Second, hotshot athletes and celebrities often attract professional hustlers who know they have the money and they're not afraid to raise the stakes.

Also, some gamblers would rather lose money than admit to playing at a higher handicap. Had they gone into a match with a 15-stroke handicap as opposed to lying about being a 7, they might have won the wager. When you lower your handicap for the sake of your ego, you penalize yourself. Any good golfer knows that a money game is won or lost beforehand by negotiating strokes.

Also, if you're going to play for money, you have to watch out for sharks. Golf courses, like casinos, are rife with hustlers. Anytime someone comes up to you with an outrageous bet, trust me, they can usually do what they bet they're going to do. Show me a guy who offers to play you with a five-iron and a rake, and I'll show you a guy who can shoot a 72 with a rake. Otherwise, he wouldn't make the bet. Those are the real hustlers to watch out for.

Titanic Thompson was a legendary golf hustler (as well as a card cheat and crooked dice thrower) who died in 1974. He was Lee Trevino's mentor when Lee was a little kid barely scraping by. Titanic's strategy was to lose a bet on a golf match, then challenge the guy to a second round, double or nothing, playing left-handed instead of right. If the unsuspecting mark didn't already know Titanic was an ambidextrous scratch golfer, they certainly learned the hard way.

A hustler who is a 7-handicap won't let his ego get in the way. He'll go into a match as a 12 and whip your butt.

I had my brief stint hustling a few golf bets, separating a few unsuspecting country club members from their Benjamins. It seemed like the right reason at the time. I can't get away with it now because I have a reputation, but in my early playing days, when I was a skinny rock 'n' roller playing in cutoffs with a beer bazooka, I'd hustle them good. I'd lose big on the first three or four holes, then end up shooting an 82 and still take home the chips.

"That's the best round I ever played, and I still lost," the losing player would grumble as he handed over a few hundred dollars. I'd be pocketing the money when someone would tap him on the shoulder and say, "He's a 9-handicap, you dummy. Couldn't you tell that by the middle of the round when he was swinging really good and the ball was going exactly where he wanted it to go?"

I'd play a $300 Nassau, a hundred dollars on the front nine, a hundred on the back nine, and a hundred for the total score. I never came in greedy and overconfident, so he wouldn't get wise. I'd let the guy win the front. Then I'd win the back *and* the total, because all of a sudden I got really good and lucky. He'd win one, I'd win one, but I took the total.

Try that in Detroit and you'll get your thumbs broken.

One of the greatest compliments I ever received was when a journalist asked Tiger Woods to rate celebrity golfers. They threw out a few names and he commented. When they mentioned "Alice Cooper," Tiger remarked, "I would not give Alice two a side." In other words, Tiger was saying, "I would not give him the extra two-shot handicap on the front nine and the back nine of the match because he would beat me." It was a very nice compliment.

People were impressed: "Wow. Alice must be really good for Tiger to say that." The truth is, Tiger could give me five a side or six a side and still clean my clock. But it was a very nice thing for him to say anyway, because it enhanced my reputation. For Tiger to say that is like Paul McCartney saying he'd love to write a song with Alice Cooper.

There are three compliments in my life I will always cherish:

1) Groucho Marx saying that Alice Cooper was the last hope for vaudeville.
2) Bob Dylan saying "I think Alice Cooper is an overlooked song-writer."
3) Tiger Woods saying he wouldn't give me two a side.

Three completely different and divergent worlds, yet I'll proudly take and accept those compliments. Of course, Tiger's put the nails in the coffin of my career as a hustler.

Because I play for the right reasons, I never get tired of the game that has brought me so much happiness. Golf inspires me so that each day I play, each round is unique. There are so many facets to the game. You never experience the same shot twice. The ball ends up in the grass differently. I could play a favorite course a thousand times and never field the same shot. Sometimes it's an eight-iron; sometimes it's a seven-iron. Sometimes there's a tree limb in the way. Sometimes there's sand. You have to know every shot in order to become a low handicapper. To shoot decent scores, I have driven, chipped, and putted literally millions of golf balls over the past twenty-five years. It's now ingrained as part of my life. My strengths in golf come from my love of (and addiction to) the game. I don't get mad at the game. I don't get mad at myself. I never throw a club. Golf isn't a misery or a frustration. Golf is the gift that keeps on giving, and for all the right reasons.

The original Alice Cooper band reenergized from living in Detroit, circa 1970.

Chapter 9

Motor City Migration

IN THE SPRING OF 1970, WE RECEIVED an offer to play at a pop festival in Detroit. We were so strapped, we had to borrow gas money to get there. They put us on the bill with a lot of strange groups I'd never heard of, local bands like Iggy and the Stooges, MC5, Frost, Bob Seger, Ted Nugent and the Amboy Dukes. And then there was us, this new band from L.A.!

We got up on stage and plugged in. Technically, I was a local boy and this was a homecoming.

"From Detroit, Alice Cooper!"

Warm applause. Interesting. We really turned it on because the audience liked us. Somebody threw a pink blow-up rabbit toy up on the stage. Then this huge biker jumped up on stage. I was afraid he was going to kill me, so I quickly threw him the pink toy rabbit.

"Kill it!" I commanded.

Next thing, he's stabbing it. The crowd loved us even more. We got the standing ovation we were bucking for. Plus, it was nice to be out of L.A. Detroit! My kind of town!

♀   ♀   ♀

The next day, we felt like fingers that fit into the Detroit glove. The Stooges, MC5, Amboy Dukes, Bob Seger, and now . . . Alice Cooper! We were in.

So according to Shep's plan, we elected to leave L.A. and move to Detroit. Times were still hard. We checked into a hotel on Woodward Avenue, and each time we ran out of money, we'd skip out and check into the next hotel. Then the next one. Then the next one. (By the way, after we

75

scored our first hit record, we went back and paid off each and every hotel. Shep insisted on it. He was opposed to leaving a trail of blood.)

Once we were settled into Detroit, we began working almost every weekend. The Detroit scene was rocking–there were lots of clubs and halls, great places like the Grande Ballroom. Just like the Phoenix days with the Spiders, we played with the top touring British bands, like the Who, Savoy Brown, and early Fleetwood Mac. We were now one of the the local bands who could draw as many fans as some of the visiting headliners. It got to where we didn't need headliners anymore; the local Detroit talent was that red hot. If you were a West Coast band on acid, beware. We're talking a no-frills shot of reality, Detroit style. You had to be tough to play Detroit.

The greatest thing was the camaraderie among the bands. There were about a half-dozen bands who ruled Detroit–and almost every one of those bands had a house. After we had money from a few shows, we rented one in Pontiac on Brown Road. The MC5 had their house in Ann Arbor. The Stooges had a home in Southfield. Band houses were like frat houses. Every weekend, after a Grande Ballroom gig, the question was Who's hosting the party this week? The Amboy Dukes? Two hundred rock 'n' roll revelers would show up. The next week, the party would be at Alice Cooper's house.

We were all pretty much friends, but at the same time, the rivalry and competition was heated. In L.A., it was about climbing up the ladder no matter who you had to step on. In Detroit, it was good old-fashioned, gloves-off, bare-knuckled, fist-in-your-face competition. The locals would show up in droves to see what was going to happen between Alice and Iggy. Last week, Iggy Stooge smeared peanut butter all over his body or rolled around on broken glass? How are we going to one-up them? Let's do something like blow a bunch of feathers around the stage. That always made a Detroit crowd stand right up.

Iggy and Alice. Alice and Iggy. Iggy was the total street-punk sex god– no shirt, his private parts sticking out of his pants. But he was a great performer. The band was so basic and raw, but it didn't matter how well they played. In fact, the Stooges made the Ramones sound like a string quartet. The Stooges were relentless, and no matter what happened to Iggy out there in the crowd–somebody in the audience might knock him out cold, whatever–the band would *never, ever* stop playing. The roadies had to revive

Iggy and set him back upon the stage, but meanwhile the band would go right into the next song. The Stooges were serious customers. I hated going on after Iggy! He wore the audience out. Musically maybe we were the better band, and visually we might have been more stunning, but the Stooges rocked.

♀ ♀ ♀

At the time, we were playing songs from our first album, *Pretties for You*, and our second album, *Easy Action*, which came out in March of 1970. We recorded it in L.A. for the Straight label, but still no radio station would touch it. Yet the band seemed more stable, back in the chips in Detroit. We lived in one big house. We had girlfriends. We were a pretty big deal around town, bringing in about three or four thousand dollars a week, which was not bad dough for a group of West Coast rejects.

In my mind, the Detroit local band scene was every bit as important as Motown Records. While Motown was mighty nationally, we were the rock of Detroit. The top fuel eliminators. The muscle cars that made the Detroit rock 'n' roll scene respectable. When you toured the Midwest (or anywhere else, for that matter) once you admitted you were from Detroit, people showed instant respect for the Motor City and the bands that came from there.

There's a certain arrogance about being a Detroit guy—especially with music and sports. To this day, if you're from Detroit, you feel a sense of pride and acceptance and respect. It was the right place to be, and at the right time—we had something different and new to offer the already-hot local scene.

It was a weird homecoming. I never thought I'd end up back in the city where I was born. Before we split L.A., I'd never heard of the Stooges or the MC5. It was as if there was a private Midwest movement going on that the rest of the country didn't know about. People in Detroit would say, "Morrison's cool, but the rest of the L.A. bands seem so feminine." Typical Detroit. Ballsy. They wanted black-leather-jacketed rock 'n' roll. It was the healthiest rock scene I've ever seen, both then and now. It was great to be back! Go Tigers!

The Alice Cooper billboard traffic-jam stunt in London's Piccadilly Circus in 1972.

Chapter 10

"Eighteen," the Chicken, and the Snake

WHILE WE WERE MAKING OUR NAME in the Detroit area, Shep was still trying to figure out an angle to break us nationally. We'd played some Zappa dates in Seattle and Vancouver along with the Guess Who. After our first two albums, we still hadn't made our *great* record yet, and the Guess Who had some catchy records–"American Woman," "She's Come Undone," "No Time." So Shep traveled to Toronto to meet with Jack Richardson, who produced the Guess Who's records at his production-company studio called Nimbus 9.

Jack Richardson wasn't exactly impressed with us. He didn't want anything to do with Alice Cooper.

But Shep was relentless. He set out to convince Jack, who probably just wanted Shep out of his hair. Shep set up meetings with a couple of concert promoters in Toronto. He was looking for anything that might get us a buzz in Richardson's ear. So while we played the clubs around town, Shep had his eye on the big prize: the Toronto Rock 'n' Roll Revival Show. Shep met with the promoters on how he might be able to help them produce this huge event held at Varsity Stadium. With his help, they ended up selling 60,000 tickets at five bucks a head to the show, which was to be headlined by John Lennon and Yoko Ono's Plastic Ono Band with Eric Clapton *and* the Doors. When they offered to compensate Shep, he deferred.

"I don't want any money. Just put Alice Cooper on between the Doors and John Lennon. That'll be my payment."

During this time, our shows ended with me hacking up feather pillows while shooting off a CO_2 tank to stir the feathers around the stage amid the strobe lights. Wherever we were, just like in Detroit, every time we did that the audience would stand up. We did it at the end of the Rock 'n' Roll

Revival Show and people loved it. John Lennon and Yoko were on the side of the stage, watching us and smiling. It was performance art to them.

But before that, during the middle of our set, someone threw a live chicken on stage. Once I saw it, I threw it back into the audience, thinking that since chickens have wings, it could fly. Wrong. The audience tore it to pieces. What was even scarier was that all along the front row were the people in wheelchairs, and they were more insane than the other fans.

The next day, the buzz of the Revival wasn't John Lennon or the Doors, but this strange Detroit band that killed a chicken on stage.

I never understood where the heck a live chicken came from in the first place. Let's see, somebody is going to the concert in 1969. He's got his wallet. His tickets. His drugs. Beer. Oh yeah! His chicken! Who would bring a chicken to a rock show? Was it on a leash? A pet perhaps?

I always suspected Shep, though I had never confronted him directly about it. Only now, as this book is being put together, he's finally confessed. Shep was the man behind the chicken incident!

There were lots of photos circulated of me throwing the chicken—and, of course, no one could tell that I honestly thought it would fly away. Of course, the overground and underground press blew the incident way out of proportion.

ALICE COOPER KILLS CHICKEN AND DRINKS BLOOD

Frank Zappa phoned me. "Alice, did you really kill a chicken?"

"Not exactly." I told him my side of the story.

"Well, don't tell anybody! Everyone hates you—that means the kids will love you."

The chicken story was the beginning of national notoriety. It's still one of the first questions people ask me today.

♀   ♀   ♀

After we got back to Detroit, Shep contacted Jack Richardson. "So? The chicken?"

"I heard about it."

"Well?"

"Look, I've got this kid working for me. He's an apprentice. He knows a little about production. I'm going to send him over to see you." We had a gig coming up in New York City at Max's Kansas City, and the kid was going to come from Toronto to watch.

Bob Ezrin was a young, classically trained kid with hair down to his shoulders. Kind of a pretty boy born in Toronto. Andy Warhol and his whole group were in the New York club scene audience that night. After Bob heard us, he came backstage.

"I really like that song 'Edgy,' " he said

" 'Edgy'? We don't do a song called 'Edgy.' "

"Yeah, you know, 'I'm edgy . . .' "

"No, Bob," I said. "That's 'I'm eighteen.' "

We had a barn that we rehearsed in back in Pontiac. Ezrin had a plan.

"We're gonna spend seven months of our lives in that barn," Ezrin said. "You'll gig on weekends so you'll have money, but for the rest of the time, we're going to work twelve hours a day and thrash out material from the time we get up in the morning until we can't stand up at night."

And we did. Bob worked us hard. For the entire seven months. He completely deconstructed Alice Cooper and built us back up again.

He first concentrated on me, setting his sights on my vocals. "Look, Alice. When you hear Jim Morrison, you know it's Jim Morrison. When you hear John Lennon, you know it's John Lennon. When I hear Alice Cooper, there's no signature sound there. People may like the live show, but you have no defining handle on your voice and the music."

Bob Ezrin taught me how to sing in a signature voice. We worked on the different voices, an Alice sound. Singing soft. Loud. Growls. Snarls. Croons. Then he worked on a guitar sound with Glen. After that, a drum sound for Neal. He retaught us how to play our instruments. Bob Ezrin became our George Martin. He came in (just like a great golf instructor) and, starting from the bottom to the top, he had us unlearn everything we knew and relearn it better. I had never worked so hard before.

Then it was time to write and put together the *Love It to Death* album with "I'm Eighteen." Pretty soon, songs began to take shape: "Is It My

Body" and "Ballad of Dwight Frye." We economized our sound and arrangements by eliminating 80 percent of the musical excess. We instituted the right key and tempo changes. We sharpened up the lyrics. "I'm Eighteen" was stripped to the bone—simple and direct, right down to the guitar and chorus hooks. And the teenage angst. Simple and raw. Like the Stooges. Tough. Arrogant. But also *funny*—the difference between us and everyone else was that we weren't taking it completely seriously.

"I'm eighteen and I LIIIIIKE it!"

After we recorded *Love It to Death* in Chicago, we sat in the studio and listened to the album. It sounded like the first *real* Alice Cooper album.

♀　♀　♀

By the time the album came out in February of '71, Frank Zappa had already dissolved his Bizarre/Straight labels. Shep, who had set up management shop in New York City, re-signed us to Warner Bros. Records.

Shep and his boys hit the phones, promoting "I'm Eighteen" to radio. One of the first deejays to play the song was a young jock in Missouri named Rush Limbaugh. Meanwhile, Rosalie Trombley, the music director at CKLW-Windsor, the powerhouse AM station across the river from Detroit, had a son who was a big Alice Cooper fan. He wanted us to play at his high school. We found out about it and gladly did the gig. Rosalie eventually made "I'm Eighteen" her Pick Hit of the Week. It became their most requested song. Then it charted. Then we were number one in Cleveland. We had a hit! We now garnered larger offers of $8,000 to $10,000 per gig. *Rolling Stone* was covering us. Could this be the same band that scared the hell out of everybody at the Cheetah in L.A.? What's this new sound?

Alice Cooper now had a hit record, which made Bob Ezrin look like a genius. (Which he was.) On top of that, we already knew how to put on a shocking and exciting live show. We had eight years of accumulated experience treading the boards. Now we had a vibrant sound and real songs to go along with the show. Warner Bros., the same label that had James Taylor and Van Morrison, suddenly had this weird album with a bubbling hit single on their hands. A lot of people, including rock music insiders, didn't really get it . . . but they liked it.

♀ ♀ ♀

I was backstage at a show in Florida, on our very first headlining U.S. tour, when this groupie came in with a small boa constrictor wrapped around her arm. It scared me— I jumped. Then I thought, *Hmmm, if I reacted that way to a snake, other people will too. Alice Cooper should have his own fifteen-foot boa constrictor on stage. It could be pure shock value—and people are going to hate it!* So we adopted a snake (instead of a chicken) into our live show.

Snakes are the easiest reptiles to take care of. They eat once a month. They're deaf. They're terrified of being dropped. They will only attack you if they think they can swallow you. God gave them the eyes and instinct to look at a guy like me and know that they definitely can't swallow me . . . so why kill me? It's in a snake's nature not to kill you. He's looking at you hoping you'll give him a rat to eat later.

When you put a snake around your neck, why do they curl around you? Simple: so they won't fall. When I put a snake around my neck, I grab him by both ends. Now he's secure and he knows he's not going to fall. Snakes are curious. They'll give you that little tongue thing because they have horrible eyesight—they're simply smelling and sensing heat. Most snakes have absolutely no reason to bite you. On stage they'll check out the audience. I find them very theatrical. Their temperaments do vary—I've had snakes that were a little more nervous than other ones, but I know how to handle them. I've never once had a snake open their mouth and try to bite me.

The bigger the snake, the less often they eat—maybe a couple of times a month—because they'll eat bigger things and digest them slower. I can look at my snake and I'll see if he's shedding. That's okay—they don't eat then. But if his eyes are glassed over, that means he's ready to eat. So I won't use him—I'll give him a rabbit or a rat and three days to digest it. The next sign of the eyes glassing over, they're ready to eat again.

My snakes have had lots of interesting names. Boa Derek. Julius Squeezer. Yvonne was our favorite, a monstrous-looking snake but the sweetest thing in the world. She never hurt anybody. She loved being picked up.

Most of my snakes grow up in captivity and are docile. One time we were booked to play in South America and I was going to bring my snake— we didn't find out until right before we left that we couldn't bring a snake into the country without it spending weeks going through quarantine. So the promoters promised us a snake.

Once I got backstage and opened up the bag, out pops this snake, snapping.

"Whoa!"

"What?"

"Where did you get this snake?"

"We went into the jungle and found him."

I couldn't use that snake. Somebody had trudged out into the jungle and picked up a snake off a tree, a snake that had never been touched by human hands. They put it in a bag and brought it backstage. They figured that's how we got our snakes. My snakes are like lambs, like babies. This snake had never seen a human being. Of course, he's going to be freaked out by putting him in front of a huge audience of screaming fans.

♀   ♀   ♀

In 1971, fueled by our big radio hit and elaborate theatrical stage show, the Alice Cooper band became one of the very first arena rock attractions! More production. We were the first band to use track lighting. We had attitude galore, and we weren't about to back down now.

But at the same time, it all was supposed to be funny. Our interviews were meant to be humorous. I wound up on several magazine covers, from *Rolling Stone* to *Forbes*. Kids absolutely loved us, while parents totally despised us.

Because of urban legends–"Alice Cooper worships the dead and is cruel to animals!"–we were instantly banned in England on our UK tour. But as "Eighteen" went top ten worldwide, and once the Brits realized there wasn't a real reason to ban us and that we weren't burned-out druggies, we sold out Wembley Arena.

While we were over in Britain, Shep's plan was to *really* stick it to the English. We hired Richard Avedon to shoot a racy fashion photo session of me lying naked with a boa constrictor wrapped around me. We blew up one of the photos of me and put it on a lorry (truck) and "stalled" the truck on Piccadilly Circus during Friday-afternoon rush hour. We made the front pages of the British papers for stopping traffic in London. The British "got it." It was an old-fashioned Hollywood-style publicity stunt, and they loved it! I guess we appealed to their dry sense of humor, because British music fans embraced us long before Americans did. They voted us as a number-one band in one of their weekly music polls over Led Zeppelin and the Stones. We came back from London as big stars, and a lot of Americans assumed we were British even though we were actually this little band from Phoenix who had traveled to Los Angeles, Detroit, Toronto, London, and then back again to the States.

The rumor mill was always our best friend. As the Alice Cooper circus pulled into the next city, there were four or five new fables of gore and excess awaiting us.

"I heard you set a German shepherd on fire on stage." Or: "I heard Alice bit the head off a bat:" They were incredibly imaginative rumors, and I could only shrug and say, "That's a good one. I haven't heard that one yet." One of my favorites was "I heard your father is Mr. Green Jeans on *Captain Kangaroo*." Man, where did they get that one?

Alice teeing off at the 2004 Kraft Nabisco Championship.
(Courtesy of the Kraft Nabisco Championship. Photo by Scott Avra)

The Fourth Step of Golf Addiction

Let the Adrenaline Flow

Sword in leg. Bright pink pants. Beauty of the desert.

The stamina of performing rock 'n' roll in front of an audience is purely adrenaline-based. When you have adrenaline pumping through you, it feels wonderful. It's by far the most powerful onstage drug. It has an addictive jolt all its own.

There have been times when I'll go on stage sick with a bad sinus headache or the flu. Before the show, I'll be sneezing and suffering. I can't picture myself playing Alice that night. I'll look around the stage. If my head is throbbing, can I sit down at a certain point and make it look like part of the show? Honestly, I'll start thinking like that.

Then I come back to reality. The thought of canceling a show or phoning it in never occurs to me. I'm a professional. The show must go on! It's part of my being. There's no such thing as making an excuse to the audience—they've just paid their hard-earned bucks to see you. If you feel horrible, they don't have to know that. I suck it up and climb on stage, and once I'm in my makeup, and the lights go down and the crowd roars, the adrenaline kicks in and takes over. Now I'm home free. Take away the audience and I'm dying again. The audience is giving me such a boost that by the end of the show, I've never felt better the whole day than during those precious two hours. As soon as the show's over, I crash-land on my hotel bed, but for those two hours the illness is gone.

I carry around a real sword on stage, a sharp one that I can stick into the stage floor, just to let the audience know that it is a real dueling sword. One night while I was on stage during a tour in Europe, I accidentally put the sword right through my thigh. It went right through my leg and out the other side—I took my hands off the sword and there it stayed, sticking in my leg. Of course, the audience thought it was a trick sword, but the band knew otherwise. I was squirting blood all over, and I thought it looked great. The audience loved it.

After I pulled the sword out and stuck it back into the floor, there were puddles of blood everywhere I walked. My pants were soaked in blood. But it really didn't hurt that much—my adrenaline level was so staggeringly high, I couldn't even react to it. (This was also back when I was still drinking, so I guess I was a little bit anesthetized from the alcohol, too.)

The next day, I could hardly limp off the bus. I wondered how I was going to be able to perform the next concert. I could barely walk for the entire day, but as soon as that night's show came along, it was as if nothing was wrong with me. I was all over that stage—proof positive that I really do live to be on stage, that when the adrenaline is pumping, nobody or nothing, not even a sword through my limb, can stop me from being up there.

Nothing that crazy has ever happened to me on the golf course, but the adrenaline should always be pumping—every game, pretend there's a crowd ready to watch you strike your drive just right. I play at home in Arizona, where golf spectators are often accused of being rowdy and out of hand. At the Phoenix Open, the sixteenth hole is affectionately known as the Frat Hole—thousands of people get loose (and maybe a little drunk) during the Pro-Am tournament. The crowd makes a lot of noise for whoever is on the tee hitting the ball. They'll cheer when you're walking up, scream out your name. It never distracts me—to be honest, it makes me feel like a hero. Adrenaline plays a major role in any golf game if there's a ton of people watching, and it puts you on your best game.

When I first started playing tournaments, I was pretty low key. I would dress exactly like everybody else. I didn't want people to notice me or to be seen as outrageous. I didn't want to stand out, because I was already Alice Cooper trying to play golf. Since I wasn't a very good player, I just wanted to blend in and be the average golfer dude so that people would accept me as just one of the guys.

Then, when I started getting better, I went to the other extreme. I dressed flamboyantly, because I found out that the more people looked at me, the better I played. It set off a wild golfer's chain reaction: The more I showed off, the more I was the center of attention; the more pressure that was put on me, the better focused I became; and the more I concentrated, the better I played. So I started going to tournaments in bright pink pants and black shirts, even though I might get razzed. Whatever you're wearing, you'd better be able to back it up.

It was my way of putting myself on the spot in order to force myself to play better. It was something totally opposite to what I was doing when I first started playing, when I was unsure of my game. As soon I gained confidence, that's when I became rock 'n' roll again. If you look as crazy as me, you'd better play good. It was like that when I'd walk on stage with the makeup on, looking as outrageous as we did when we played in Detroit. You'd better deliver, boy, or they're going to laugh you right off the stage.

Whenever I play shows with a band as legendary as the Rolling Stones, trust me, I'll be on my best game that night. I'm going to be so focused, it has to be a good show. I'm playing with the champs. I may not steal the spotlight from Mick and Keith, Charlie and Ronnie, but I'm going to give it my best shot. I'm certainly not going to wilt into a wallflower. If you're Charles Barkley with the big mouth, and you can score thirty points a game and jam the rock in the hoop, then go for it! Because you can back it up. If you're Muhammad Ali and you're reciting poetry about your opponent, making fun of him, *and* you can knock him out when you say you're going to, then great. Live it up! These are the guys who inspire me.

In this game, amateurs are not good enough to really trash-talk. We just want to get it on the green. We just want to get it in the hole somehow. We just want to satisfy our addiction with a few good shots and avoid the Golf Monster.

Guys like John Daly can trash-talk. If he tells you that he's going to hit it over that tree, bounce it off the cement, and land it a few yards next to the hole, he'll do it. People love that. It's like Babe Ruth pointing to center field, then parking a long home run into the center-field bleachers. That's great if you can do it; if not, don't open your mouth! I think there are times when I'm playing so consistent that, yes, I may let my ego loose and show off a little bit. But it's all for show, and generally I'm not much of a golf trash-talker or a showman on the links. On stage as Alice, it's a whole different story.

There have been times when someone challenged me: "You can't hit over that lake. That's 260 yards. You can't possibly hit it that far." I'll look at the lake, and if I know how I'm hitting the ball that day and the adrenaline is pumping and I'm really confident, I'll go for it. There are also days when I won't do it because I know my swing isn't fluid. Still, the days when I'm hitting the ball well, I feel as if I can hit the ball as far as anybody.

Let the adrenaline flow at all times. If you're nailing the ball on every level, get into the zone, stay there, and let it flow.

Know your best time of day to play. I'm much more effective as an early bird, so I play in the morning. If I get up when the sun is coming up, I'll play great. There's something about how nature erases the mental blackboard every time I wake up fresh in the morning.

I don't like playing at noon. If I'm in a tournament and my tee-off time is 12:10, that's too much time for me to think. That means I'll have to get out there at about 10:30, hit some warm-up balls, putt a little bit to get a feel of the greens, maybe sign a bunch of autographs . . . then, by the time I get to the first tee, half my energy and concentration is sapped. Signing autographs all day on a celebrity golf course takes more of your energy than hitting that golf ball.

But in the morning, I tee up without as much as a warm-up shot. I'm pumped. All my adrenaline is popping. Everything seems new. I haven't had the chance to get irritated with anybody. No lousy phone calls, indigestion, or other sidetracks and hassles. The morning is pure. To me, that's the greatest part of the day.

When I get up and play at 6:30 in the morning, and I'm in the desert with the Arizona sun coming up, it's a beautiful and inspirational sight to behold. And it's quiet. When I'm in the middle of the desert at the beginning of the day, I can't imagine playing any other time. Most of the guys on the course out that early look at each other and we're all thinking the same thing: *Isn't this the life, getting up early in the morning?*

I'll purposely loft a ball into the desert just so I can venture out into the dry air and utter a golfer's prayer: "This is great. What a great desert. What a great time this is." Just to share a few seconds of private meditation. To me, part of the game of golf involves giving thanks and acknowledging the beauty of my surroundings. I'm blessed that golf is a game where I can enjoy the beauty of the desert.

Whoever thought an addiction could be so peaceful?

Alice models the controversial paper panties
wrapped around the *School's Out* album.

Chapter 11

School's Out Forever

UNDER THE TUTELAGE OF BOB EZRIN, we now crafted better songs. Hit songs, the stuff that will put the icing on the cake. Nobody was going to care about Alice Cooper if we didn't have hit records. Critics and writers could have dismissed us as a novelty act. "Don't worry. Alice Cooper will soon go away. People will tire of this character and forget about him. His fifteen minutes are almost up."

But once you factor in hit records, then the game changes. It was much harder to write a hit record back then than it is now. When "I'm Eighteen" became a Top Forty hit, we were in competition with the best: the Supremes, Carole King, the Rolling Stones, the Bee Gees, the Jackson Five, Simon & Garfunkel, Dean Martin—whoever occupied the charts at a given moment.

"No More Mr. Nice Guy." "School's Out." "Elected." "I Never Cry." "You and Me." "How You Gonna See Me Now?" "Poison." They were all Top Forty hit records. Bob Dylan mentioned in a *Rolling Stone* interview that Alice Cooper was an overlooked songwriter. Then John Lennon said his favorite song was "Elected." Now we had a Beatle and Bob Dylan praising us. Who would have believed it? We gained more and more credibility.

When we first started doing press interviews, I sort of winged it. I cited my high school influences, Dalí and surrealism. As the villain of rock 'n' roll, I was making it all up as we went along. Feeding the press often meant giving them lines like:

"The sicker our fans get, the sicker we'll get."

"Rock music is sex music and violent music."

"We are the group who drove a stake through the heart of the Love Generation."

"I've got a Peter Pan complex with a Captain Hook personality."

Parents really hated us. But the kids knew. Alice was going out of his way to piss off the status quo–mongers.

Meanwhile, back in Arizona, my mom and dad were seeing their son on magazine covers, getting a slew of top-ten hit records. I was featured everywhere, even in women's publications like *Cosmopolitan* and *Redbook,* in articles like "Should You Let Your Kids See Alice Cooper?" My father the pastor was getting called on the carpet. The press was knocking on my parents' door.

Finally, my mom and dad flew out to Omaha to watch a big concert. *Rolling Stone* was there to do a story on us. They printed pictures of me and my mom and dad backstage. After so much press speculation about how he felt about his son, my dad laid it on the line to them: "I know my son. I know who this Alice Cooper is. He's as normal as anyone else, except that he's got a very artistic way of expressing himself. He's no drug-addled Satanist. I understand his sense of humor."

Wow. My dad stood up for me. I was deeply moved—but hardly surprised, given the kind of man he was.

When *Love It to Death,* our first album produced by Bob Ezrin, became a hit album, we were as surprised as anybody. Back then, you were normally contracted to record and release two albums of material per year, not one album every three years like today. Then, after you recorded your album, you toured your butt off, came back, cranked out another album's worth of songs in the studio, then you toured again, then did *another* album and toured some more. It was a seemingly endless, exhaustive cycle, but we embraced it and accumulated an impressive catalog of songs.

So, as soon as the Love It to Death tour was over, we were back in the studio working on our follow-up. We already had a few ideas for songs, and once again, Bob Ezrin slapped them into shape, turning them into polished gems. We were out to prove to ourselves that we were a real band rather than just a theatrical act. We had one song, "Halo of Flies," a seven-minute piece designed to show the Emerson, Lake & Palmer and the King Crimson fans and the other prog rockers that we could play our instruments. "Halo of Flies" as a single actually went to number one in Holland. The straight press, the music press, and recording industry insiders got tired of resisting. Alice Cooper couldn't *accidentally* cut five platinum albums in a row. Maybe there was something to this group.

Killer, with "Be My Lover" and "Under My Wheels," was the sixth-biggest-selling album of 1971. It's our best album, according to a lot of critics, as far as pure rock 'n' roll goes. I agree with that, because it was an extension of *Love It to Death*—the songs came quick and easy. We would write and arrange them, and then Bob would throw in a few clever ideas. Maybe he'd add a piano part or an oboe here or a cello there.

At first we would say, "Oboes and cellos? Not on our records you don't."

"You're not even going to hear them," Ezrin clarified, "but they're going to be there. Wait and see. They're going to back up the bass line."

We had no idea what Bob was talking about, but the end result made our tones richer. We learned that producers use little tricks to make an album sound fuller, using instruments and devices we never dreamed of.

As band members, we wrote separately and together. Mike Bruce wrote "Be My Lover," with simple chords and rhythm. Dennis used a more complex psychedelic approach, coming in with songs like "Under My Wheels." As a lyricist, I tried to be specific and not as abstract as Dennis. I liked my lyrics to be more direct and tell a story in three minutes. I patterned my writing after Ray Davies of the Kinks, who could tell an entire life story in three minutes, whereas Dennis was more like e.e. cummings and let his lyrics float along and allow the audience to invent their own story.

Whenever a band song came in that was a little too "out there," I would clear things up a bit. Since I was the guy who usually wrote the lyrics and sang the songs, that was my job. Thanks to working with Ezrin, soon I could sit and hear all the parts in my head. Songwriting became easy. Ezrin taught me a few formulas. Verse, B-section, verse, B-section, half-chorus, guitar, chorus, chorus, out. Or a little bit different structure: verse, B-section, chorus, verse, B-section, chorus, break, chorus, chorus, out. There were certain formulas to adhere to when making a hit record . . . but on the other hand, since we were Alice Cooper, we couldn't afford to be too predictable.

♀   ♀   ♀

At that time, "I'm Eighteen" was serving as our first and primary signature song. Every successful band wanted one: The Stones had "Satisfaction" (even though they'd written twenty songs that were better); "My Generation" was the Who's anthem. While "I'm Eighteen" was a strong hit, we still weren't satisfied. We lacked the definitive Alice Cooper signature tune. So we set out to rectify the situation.

Question: What are the two happiest moments in a young person's life?

Answer: Christmas morning and the last day of school.

I thought back to my own school days, looking at the clock. Three minutes left before three months of summer vacation. I remembered that anticipation, as the seconds ticked down. If we could only write a song capturing those final climactic three minutes of the last day of school.

So we did. The song was called "School's Out," and the opening guitar riff was recorded to sound like someone shaking their finger at you: "Na, Na, Naaaa, Na, Na, Naaa, Na, Na, Na, Na." Like a little kid "na-na-nanny-ing" at the world, but done on a guitar. We wanted to re-create that sneering and snotty vibe: "I don't have to go to school anymore . . . no more teachers, no more books, no more teachers' dirty looks . . . out for summer, out 'til fall, we might not come back at all . . . got no class, got no principles, got no innocence . . . "

"School's Out" was pure punk, but as catchy as pop. We added a rhythm at the bottom of the song that was a cross between Ravel's *Bolero* and "Beck's Bolero." The whole band wrote it together. I penned the lyrics, and once again, Bob Ezrin was there directing us and egging us on. He added in the children's voices, a trick he would repeat years later when he produced Pink Floyd's "Another Brick in the Wall."

"School's Out" was written in a rock era where you couldn't predict what an immediate hit was going to be. Yet as soon as *we* heard it, we looked at each other and gasped, "This is gonna be a monster."

It was an immediate hit. The single went straight into the American top ten as soon as it was released. It also shot to number one in England. It didn't need any special hype or promotion—it nailed the experience of being released from an educational government institution, that elated feeling of freedom, and kids everywhere got it.

Now there was no doubt. Alice Cooper was for real. Our remaining detractors had been silenced for good. You couldn't argue. Once "School's Out" hit the *Billboard* Top Ten, it became the definitive Alice Cooper anthem.

♀   ♀   ♀

The *School's Out* album was an example of fun and excessive packaging. We worked with a group of graphic artists who did all of our album covers. Those guys were a lot like us. We worked well together, throwing out ideas. What if a kid lifted up his desk on Monday after the weekend? What would he find? What if he produced a pair of panties? Then he was *the guy*! What else might be inside the desk? A switchblade? Notebooks? I had an idea.

"Let's wrap the next record inside a pair of pink panties instead of a dust cover." A typical Alice Cooper formula: Kids will love it; parents will hate it.

The entire concept changed: The album cover would transform into a desk that would actually unfold so you could open it. We scratched our own names into this desk that they would take a picture of for the cover. The original carved desk now lives in a Hard Rock Café.

It had gotten to the point where our label, Warner Bros., was telling us, "Do what you guys do." And their art department agreed: "Tell us when it's done." When we brought the package in and presented it to them, everyone laughed. It was Alice Cooper—and coming off two platinum albums, nobody was going to say no to us. They liked our concepts. Three of the original band members, Dennis, John Speer (our first drummer), and I—were all art majors. I probably would have worked as a graphic artist if I didn't sing the songs.

Warner Bros. released *School's Out* in July of 1972, right after school was out. You couldn't buy the kind of publicity we received. The album was soon banned. Why? The panties the record was wrapped in didn't conform to Federal Trade Commission standards—they weren't fireproof!

Of course, my response was "Who would be lighting a cigarette or a match down there anyway?"

So now we had 100,000 pairs of pink, white, or blue paper panties wrapped around the first pressings of *School's Out* albums that were considered a fire hazard by the U.S. government. Today the album pressings with the panties are collectibles on Goldmine and eBay. Sometimes the best thing is to get banned. It was another Alice Cooperism that went on to shape our destiny and reputation.

Alice and Michael Bruce in the back of a police escort car in South America
during the 1973 Billion Dollar Babies tour.

Chapter 12

Alice as Macumba!

SCHOOL'S OUT WAS AN ARTISTIC ROCK LANDSLIDE suc-cess. We were bigger than ever. I strolled on stage wearing a top hat and cane, and kids started wearing top hats and makeup on the back streets of London. People actually wanted to look like Alice Cooper. British football hooligans dressed like us. We helped change the style and the look of rebellious kids all over the world. We influenced major cine-matic pop culture works and major musical trends. For instance, John Lydon, a.k.a. Johnny Rotten of the Sex Pistols, frequently cites Alice Cooper as a major musical influence. In fact, when he auditioned to become the lead singer of the Sex Pistols, he did so by miming and gyrat-ing (not singing!) to "I'm Eighteen" playing on a jukebox. John knew all the words to my songs. He used to sit on the couch at home in London's Finsbury Park and listen to Alice Cooper records with his mother. John and Sid Vicious used to busk in the London tube stations, singing "I Love the Dead."

The Rocky Horror Picture Show was also bolstered by Alice Cooper imagery. I once saw the director's notes for the movie, and sprinkled throughout the margins was comments like "à la Alice Cooper." It was funny how much of a pop icon Alice had rapidly become. For the band—the top hat, slathered-on makeup, black lingerie and gloves, cane—it was just what we did. Alice had tentacles reaching into the outer reaches of art, movies, and popular culture.

Next came *Billion Dollar Babies* in February 1973. That was us making total fun of ourselves. We're Billion Dollar Babies, a bunch of "babies" from Phoenix that large multinational corporations (starting with our record company) were now throwing money at. The same guys who couldn't get a

99

gig because we were too weird . . . and now, everybody wanted a piece of us. The cover was fashioned as a giant wallet with cash strewn, and babies with eye makeup. We were laughing at our audience and at ourselves and at the circus spectacle and absurdity of our success.

While we were recording the title track for the album, Donovan was in the next studio. I was drunk enough to stagger next door and walk into his studio.

"Hey, Don, I love what you're doing. Now come in here and sing some real rock 'n' roll." I showed him the lyrics. "I promise your fans will love this."

So instead of Mick Jagger or Marc Bolan from T.Rex, we chose Donovan to guest-star on our record. And he loved it. We had so much fun singing together on that track.

"Do you want me to sing evil?" he asked.

"No," I said. "Sing it with a snobby, pinky-in-the-air, upper-class British accent. I'll be right next to you with my evil voice. 'We go dancing nightly in the attic.' " Such a great duet.

Then Bob Ezrin brought in another song called "Hello, Hooray," written by one Rolf Kempf, a guy in Canada who was struck with polio as a child. Judy Collins (of all people) recorded the tune before we covered it. We wanted our version to sound like Alice Cooper meets *Cabaret*, complete with that bawdy pre–World War II German burlesque sound from when Deutschland was oblivious and drinking, carousing and cross-dressing its way to decadent destruction. When Bob brought it in, we all agreed it was important to add the big fat chords and a grand bravado intro. It became the perfect opening salvo for our live concert show. Once the audience heard the opening two notes, they went crazy. Then the lights would come up. Voilà! Show time! I thought the fact that we didn't write the song was even cooler. Every once in a while, I'll still open the show with that song.

To me, recording studios were playgrounds where I could let loose and have a little fun. And not just at our sessions, either. I remember when the Doors were holed up at a studio on the corner of Sunset Boulevard and Highland Avenue. The place was called TTG, which allegedly stood for Two Terrible Guys. This was around 1967 when they were recording *Waiting For the Sun.* At the same time the Doors were at TTG, Frank Zappa and the Mothers of Invention were recording upstairs in the big studio. So for kicks and danger, Jim and I used to hang from the upstairs studio railing, off the second-floor landing, dangling about 25 feet from the floor. Jim Morrison, who, like Keith Moon, knew no fear when it came to a dare, was a great rock star and poet and sometimes just a big kid fueled by drugs and alcohol.

♀   ♀   ♀

In 1973, I was drinking fairly heavily, but not dangerously. I drank lots and lots of beer, but I was eating well, too. I was in pretty good shape to tour when we started the Billion Dollar Babies Tour. Shep told us that South America was calling about staging a big concert in São Paulo. Population: 19 million people.

I said, "Let's go down and do the show. We seem to have played every-place else. Why not Brazil?" We didn't know what to expect.

Once we arrived in São Paulo, we realized the promoters had already sold 158,000 tickets. Not outdoors at a soccer stadium, but an indoor venue! The place was seven times bigger than Madison Square Garden. Other bands had played there but apparently didn't sell as many tickets. Kiss played there and sold about 140,000 tickets.

I guess we didn't know how big we were there. Once we motorcaded into the city, I was furnished with eight bodyguards—muscled, James Bond–type guys. The press was everywhere. Coopermania was going strong in São Paulo. My personal driver commandeered the streets like a Formula One racer. He was also packing serious heat. He might have been an ex–naval intelligence guy; he ran the whole security team. Just to get to the hotel, we changed cars three times. First we would drive down into an underground parking lot and switch cars. Then I was stashed under-neath a blanket before we'd pull out. One car would go one way and we'd go the other. The press would follow the wrong car and we'd head off in the opposite direction. But once we got to the hotel, more press were waiting.

We held a press conference and 30,000 people showed up. Two people got killed at that press conference, stabbed in the bathrooms. The army was there. A baby was born. C'mon! This was supposed to be just pre–rock concert hype.

What was going on? Shep and I figured that maybe they didn't get that many major concerts in Brazil. "Wow, we're as big as the Beatles down here! What's up with that?"

Eventually, we figured it out. Picture what I look like at the time: the black makeup, holding up a huge serpent. Apparently, a significant percentage of people who live below the equator believe in macumba, the Brazilian equivalent to Santeria. Some who publicly practiced Catholicism were privately into macumba. So not only was I rock star, I was perceived as some sort of macumba priest or apparition. The loud music, the horror images, the urban legend and rumors that followed us—it all fed into the macumba vibe. The front page of the paper had a picture of me with my huge snake, wearing full makeup. Emblazoned in huge letters across the picture: "Macumba!"

As far as I was concerned, I was just playing a character. But to the people of São Paulo, our appearance had deeper, more spiritual implications. We didn't even know what macumba was, much less that we were inadvertently incorporating some sort of religious symbol into our records and concerts. But we were macumba personified.

The concert itself was impossible. With 158,000 Brazilians indoors, when they clapped their hands in unison, the result was a deafening din. Throw in the screaming and partying and you've got utter voluminous chaos. We couldn't hear a single note on stage because of the strange barrage of white noise. Once the band started playing, I became disoriented. Forget the monitors and sound system—I couldn't tell where we were in the song! I tried standing next to an amp to hear where we were. Then I tried looking over and spotting the guitar chords just to get through "I'm Eighteen." We played about forty-five minutes. It wasn't so much a concert as just a raw display of rock 'n' roll. But it was quite an event.

Weeks later, I saw a photo of the band on stage. The army was stationed all along the front of the stage. The audience was on the floor. Upon closer inspection, I noticed a guy in the audience pointing a pistol at the stage. There was a policeman standing in front of him with his holster empty. The guy must have taken the pistol out and aimed it at me. Nobody noticed the gunman until later when we saw the photograph. Perhaps it had something to do with macumba, but to me, it looked more like an assassination attempt.

After playing that momentous gig in São Paulo, *The Guinness Book of World Records* gave us the world record for playing in front of the largest indoor audience ever. The Alice Cooper band had invented arena rock and become the ultimate road warrior rock machine.

Celebrity group shot at the 2004 Michael Douglas & Friends Golf Tournament in Cascata Golf Club in Boulder City, Nevada.
Left to right: Kyle MacLachlan, Shelby Lynne, Luke Wilson, Mark Wahlberg, William Petersen, Leslie Nielsen, Robert Wagner, Michael Douglas, Andy Garcia, Martin Sheen, Haley Joel Osment, Heather Locklear, Kenny G, Alice Cooper, Tom Arnold, and Joe Pesci. (Courtesy of Michael Douglas & Friends Tournament)

The Fifth Step of Golf Addiction

Play on the Road! Play All Over the World!

Moscow City Golf Club. Alice Cooper: 009.
Golfing in the midnight sun.

Whenever you hit the road, take your clubs along for the ride! In my line of work as a touring rock star, I've played on the greatest golf courses in the world. Every year I tour the United States, Europe, and various points around the world. Like me, many of you travel nationwide and worldwide because of your job. With tens of thousands of golf courses in the world, you owe it to yourself to give your game a boost and play at as many exotic courses as you can.

I've played a lot of different places, including almost all of the courses rated in the Top 100—all except the Augusta National Golf Club, home of the Masters Tournament. Although I've been invited to play Augusta, the two times I was serious about going was when they had a tornado and a flood in the region. I figure the man upstairs was trying to tell me something. If you ask anyone in Middle America where they would like to play, most likely they'll answer Pebble Beach or Augusta. I've played Pebble Beach many times at the AT&T Tournament, the biggest Pro-Am celebrity tournament in the world. When you play that one, you've arrived! And could you find a more pristine place to put a golf course than Pebble Beach? The resort atmosphere, the crashing waves of the Pacific next to the bunkers and splendid greens—it's perfect. The coastline landscape is so breathtaking that it doesn't matter what you shoot.

Certain courses are fun to play at, just to experience their complexity. Some are ridiculously hard because of distance. Some courses are just designed to make even players like Jim Furyk sweat.

Every course has its own distinct personality. That's the amazing thing about golf. Every tennis court looks the same to me. Every basketball court and football field looks the same to me. Every baseball stadium, the actual playing field, is basically regulation. But every golf course is a total one-of-a-kind design. Every hole is designed to conform to the contour of a unique environment. The course designer decides where the sand traps belong, and—look out!—if there's a big tree in your way, you'll have to cut a shot around it. There's never a dull moment in golf where you have the same cookie-cutter shot.

I once played a club called Whistling Straits in a town called Kohler on the Wisconsin coastline. It's as scenic a walk as Pebble Beach; it looks like a little bit of Ireland in the good ole USA. It was one of the finest-looking courses I've ever seen, and I never want to play it again. If you missed your shot to the left or right, too long or too short, there was no bailout. If I hit it short, I was in weeds that were two feet high. If I hit it right, I was on the rough. If I hit it left, I was in sand that was impossible to get out of. In other words, one of the toughest courses I've been on in a long while. I walked away from that beautiful place with an 86 score, high for me.

The lesson of Whistling Straits is: Know when to walk away. If you're turning pro, then Whistling Straits is probably okay. The greatest PGA players in the world can play Whistling Straits and walk away over par by five or six shots. But even for ranked amateurs, it's hard. I'm still not good enough to play that course. I found it extremely difficult.

Some of my most memorable golf experiences have been overseas. I once played a couple of shows in Moscow during the late 1990s, after the Communist Party had broken up and Moscow had turned into a bit of a party-hearty city. It was my first time there, and my golfing itch needed to be scratched. So, of course, when we arrived my first question was "Are there any golf courses around here?"

Turned out there was only one decent golf course in the greater Moscow area. With nearly 9 million people living in the city, fewer than 24,000 people actually played. Only the elite played golf at the Moscow City Golf Club, founded in 1987.

So they drove me out to a beautiful, quaint little nine-hole course. It reminded me of a really nice municipal course. When I got there, they made me an honorary member! My locker number is 009. Guess whose locker is two doors down? That's right, Sean Connery: locker 007! When they gave him his membership card, it read, "From Russia, With Love. 007." Now I'm 009.

The two young guys who were the resident pros were okay golfers, but they really wanted to play an American rock 'n' roller for some rubles. So I took five hundred rubles off each guy, but after the match, I gave them back their money. I knew they didn't earn too many rubles working as golf pros in Russia. In exchange, they gave me some golf souvenirs for my friends back home. Moscow City Golf Club shirts!

Of course, now that Moscow is a super cosmopolitan city, they've built an amazing and luxurious $40 million course, the Moscow Golf and Country Club, founded in 1994, designed by the famous golf architect Robert Trent Jones, Jr. I haven't played it yet, but I look forward to teeing off on my next trip to Russia. It's supposed to be top of the line.

Another unusual place I would recommend to tee off is in Iceland. We landed on the island at midnight, and I was out on the tee at two in the morning. It was still broad daylight. My band couldn't get over it—me playing in the daylight at 2 A.M. Now, that's a golf addiction.

We did the same thing after our concert in Oulu, Finland. We finished the show at one o'clock in the morning, and we were out on the tee by two-thirty. Again, broad daylight. I still had my makeup on.

If you think playing in Phoenix is hot, try golfing in Bangkok. It was over 100 degrees outside, with 90 percent humidity. I almost couldn't breathe. I've also played in South America, which is interesting because they send the kids out in front of you to beat the bunkers with sticks. There are poisonous snakes that love to lounge in the hot sand. Next, the kids run up on the green, where monkeys come down from the jungle rough surrounding the course and grab your ball and run back up into the trees. So the kids patrol the green to shoo the monkeys away while you're putting your ball into the cup. I gave each youngster a tip that amounted to about a week's wages.

I've played golf on every continent that I've ever visited. On my 2006 tour, I played in Australia, New Zealand, everywhere in Europe from the north of Finland to southern Spain, all across Canada, in Mexico and Brazil and Argentina and Chile. I have two favorite pastimes when I'm overseas: playing golf and watching films. Both experiences are so different everywhere you go.

I look forward to playing outside of the United States more. There are still plenty of places left to go. I have yet to tee off in India, Saudi Arabia, Israel, and especially Dubai, where golf is said to be getting quite popular.

Some countries actually view golf as a game primarily designed for exercise. What a concept! The Europeans, especially the Germans, feel you should actually walk from hole to hole and carry your own bag. They rarely use electric carts. I find that kind of odd—if I have a show that night, I can't walk five miles carrying my clubs, then perform that evening. I have to save my legs for the stage.

I always wonder when people tell me they're going to Scotland on a golfing holiday. I know, that's where the game was actually invented, but it's a tough locale to play. The weather is often windy, with cold temperatures to endure. I've played all the main courses in Scotland while touring with the band—landmark courses like St. Andrews, Royal Troon, Muirfield, and Turnberry— but I prefer going to a warmer climate like Maui to play thirty-six holes a day in the most beautiful weather in the world, go swimming, lie in the sun, and enjoy some incredible food.

Maybe I'm too Westernized. After experiencing golf all over the world, I still prefer to sit in the hot sun and the dry Arizona heat in a golf cart with a misting system, with my GPS computer system flashing the distance from the hole, and an ice chest full of Diet Cokes stashed in the back. Now, that's golf, whether you're a straight-arrow corporate guy or a rock 'n' roll freak like me.

Alice on the road playing poker with ex–Turtles vocalist Mark Volman.

Chapter 13

The New Millionaires

THE SUITS DIDN'T HAVE ANY RESPECT for Alice Cooper until I made it onto the cover of *Forbes* magazine in 1974. The cover headline read "The New Millionaires." Suddenly, the business world wanted to know about me because now I was speaking their language: not music, not theater, but m-o-n-e-y. *Forbes* made a big deal about how Alice Cooper's road shows were raking in some of the biggest ticket sales ever. Seeing those numbers impressed the suits. After that, whenever I got onto an airplane in my torn Levi's and cutoff shirt, CEOs in the first-class cabin would smile and welcome me instead of cowering in their seats hoping I'd sit somewhere else. The money talked loud, and eventually golf would speak even louder.

One day in 1973, I was lying around bored in Malibu, drinking beer and watching TV, when I got a call from Joe Gannon, my lighting and production guy. He wanted to know if I was interested in going out with him and a couple of guys for a round of golf.

Golf?

"Joe, I've never played golf! Why would I want to play golf?" He assured me it was no big deal. Besides, it would get me out of the house. Joe drove me and a couple other guys to the Santa Clarita Valley, north of San Fernando Valley, to a place called the Valencia Country Club.

When we got ready to tee off at the first hole, I had more than a few cold beers in me. I was loose. Joe teed up the ball and handed me his seven-iron, and without ever holding a club in my life, I took a swing at the ball and watched it sail 160 yards toward the first flag.

"Not bad, Alice," said Joe as he watched my ball sail and drop onto the middle of the fairway. "That's a really straight swing. Who taught you how to do that?"

I was as surprised as he was that I could hit the ball so straight. "I dunno, Joe. It just happened. I've never had a lesson in my life."

I started hanging out with Joe and his golfing friends at the driving range or the country club. I wasn't a real player in the earliest days. Technically, I wasn't golfing; I was merely whacking at the ball. I didn't know how to keep score, and I certainly couldn't distinguish a seven-iron from a five-iron—somebody like Joe would have to show me. Even though I showed early natural ability, I was squarely in the hackers' camp. Rock 'n' roll was my thing, not a silly game like golf. Little did I know how radically that would change later on in my life.

What set the Alice Cooper Band apart from all of the other bands during the early-1970s hard-rock era was how tight the band was, both as a live act and as a gang. We never went anywhere without each other. Even after a couple of platinum records, there was still the risk of walking into some tavern and having someone beat you up (or try to kill you). We were still considered outcast freaks, as opposed to hippies. Our hair was ridiculously long, nearly down to our waists. Only, with money we could now command respect and live the high life.

⛳   ⛳   ⛳

We were living on the road, and inside the private jets we could now afford to hire to fly us from show to show. We were virtual prisoners inside airport bars, hotels, and countless Holiday Inns. After *Love It to Death* and *Killer,* when we got our first big royalty checks in 1972, mine was for $130,000. I didn't really live anywhere. I didn't have a wife. But who knew how long this prosperity would last? So, of course, like a good rock star I planned to buy a couple Ferraris with my first big check.

Not on Shep's watch.

"You're going to buy a house. That way, if everything falls through, at least you'll have a place to live. Maybe you can go back to school." Shep was always thinking bottom line and worst-case scenario.

But the money kept pouring in. And pouring in. More and more money, to the point where I now had to deal with the reality that I was getting good at making and spending money. But I was useless when it came to investing or saving it. So I put my entire financial life completely in Shep's hands. We made a deal.

"I'll do the music and the art thing. You do the money." It was a risky procedure for most people, I realize, but since the day we met, my trust in Shep has always paid off.

Every band will tell you. There are times when things go up and things go down. Since that day, there have been times when I was totally broke . . . or so I thought. Several times I've come to Shep with my head in my hands. "Shep, I know there's no money left."

And he's always said something like "Yeah, well, maybe that's why I put away a few bucks and bought some stock for you. Oh, and by the way, you also own some land in Minnesota."

As a result, there has never been a time since I've joined forces with Shep where I didn't have money. He *always* made sure I was covered. Thanks to Shep, my wife and I have enjoyed forty years of living well. Shep has stood guard over me, my family, and my assets. Not an easy thing to do, especially when I was an alcoholic.

"Tell Sheryl I'm not going to let you touch any of this," he would say. "Thirty years from now, you're going to be really happy that you don't know this money exists." And, of course, he was dead right. Of course, I now see my own financial statements. Our accountants are accountable to each other. I now know where the money is. What I don't know is what I make per night or how much we earned on T-shirts. Sometimes that's what kills an artist's creativity. When you're more concerned about 34 percent of T-shirt revenues, it can interfere with your art.

To this day, we've kept to our original deal. I don't even know what I pay my band or what we take in every week. By the end of each tour, I'll know what we've cleared after expenses, but the day-to-day is in his hands.

Our relationship is legendary in the world of show business. I've never questioned Shep—I've never had to. He realizes the value of a relationship with trust. That's why I tell him, wherever your money goes, put mine in the same place. I'll ride the train with him. And that's the relationship we've *always* had. People have warned me about giving a manager that much control, but I'm lucky—there's no reason for me to worry. If I have money, Shep has money. If Shep has money, I have money. And if he came to me tomorrow and said, "Alice, all the money is gone," I'd only say, "Gee, Shep, we'd better go out and make some more."

Alice dressed in gold lamé pants with snake in 1972 during the School's Out tour.

Chapter 14

Sold-Out Arenas

W E PLAYED WITH LED ZEPPELIN on one of their first shows in the United States. It was Alice Cooper and Led Zeppelin at the Whisky a Go Go—a cherry gig. It was their very first United States tour, and their first gig in Hollywood. I still have a photograph of the marquee: Alice Cooper, Led Zeppelin. Four nights of rockin' at the Whisky. We knew Zeppelin very well and we all got along. Robert Plant and I are still very good friends, and I see Jimmy Page on occasion. In fact, he has a son the same age as mine. We're both proud rock 'n' roll dads.

Guys in rock bands felt immortal back in the 1960s, and especially during the decadent 1970s. Nothing could bring us down—not drugs, not alcohol, not even excessive fame. But in reality, when a band couldn't get any bigger—other than the Beatles and the Stones—they had to learn to ride the roller coaster. You're up one day and down the next, and then way up the day after that. Or else a new band like Jethro Tull from Britain comes along and you've got to deal with them. A lot of guys fall off the roller coaster. Egos collapse when somebody comes out with something bigger. A lot of bands didn't know what to do.

Peter Frampton was like that. He had sold 8 million copies of *Frampton Comes Alive* in 1976—and about 16 million to date. After his very next album sold in the neighborhood of 5 million, he wanted to jump off a cliff. His managers, Dee Anthony and Frank Barcelona, asked me to go talk to him.

"My last album's only sold 4 million so far," Peter pined.

I sat him down. "Get yourself together. Your live album was an achievement, something you're never going to equal. Get that in your head. Three million albums is still considered phenomenal. Do you know how hard it is to sell three million records? Did you really think you were going to sell 10 million records every time out?" I nearly slapped him. But I wondered if he listened to me, because later on his problems with fame culminated with a near-fatal automobile accident in the Bahamas.

♀   ♀   ♀

I was happy with the fact that the Alice Cooper Band got as far as we did. Whenever my ego would surface, all I had to do was to reflect back to the days when we were living in the Chambers Brothers' basement or playing for spaghetti dinners—and then, two years later, we headlined Wembley Arena in London. It was quite a jump. But I think I've always maintained a pretty good sense of reality and humility, remembering that it could all go away tomorrow. My plan: Keep writing great songs and keep staging remarkable shows!

When we began writing and recording *Muscle of Love,* we all sat down as usual and pooled our ideas. All of a sudden, I could feel the band start to get more and more serious about the material. Perhaps a little too serious.

"We've got to make these songs more . . . "

"More what?" I asked.

"More us." .

Suddenly, the songs started becoming more and more slick and commercial. More deliberate. I noticed the difference right away, but I thought, *Okay, let's see how it goes.* Looking back, I can't think of too many songs on *Muscle of Love* that I'm crazy about. The songs became less reckless and less inventive. There were a lot of compositions where I basically felt like I was going, "Okay, if you guys really like it that way." I could tell that the band was starting to fade. Either we needed to rest or we needed to take time off. We had been riding a tremendous wave for a long time.

Maybe it was time for the band to back off for a while and recharge—which is always a dangerous thing to do. When you're that big, backing away takes tremendous courage. It means that while you're away, somebody can take your place. A lot of new bands, American and British, were on the way up or had already arrived: Aerosmith, Kiss, Genesis. But the fact remained: We still needed to rest and reflect artistically.

Unfortunately, we didn't. The price I would pay later would be practically immeasurable.

At the time, I didn't have the wisdom I later imparted on Peter Frampton. We decided that *Muscle of Love* had to be bigger than *Billion Dollar Babies,* and when it wasn't, egos began to surface. Pretty soon I sensed jealousy.

"Why is it always Alice doing the interviews?" someone asked.

I was always the one who was willing to get up at seven in the morning and be funny. I worked the interview thing better than anybody. The guys used to want me to do it, to be glad to not have to. Now it was "How come nobody interviews us?"

Honestly, at the time, I was concerned what they might say to a journalist. Loose lips sink ships, and I felt they were inexperienced in dealing with the press. I defended my role in the band, while they groused about my abilities as a singer and front man. "While you guys are hanging out backstage, I'm talking to five press guys. While you're out running around with your girlfriends, I'm taping a TV interview. These things don't do themselves."

The reason the press spoke to me was that I was the most available. Being Alice was my job. In 1974, I even legally changed my name to Alice Cooper to protect the brand name. Finally, I'd had it.

"Look, if you guys want to do the interviews, I would be more than happy to sleep in."

That stopped it really quickly. With our hectic touring schedules, nobody wanted to get up before noon—and by noon I had already finished five interviews. So the dissent and the arguing petered out.

In my eyes, the Alice Cooper band never broke up. There wasn't any yelling. Nobody accused anyone of anything or pointed fingers. The other band members contributed ample material. Neal was writing songs. Mike was writing songs. Dennis was writing songs.

But maybe it *was* time for a break. Then Michael Bruce talked to Shep about his plans to record a solo album. Shep warned him that such a move might jeopardize the band, but Michael decided to ignore the warning. Once that happened, Michael opened the door for the others to start thinking about recording solo albums.

Alice in a white tux and top hat during the 1975 Welcome to My Nightmare tour.
(Ken Ballard)

Chapter 15

Welcome to My Nightmare

THERE WAS ALL SORTS OF COMPETITION out there ready and willing to cash in our coupons. I guess bands like Kiss thought, *If one Alice Cooper works, then four ought to really do well.* Neil Bogart, who ran Casablanca Records, Kiss's label, admired Shep, so we were very aware of Kiss before they happened. Every single thing that they did was something that we had done—when we did the rock 'n' roll carnival, they then did the rock 'n' roll circus. In the beginning of Kiss, we had helped set them up with our road crew and even gave them information about their makeup. Our producer, Bob Ezrin, produced their 1976 *Destroyer* album. What can you do? Imitation is the most sincere form of flattery.

After a run of platinum albums, a lot of the money we made as a group went right back into our shows. After every tour, after the *School's Out* and *Billion Dollar Babies* releases, after every top ten album, we had to maintain our Alice Cooper brand by creating bigger and better concerts to stay ahead of the pack. Sharper guillotines. Bigger gallows. That proved expensive. After 1973's *Muscle of Love* album and tour, and after our 1974 *Greatest Hits* album, things got to the point where the band had had it. But Shep and I were still raring to go. I was enthusiastic about Alice Cooper's future, but the band had different sentiments.

I met with the guys one day and put it out there. "I've got a great idea for our next album," I told the band. "It's going to be the biggest rock production ever. But it's going to cost us a ton of money."

I felt a collective cringe in the room. The band felt the opposite. No, no, no. They wanted a smaller, more compact, and a more basic and safer show. Let's not spend all the money. Let's get back to our roots! The ride is almost over. Let's put on the brakes. We want our money.

119

I still saw things differently. "Everybody wants to be us! Why can't we take it to the next level?"

Neal wanted to do a solo album. Mike wanted to do a solo album. But Shep and I were gazing down the road toward the great unknown.

"Shep and I are going to put every penny into this new idea. Are you guys in or out?"

None of the other band members wanted to take the ride with me as lead singer. After seven years of slaving, seven hard years on the road, they were tired. The last thing they wanted to hear was that Alice and Shep were planning the production of all productions, a tour that would make our other tours look tired and silly. The rest of the band balked and backed out. Shep and I said, "Okay. We're pushing onward."

Welcome to My Nightmare was our baby. I still had Shep and Ezrin, my kindred spirits. Bob was the kind of guy who, when I said, *"Welcome to My Nightmare,"* he was already orchestrating ideas in his head. Once we laid out the concept—the inability of a child to wake up from a nightmare, starring Alice—I brought songs in to Ezrin. Then we transformed each song within a seamless musical total concept that fit inside our story line. Bob could take my songs to a place where they had not gone before musically. Once I heard *his* ideas, then Ezrin would add strange arrangements, dissonant strings, and touches that augmented and fortified each new song.

After our unsuccessful meeting with the band, Bob asked me if I was willing to use other musicians. I told him we could now use anybody we wanted. Then Shep found a clause in our recording contract that stated that if we recorded "a soundtrack," we didn't necessarily have to release it on the Warner Bros. label. We decided to use that loophole, since Atlantic Records was more than willing to hand us a larger chunk of money to be on their label.

We picked out Steve Hunter and Dick Wagner, the two lead guitarists from Lou Reed's fine group, who had been spectacular on his live *Rock N Roll Animal* album. Even better, Dick was from Detroit. Wagner and Hunter turned out to be the best American lead-guitar tandems out there, comparable to Beck and Page. Listen to their live stuff or watch the *Nightmare* video—their guitar work was so unbelievable that when we turned them loose to play extended guitar solos, it was a major departure from the original Alice Cooper band. It was fresh, driving, and best of all, it worked.

We put together a super lineup of session players, and when we played the new songs live, they sounded a little more majestic, like Queen. Nobody had ever heard Alice Cooper in front of a band as tight and precise as this.

Still, I was worried. I asked Ezrin, "Do you know what a tremendous gamble this is? Alice Cooper with a new band? Our fans are either going to love it or kill it. We could be out on our butts after this record."

        ♀   ♀   ♀

One particularly memorable recording session came when we added an orchestra to the ballad "Only Women Bleed." We were recording the string sections in Toronto with the Toronto Symphony, which consisted of about seventy extremely skeptical maestros between the ages of sixty-five and eighty-five who really didn't want to be there. "Who's this young kid with long hair directing us?"

Bob got his charts out to conduct the gorgeous string arrangement. He cued the orchestra and they began playing their parts beautifully.

But Bob waved the full orchestra to a stop. "Third cello, I believe your fourth string is flat."

Everybody stopped as the cellist plucked his string. "I'm sorry," the cellist said, "You're right, it was flat."

Suddenly, the musicians respected their young conductor. That guy can hear everything! They recorded his charts and performed magnificently. I was completely impressed.

After the session, I turned to Bob, exclaiming, "Wow! That was amazing. How did you hear that flat string on the cello?"

"I couldn't. I knew they weren't going to listen to me, so when they took their break, I walked over and detuned it. It was the only way they were going to respect me."

        ♀   ♀   ♀

The next problem. How were we going to turn this project into a soundtrack? Or better yet, a soundtrack to what?

We found a guy in Toronto working with a technology called video. We now had a plan to take every song and shoot each one as a small vignette, then put it all together. Now, technically, the album would be a soundtrack to this thing called a rock video. But who would play it? There was no MTV. *Midnight Special? Don Kirshner's Rock Concert?* Video was a brand-new medium. It ended up airing on the ABC television network. It was the first long-form video album ever, released before the genre even existed.

We shot the video for five days in Toronto with Vincent Price and a whole cast of dancers and musicians. The guy who shot the video didn't even know what to charge us. We settled on $20,000. Today we might spend millions on something of that magnitude. The ball began rolling really fast. After the music and video were done, we auditioned dancers and choreographers from *West Side Story* for the tour. Disney was building our props. It was five grueling months of rehearsal and recording. Ten, twelve, fourteen hours a day. We needed to synch up the music and the dancers, make sure all the set pieces worked, rehearse everyone over and over again.

I know now I should have taken a break like the other band members. I was exhausted before the tour even started, and once the tour began, it never ended. Once we sold out the first set of dates, that became my fuel to go on.

At times, while we were putting it together, Shep and I would look at each other, shudder, and say, "What are we getting ourselves into? If this thing falls apart, we are flat broke. If it doesn't work, if it's truly over and nobody wants us, we are so dead."

But we didn't die.

Welcome to My Nightmare was a big breakthrough. When the album was released in February of '75, it took off like a rocket. Then, once the critics saw the live show, the biggest rock production of all time, they loved it as well. It was my first solo album and a huge gamble, but it worked, and it remains one of the most iconic Alice Cooper moments in history.

♀   ♀   ♀

When I reflect back on *Nightmare,* it was a lot on the shoulders of one skinny guy. I get exhausted just thinking about it. At the time, I didn't take my own advice. I let the adrenaline and the ego carry me. Shep called me with the good news. "We've sold out two hundred shows. We're maxed. We can't fit another show or sell another ticket if we tried." I could not argue with the words "sold out." I couldn't jump off the train while it was running full steam. And as the show gained momentum, the tour got bigger and bigger and bigger.

Nightmare toured for over two years straight. After a little time off, I'd get the call. We'd just sold out an additional twenty-eight shows in North America, 20,000 tickets a show. After that, we booked a European tour for double the dollars we were getting in America.

In 1975, I was supposed to tour Australia, but I was banned. According to the government labor and immigration minister, I was a bad influence on the impressionable Australian youth. "I am not going to allow a degenerate who could powerfully influence the young and weak-minded to enter this country and stage this sort of exhibition here." I maintained that our show wasn't anywhere near as bloody as *King Lear* or *Macbeth,* which were considered required reading in every high school in America.

Sometimes I would do nice things, just to throw off my critics. In August of '75, I grew a mustache and found time to assemble and join 300 volunteer Alice Cooper fans who worked for a day to clear away garbage out of Manhattan's Riverside Park. I figured the deed would keep everyone off guard while at the same time emphasize that neither Alice Cooper nor his legions of young fans were necessarily rock monsters. We were capable of being Mr. Nice Guys, too.

Before going back into the studio to record the next album, I presented Vincent Price with a gold record for his contributions to my *Welcome to My Nightmare* album on *Dinah!,* Dinah Shore's popular daytime show.

Then I released *Alice Cooper Goes to Hell* in 1976, except the thirty-city tour was canceled after I was rushed to UCLA Medical Center with anemia. The following year, my next album was *Lace and Whiskey,* and I did tour heavily on that.

Finally, in 1978, at the end of my King of the Silver Screen tour promoting my *Lace and Whiskey* album, I staggered back to my house in star-studded Malibu. I couldn't believe it! No more shows. I was worn to a nub.

I was flat-out exhausted from the constant recording and touring, no time off, and nonstop drinking. I finally had nothing to do. I didn't have to put on that costume again. That felt great!

Then the phone rang. It was Shep.

"Alice, we gotta be in Vegas."

"Vegas? For *what*?"

"We owe Warner Bros. a live album. We gotta tape some live shows in Vegas. We'll cut it there."

I thought about it. "No."

It was the first time I had ever said no to Shep. He couldn't believe his ears.

"What?"

"No. I can't do it. I can't get up. I won't put the costume on again. I can't go up on stage and do the album ever again."

I put the phone down.

Another call. Shep again.

"You know who's producing this show? The Mafia. They've got Joe Gannon tied to a chair. They're gonna kill him unless you do it."

"I feel sorry for Joe."

"I'm not kidding. They've already slapped him around."

We had a fabulous road crew at the time. Besides Joe, there was Hot Ralphie Cafuoco, Fat Frankie Scinlaro, Space Lattanzio, Junior Sirico, Ralphie Febre. These were real Brooklyn guys. They all went to school together, and some of them even served in Vietnam together. These guys walked right out of the movie *Saturday Night Fever*. I know they would have taken a bullet for me.

"No!"

I kept resisting, but finally, Ralphie Febre and Hot Ralphie Cafuoco literally broke through the front door, threw me in a car, and drove me straight to Vegas. Somehow they pushed me up on stage. Then we recorded the live album, called *The Alice Cooper Show*.

Of course, the Joe Gannon story was a lie. He wasn't tied up or threatened by the Mafia. It was all a ruse to get me to Vegas no matter what it took.

Shep told the road guys, "If you have to knock Alice over the head, do it. Just get him here." We would have been sued if we didn't record and release another album for Warner Bros.

To this day, every time I'm asked to sign that live album, *The Alice Cooper Show,* I look up and say, "I hate this album."

The band plays great on it. I'm fine on it, I suppose. As usual, once I got on stage, I became Alice. But doing those shows at the Aladdin Hotel in Las Vegas in 1977 was sheer hell. Between the exhaustion and the heavy bouts of drinking, I was about to pay a massive price for all my hard work and success.

The next stage of my life was the most frightening ever. I would soon be confronting demons and nightmares I could never have imagined.

Alice Cooper, Golf Monster, at the Arizona Biltmore Golf Course
in November 2006.

The Sixth Step of Golf Addiction

Confront Your Demons and Defeat Them

The Sh*nks. The Unsh*nkable Alice Cooper.

There's a word in the golf glossary that you must *never, ever* utter on a course. It's a word so vile, so feared, and so evil, I hesitate to include it in this book.

(Cue music: Mike Oldfield's "Tubular Bells" from *The Exorcist*.)

SHANK.

A sh*nk is when you swing and the hosel of your club hits the ball and it goes to the right. It is the worst feeling. An eerie vibration runs through your hands, and you never want to hit another ball for the rest of your life. Sh*nking the ball is the most embarrassing moment in golf imaginable. Especially during a tournament, when people are watching.

Welcome to my nightmare, Mr. Golf Monster. The dreaded sh*nk.

Don't even say the word in front of people on a golf course. If you say it, you'll sh*nk it. Ask any golfer. If you want a dirty look from somebody, say the word in the middle of their golf game. It's like giving them the evil eye. It's the curse of the course. And if you sh*nk it once, you're going to sh*nk it a whole bunch of times afterward. Again and again. You can't get out of it. It's like biting the inside of your cheek: You don't want to, but you keep doing it. It's maddening, hellacious, demonic.

But you must bravely face your demons. And defeat them.

The worst thing about the sh*nks is that they eliminate your confidence. Worse, you no longer believe in your swing. The less you believe in your swing, the more you'll sh*nk the ball.

You're in front of 20,000 people. You're on a par three, getting ready to hit the ball. You sh*nk it. Everybody laughs. What do you do? Confront your demons! Tee up another one. Oh, no—you sh*nk it again. Now the gallery is dying laughing. Just remain strong and steadfast, and keep swinging.

In order to successfully defeat those demons, you have to keep hitting the ball, no matter how painful, until you woefully crawl out of the sh*nks. The only way out is to *play* your way out. Five or six shots, more if that's what it takes, until the sh*nks are gone. It's like a demon (or my onstage alter ego Alice) has taken over your club—and the only way to exorcise the demon is to regain your rhythm and confidence, until you find something in your swing that rescues you and drives the demons screaming away from your driver.

The sh*nks are an unexplainable paranormal phenomenon. Yet every golfer, pro and amateur, has gone through them. I've seen guys sh*nk on TV. Tiger once had a shot into a par five, an easy six-iron shot to get back into the hunt, but he hit it right on the hosel and sh*nked it into a tree. Everyone in the golf world gasped. We collectively felt his pain.

Tiger Woods sh*nked a ball!

It was like Sinatra hitting a flat note. But it happens.

Now, every time I'm up and I take the club back, buried in the deepest and darkest recesses of my brain is the ghastly thought *Keep your hands in front. Don't flip your hands over. Don't sh*nk it!*

Alcohol has nothing on the sh*nks. Compared to them, whipping alcohol was easy.

I'm open to new golf technology. If it seems logical to my game, I'll try it. I found out at some point that there's a club out called the "face forward wedge," where the hosel is eliminated from the face of the club. The club face is designed with a traditional shape, except that the hosel is positioned above and away from the leading edge, making it impossible to hit the hosel.

Voilà! A sh*nk-proof club.

Actually, Glen Campbell saw them on TV and ordered me a set. They're ugly. And they work. So when I play tournaments, and if I get into a situation where I need to chip the ball *and* eliminate the terror of sh*nking the ball in front of a lot of spectators, I'll take out one of my ugly Glen Campbell wedges and freely hit the ball up there and get back in the game. Hit the ball, Alice!

I'm trying to talk Callaway into building an entire "face forward" set of clubs. My point is this: How many people, amateur and pro, are terrified of sh*nking the ball? Why not build a set of clubs that makes you unsh*nkable? If Callaway built me a sh*nk-proof set of irons, I would play even more golf than I play now. Now, there's a frightening testament to addiction.

Outside the Troubadour in Los Angeles in 1974.
Left to right: John Lennon, Anne Murray, Harry Nilsson, Alice Cooper,
and Micky Dolenz—right around the "Lair of the Vampires" era.

Chapter 16

The Lair of the Vampires

I WAS LIVING IN A MANSION IN MALIBU in 1975. Beer and success went hand in hand, while whiskey waited in the wings. The phenomenal acceptance of *Nightmare* was coming at me fast, like a speeding meteorite. There were musicians and celebrities in our dressing room at the end of every show—John Lennon, David Cassidy, Lou Reed, Todd Rundgren, the Doors, Aerosmith, Andy Warhol. I was on constant tour. The original band was history. Now I was surrounded by topflight session musicians, an able road crew, a private jet, and Shep's management organization that saw to our every need, 24/7.

As soon as I opened my eyes in the morning, my first reflex was to reach over and grab a cold beer from a cooler stash I had an arm's length from my bed. Then there was more beer on the jet. More and more beer all day. The world was at my feet. I wasn't shooting heroin and I wasn't snorting cocaine—none of that evil stuff. It was just beer. Except nobody noticed that I was drinking more than a couple six-packs a day.

Even when I was drinking at my heaviest, I *was* Mr. Nice Guy. I wasn't an angry, difficult, mean, or fighting drunk. I was a nice guy drunk—a rich, successful, respectable drunk—and I subconsciously credited the alcohol for giving me the fame and gold records, and the drive and courage to succeed. But I was also a pitiful guy. I couldn't say no to anybody about anything, because I hated conflict. I wish I could have said no to alcohol, but instead, I became the most functional alcoholic you could ever meet—a virtual touring and recording machine. Push me on stage or in a studio, and I'd never miss a word to a song. Put me in a movie and I never flubbed a line. I could do *The Tonight Show* (and I did twice) and be as lucid as any of Johnny's sober guests. You'd never imagine I was a drunk. Those closest to me didn't realize how much I was drinking.

Pretty soon I was drinking up to a case of beer a day.

It got to the point where I perfected (and rationalized) my alcoholism so well, I played by a set of ground rules. I'd get up in the morning and, after a cold brew, I'd promise myself, "Okay, I won't drink hard liquor until after ten o'clock at night." Then pretty soon the ground rules shifted. I wouldn't start drinking whiskey until *nine* o'clock. Then *eight* o'clock. It went on like that. Soon I promised myself I would not drink the hard stuff until noon.

Eventually, though, the beer had no effect on me. In order to get high, I now needed to get up in the morning and have a few beers, then pour myself a glass of Coca-Cola and add in about three or four shots of Seagram's VO. That became my new drink, my poison. That's how I started my day.

♀   ♀   ♀

I say I was a functional drunk, but suddenly, looking back, I realize maybe I wasn't functional all the time. In July of '75, during the Nightmare tour, I fell off the stage in front of 17,000 people while chasing the "nightmares" into their ten-foot toy box. It took fifteen stitches to the head to sew me back up. Against doctor's orders, I took the stage again three days later, but collapsed after about twenty-five minutes. But generally, I soldiered on like a good rock star.

The corrosive effect of drinking caught up with me. During the Nightmare tour, as I was drinking more and more whiskey, it got harder and harder to muster up the energy and desire to put on my costume and do the show, which was very complicated and strenuous. It was a tough show, as tough as any Broadway production, only we were doing it on the road (a new city nearly every night) and I was in nearly every scene and sequence. It was a two-hour show of dancing, performing, climbing, acting, special effects, and several costume changes by fifteen cast members who played different parts. In fact, that's how I met my wife, Sheryl Goddard. We hired her on as an eighteen-year-old dancer.

Of course, we were bringing in tons of money. We had to. The overhead was so high, Shep and I couldn't slow down. And since I was a natural actor, I never let anyone peek behind my personal facade and see the toll that alcohol was slowly and steadily taking on my health. Nobody knew I was throwing up blood first thing every morning. Or that my days were turning dark and depressing.

My professional gamble paid off, but at what price? During the Nightmare marathon, when I was on the verge of collapse, I would walk into my dressing room and gaze at my costume all laid out . . . and it would take half a bottle of whiskey just to get myself into that costume. Soon I hated the taste of VO, and my inner soul began to equate the costume with death. I should have been in a hospital a year into the Nightmare tour. Actually, I should have been in the hospital after *Billion Dollar Babies*. But the long-distance runner inside egged me on. Each day was another race to endure. I toured and recorded constantly. *Welcome to My Nightmare* morphed into other concept albums, like *Alice Cooper Goes to Hell* and *Lace and Whiskey*.

"You can do it. Get up and have a drink. Then you'll feel better."

Toward the beginning of Nightmare, I was in good shape and eating properly. But toward the end, I would go days without eating. I was living on drink. My stomach was raw. I developed pancreatitis, a condition where my digestive enzymes were attacking my own stomach. In other words, I was eating myself alive as the alcohol tricked my body into thinking I was well fed. Eventually, I couldn't even get out of bed. All I did was lie there and watch cartoons and drink until show time.

Normally, I was the first guy up and running around, getting everybody going. Now I was no longer me. My health had deteriorated badly; I had zero potassium in my system. I was running on empty on every level. What was particularly sad was that even though I loathed the taste of VO, I still needed it. It was later that I learned that someone might drink a fifth of whiskey a day but technically not be considered an alcoholic, whereas someone else who might have three beers a day could be a total alcoholic. It's not how much you drink, but *why* you drink.

Alcoholism is a tricky monster. It feeds on itself, snowballing and gathering momentum until it devours you. The more you drink, the better you feel, then the worse you feel. The illusion of One More Drink is that, with more alcohol, I could feel well enough not to dwell on the roots of my depression or the fact that my stomach was a mess. Just take a drink, do the show. Tomorrow you'll wake up and, once you drink again, everything will be great.

I'd ask myself, "Can I stop drinking? Of course I can stop drinking!" But if you took my alcohol away, I couldn't walk from my bed to the door.

I became the classic alcoholic, if there is such a species, because I was using alcohol to self-medicate and sustain my productivity. If there were five interviews to do and you gave me my beer and whiskey, I could do them all. If I had a show to do that night, I would keep drinking. But take away the alcohol and it's no show, no interview, no production . . . no life.

That's when you know you're truly an alcoholic.

♀   ♀   ♀

There was a time when drinking was recreational fun. We were never one of those bands who trashed hotel rooms, but our friends would. Like if the Faces or the Who came into town, we would visit them and they would destroy their rooms. I might have thrown a lamp around or something, but we just weren't into destroying rooms; it wasn't our thing. We were so tired after doing the shows, we didn't have the energy to destroy rooms. But the Who, Led Zeppelin, and the Faces were experts at it.

The Who were close friends from our early days playing and hanging out together in Los Angeles and Detroit. When we went to London for the first time, they took us to their club to stage a drinking contest. They heard we were celebrated drinkers. I can remember it clearly. We all sat at a long rectangular table. I sat across from Pete Townshend, Neal Smith sat across from Keith Moon, Dennis was across from John Entwistle. Pete drank Rémy cognac, and I drank my Seagram's VO. The deal was, we'd drink half a bottle, then switch, so I had to drink the remaining Rémy and Pete had to finish the VO. Then Bob Ezrin came in. He had just eaten a full meal, a pepper steak or something. After drinking nearly a full bottle of scotch with

Entwistle, Ezrin literally projectile-vomited about three feet across the table, splattering bile and blowing chunks all over the Who, who just sat there with vomit all over them. It was like something out of a Monty Python movie or the *The Exorcist*. What I admired was that the guys never flinched. They simply ordered another drink.

I thought, *Man, these guys are good.*

There wasn't a time when anybody had to pick Alice up off the floor. I was never that kind of falling-down drunk. Not that I remember, anyway. Instead, I was the Dean Martin Golden Buzz–type guy, drinking late at night with Harry Nilsson or John Lennon (those guys could really drink).

When I lived in Hollywood around 1975–1976, we made the Rainbow Bar and Grill on Sunset Boulevard our nightly drinking sanctuary. Go to the Rainbow today and there's still a plaque there that reads "Lair of the Vampires."

The Lair was the room upstairs, a bona fide drinking club. In the old days of Hollywood, John Barrymore, W. C. Fields, and Errol Flynn had their own drinking club. According to Errol Flynn's memoirs, when Barrymore died, film director Raoul Walsh stole his body, sat him at the Barrymore table, and toasted him, even though he was dead as a doornail.

Our club was a modern-day version. President, Alice Cooper. Vice President, Keith Moon. Secretary, Harry Nilsson. If anyone had to do a show or movie, he would announce it to the Vampires—I would say that I had two weeks of shows coming up, so someone else would have to take over as President. Nilsson would gladly step in. Since we were all going to drink anyway, we figured we might as well all drink together. It was a "last man standing" kind of drinking club. We would all show up, go to the top of the stairs, and all night you would see nothing but rock stars and celebrities drinking and looking down upon the nightclub audience. Every night we'd wait to see what Keith Moon was going to do. One night, he showed up dressed as a nun. The next night, he came dressed in full-out Nazi regalia (with riding crop) as Adolf Hitler. The next night, he was a French maid. By the end, we were crawling downstairs, somehow getting into a car with someone driving us home. Next night, it was back to the Lair.

The Rainbow was an ultracool nightclub, and we were notorious patrons. At the time, we all were very functional. The membership included only household entertainment names. John Belushi was a member. Jack Nicholson would show up every once in a while. Anyone who was playing Los Angeles became an Honorary Vampire. We even had a softball team.

I remember Bruce Springsteen was invited up one night. It was when the press had billed him as the "New Dylan."

"Sit down, Bruce," I told him. "I've got to talk to you about something important." Bruce was wearing cowboy boots. Bernie Taupin, who was a Vampire at the time, was sitting to the other side of him.

"Look, you're really talented," I said. "But whatever you do, don't let them sell you as the next Bob Dylan. That's suicide. You're Bruce Springsteen, not Bob Dylan."

Then Bernie tapped him on the shoulder. "Bruce, I've got to tell you something." Bernie started talking to Bruce. While his attention was on Bernie, I poured my drink into his cowboy boot.

After Bernie, I got his attention back. Bruce would turn to me, and Bernie would pour his drink into Bruce's other boot. By the end of the night, the poor guy was sloshing around. The whole room was in hysterics.

Bernie and I were the best of friends. Inseparable. Looking back, it was some of the most fun times of my life. It was also right before things started caving in. A lot of those guys eventually died. Harry Nilsson. Keith Moon. John Belushi. I guess I was one of the few survivors out of that bunch. You can't drink like that and not know that at some point it's going to catch up with you. VO Canadian Club and Coke. That's all I drank as a Vampire. Beer during the day, whiskey at night.

We had our very own waitress, a blond gum chewer named Schottzie. Schottzie was great because she took care of us and never took any crap.

"Harry, you've had enough."

"John, you're out of line."

"Alice, you haven't had anything all night. What's your problem?"

"I'm on penicillin."

Schottzie was like our mother and the perfect waitress. We listened to her when she'd lay down the law and grab our car keys. I would find a ride out front, then I'd slip her a hundred dollars.

I look back at my drinking club days as another life long ago. They were great times, but they were also the lost years. But it's funny, the Vampires were all extremely productive during that time. Harry Nilsson was cutting his *Nilsson Schmilsson* records. Jack Nicholson was making great movies. Bernie was writing hits with Elton John. Belushi was a Blues Brother and a cast member on *Saturday Night Live*. We were all riding a huge wave of celebrity. I could go anywhere in the world and people would recognize me. We felt immortal. Yet in the back of our minds, we knew we couldn't live like that forever. It could end at any time, so we'd better party hard and live each night like it was our last. And for some of us, it was.

Alice and Groucho Marx attend a movie screening together in 1974.

Chapter 17

Rocky, the King, Clouseau, the Dalí, and Groucho

ALICE COOPER TRANSCENDED THE ROCK 'N' ROLL scene by intersecting it with the world of art and showbiz legends. My influences weren't just rock stars, but artists and cultural icons. Salvador Dalí, an early and lasting influence, was a big fan. Groucho Marx saw my Alice act as vaudeville taken to the next logical and modern extreme. Fred Astaire saw our dancing and noted that our choreography was rooted in *West Side Story,* not schlock. Andy Warhol was in love with our celebrity (or, for that matter, anybody's celebrity).

Andy Warhol was a permanent fixture at Max's Kansas City and Studio 54. He was the darling of the New York underground. We became acquaintances at this time, mostly because of my notorious infamy and out of pure curiosity. Andy was a media gourmet and I was on the cover of every single magazine, which meant he had to have Polaroids of us together. That was his addiction. I bought his *Electric Chair in Red* painting at the Factory in 1973 or 1974, for $2,000. That painting seemed to be appropriate, because in my stage show I was electrocuted in an electric chair every night. I still own that painting.

Andy was hard to get to know. He wasn't like the personable John Lennon, the surreal Salvador Dalí, or the chummy Peter Sellers who you could really be friends with. Andy was at the center of his own universe, with lots of strange little satellites revolving around him. He would only really recognize you if you were glamorous or hugely famous, and he didn't play golf.

Shep was managing Raquel Welch in 1975, during an era when movie stars had to be linked with a rock star—Faye Dunaway was married to Peter Wolf from the J. Geils Band. And then Raquel Welch fell in love with Alice Cooper.

I'm thinking, *What?!?!?!*

It wasn't that I didn't like her—I just wasn't ready. Here's Raquel Welch, in her prime. She'd call me over to her house, her assistant saying something like "She needs to see you." I'd walk into her room and the door would close, locking me in. It was the silliest thing. I was this kind of straggly Keith Richards type, this sloppy disheveled rock star. She was beautiful and voluptuous. And I honestly wasn't interested. It sounds crazy, but I was in love with this skinny ballerina named Sheryl whom I'd met on the Nightmare tour. My friends couldn't believe it.

"You mean you're not bedding Raquel Welch because you're in love with a dancer?"

Raquel couldn't understand it, either. Didn't I understand who she was? Battleship-sized breasts! She was the hottest woman in the world! The fact that I wasn't interested drove her crazy. *Nobody* said no to Raquel Welch.

One day I was playing golf at the Doral Golf Resort in Miami. I got paired up with three straight business guys who really didn't want to be with me. They were three heavy CEO types, and I had hair down to my ass and I was wearing cutoff shorts. We were getting ready to tee off, and I felt these guys rolling their eyes behind my back. And then, all of a sudden, here comes Raquel Welch in a golf cart.

"Alice, Alice, I'm your caddy today!"

"Rocky, go away, will ya? Can't you see I'm playing golf?"

These guys looked at me.

"You just sent Raquel Welch away."

I shook my head. "I know, but she drives me crazy."

After that, they looked at me like I was a god.

Much later, Raquel invited Sheryl and me to her show at the Fontainebleau. It was a brilliant stage show, and Rocky was absolutely killer on stage. She's quite the song-and-dance girl. She's really good at it. Most people don't realize how amazing she is live on stage—she can really nail an audience. Our seats were right up front, and Raquel said to the crowd, "I have to introduce one of my friends. Alice Cooper is here tonight."

There was a bottle of wine at our table, and as she bent over to kiss me, she knocked the wine all over Sheryl with her boobs. Sheryl was covered in wine as Raquel apologized. To this day, I say to Sheryl, "You know, I threw Raquel Welch overboard for you."

"Yeah, and it was the smartest thing you ever did."

♀ ♀ ♀

Liza Minnelli and I were really good friends. Let's just say we hung out. One day while we were in Vegas, we got a call that Elvis Presley wanted to meet us. *Elvis? Are you kidding? Cool!* We got into the elevator and it's me, Liza Minnelli, Linda Lovelace, and Chubby Checker all going up to meet Elvis. Quite the foursome. Every night that he was in Vegas, somebody got an audience with Elvis, and I guess that night we were the lucky ones. As we got off the elevator, Elvis's bodyguards searched us. Then Elvis appeared.

"Hello, guys, it's good to see you."

I couldn't believe my eyes. I mean, it was *Elvis*. And this was when he was sharp and slim. He looked great.

"Hey, man," he said to me, "you're that cat with the snake, ain'tcha? I think that's cool, man." We chatted for a little bit, and then he said, "Hey, Alice, you're from Detroit, right?"

"Yes, Elvis."

"I wanna show you something. You've been around guns, haven't you?"

"Not really." It was hard picturing my father with a gun.

We went into the kitchen. It was just me and Elvis—no bodyguards, no entourage. He opened a drawer, pulled out a loaded .38, and handed it to me.

"Go ahead. Point it at me."

I stood there with a loaded .38 pointed at Elvis Presley. For one brief moment, the mischievous little devil on my left soldier whispered in my ear, "Shoot him."

Why?

"Because it'll be the biggest story ever in rock 'n' roll. Alice Cooper shoots Elvis. Shoot him and let's get outta here!"

Then the other voice, the angel, said, "What are you doing? You've got a loaded gun on Elvis Presley!"

If Elvis's guys had walked in, they would have surely killed me.

Then Elvis said. "Okay, now this is what you do, man." He did this karate spin thing where he knocked the gun out of my hand. Pretty soon I was down on the floor with his boot on my throat.

"That's great, Elvis," I said, my voice muffled and my face beet red. "Can I get up now?"

"I didn't hurt you, did I?"

"No, Elvis, I'm fine."

Then he says, "Hey, man, I wanna show you my most prized possession."

I followed Elvis into his bedroom, and he closed the door and locked it. I thought, *Now I'm in Elvis's bedroom. I don't really know this guy. What's the deal? Is he some kind of demented hillbilly?*

"Come over here and sit down."

I was sitting on Elvis's bed. He opened up a drawer in the nightstand and took out some papers—it was a police report.

"I was leaving the Hilton the other night," Elvis said. "My boys and I were going out to play some pool, so they closed the pool hall for us and we went in. As we were leaving, these four old boys were out there, waiting for me. 'Hey, tough guy,' they said. So my boys came around, but I said, 'No, I'll take care of it.' "

According to the report, Elvis kicked the hell out of all four guys because he *really* was a karate expert.

"I wanna show you this particular part about this guy here. I kicked him and broke his knee. Then I swung around and hit the other guy with my elbow and broke his jaw."

Elvis was so proud, showing me the report with the details about broken jaws and knees.

"Then I turned around and I cracked this guy and I beat his head in."

I nodded, thinking, *Great, Elvis. This is your most prized possession? These police reports?* I realized that this was Elvis's only contact with the outside world. This stupid fight. He was never, ever out of the sight of the Colonel or his boys. But this fight was something he did on his own, without his boys. How sad this man was. I almost said, "Hey, Elvis, you gotta get outta this lifestyle. Let's get up in the morning and go play some golf. Let's go to the movies. Let's sign some autographs and stuff. Let's live! Get a life! These are things I can do every day. You don't need fifteen bodyguards around you."

But life was sheltered for Elvis. He couldn't move without his entourage. What a mindblower—I was sad for him the rest of the night. I decided I never wanted to be that famous. It was debilitating. No wonder he was going insane—he was such a big star that he had no life. He could have had anything he wanted in that room, up there in his suite. He could have all the drugs he wanted, all the televisions to shoot. But he couldn't go out.

Months later, I was running down Benedict Canyon, getting into shape for another tour, when I saw this gleaming Stutz Bearcat coming down the street. Elvis popped his head out.

"Hey, Alice!"

"Hey, Elvis! How you doing?"

"Hey, man, let's you and me get together and go out."

Suddenly, a hand pulled him back in. The guys wouldn't even let Elvis pop his head out of the car.

I later called Shep. "How can we help this guy?"

But there was no way. Elvis was impenetrable.

Incidentally, a weird thing happened later in the evening of the Elvis police report incident. Liza got a call that Linda Lovelace was in jail for cocaine possession. After *Deep Throat* made porn history, somebody had gotten the idea of Linda planning a Vegas show—this bust meant her show would never happen. She seemed like a very sad person, and I felt sorry for her. Maybe she was doing coke. Maybe she was framed. It just seemed weird how it all came down. At that time, the people in charge were trying to clean up Vegas's image, and Linda's show gets canceled . . . it seemed very suspect.

♀ ♀ ♀

After movies like *The Pink Panther* and *A Shot in the Dark* came out, Inspector Jacques Clouseau became one of my heroes. I knew Peter Sellers's work from *Dr. Strangelove* all the way back to *The Goon Show*. Sellers showed up backstage at one of our shows in London after it got back to him that I was a big fan. We got to be really good friends. He called me Inspector Maurice

Escargot, and Sheryl was Nicole. Together, we were his Thin Man, Nick and Nora Charles, and he'd call whenever we played London.

"Hello," he would say in character in a comically heavy French accent.

"Clouseau?" I'd ask.

"Yes! Escargot? We must go out gambling tonight. I vill pick you up at 7:32."

"Seven-thirty-two?"

"Yes, I am on a case, and I do not have a minute to lose." Click.

We stayed at the Savoy Hotel. I'd be wearing a tuxedo, and Sheryl would be dressed in an evening gown. Peter would show up. We all carried plastic dart guns with plunger darts. There would be a knock at the door. We'd open the door and Peter would jump out.

"Escargot, you swine!!" Then he'd dive behind the couch.

Sheryl would turn and yell, "Clouseau!" Then she'd shoot a dart at him. Boing! Right on the forehead. Then off we'd go to gamble and have dinner.

You never knew when Peter would turn into Clouseau. One particular night, Peter was with a girl with long blond, flowing hair. She wore a beautiful white gown with a long train behind it. The four of us showed up at the White Elephant, the most exclusive gambling club in London—formal dress was required. Peter was a regular there. As we were seated for dinner, Peter dropped his napkin to the floor.

"Oh, dear," he said in his Clouseau voice. "I seem to have dropped my napkin."

As he bent down for the napkin—splat!—he fell face first into his plate of spaghetti. Then he sat up.

"Oh, how stupid of me." The waiter rolls his eyes as Peter reaches to wipe his face. But it's not his napkin—it's the train of the girl's dress.

The blonde screams, "What are you doing?"

"I'm so sorry." Then Peter abruptly stands up and flips the entire table over.

It was like being in the middle of *The Pink Panther*. The waiters were used to his antics. They calmly said, "Mr. Sellers, your other table is ready."

"Ah! Thank you." Then we all sat down at a new table and finished our dinner.

Every time we finished a show in London, the first thing I'd ask was "Where's Peter?"

We were in London when he had his heart attack. So we sent him a telegram.

"Don't worry Clouseau. Stop. We are on the case. Stop. Signed Escargot and Nicole." They told me it was the final communication he received. He laughed and then he closed his eyes.

When Peter Sellers died, one of my best friends was gone.

♀   ♀   ♀

The first time I met Salvador Dalí was in 1973. He had contacted us about me being the subject of a moving hologram, The First Cylindric Chromo Hologram Portrait of Alice Cooper's Brain. As an art major, Salvador Dalí was a huge inspiration for me. He influenced the band in so many ways. Whenever he called up Shep, he would say,

"Hello, Mr. Blemmings."

"My name is Shep Gordon."

"Yes, Mr. Blemmings." For some unknown reason, he always called Shep Mr. Blemmings.

I guess Dalí saw Alice as surrealistic art. He knew our show, and maybe he could relate to the surrealistic influences: Alice's crutch, a baby doll, a sword with money on it, a snake, a guillotine, the gallows.

He wanted to meet, so we booked a table at the St. Moritz Hotel in New York. Shep and I got there early. I was excited because this would be the first time I would get to meet my idol.

Whenever you saw Dalí, his entourage arrived in waves. First, five or six guys or girls would show up, strange androgynous creatures. Then his wife, Gala, would arrive with her entourage, dressed in a man's tuxedo with white spats, white gloves, cane, and a top hat. She was the businessperson, the brains behind Dalí's enterprises, so she spoke to Shep because she realized he was my business guy.

Then, finally, Dalí made his entrance. There were ten people at our table. He looked around. He wore the famous upturned mustache, giraffe-skin pants, a zebra jacket, Aladdin shoes that curled at the toes, purple socks that Elvis gave him (that he frequently wore), and a dandy cane.

"I am the Dalí!"

He sat down and ordered everyone a Scorpion. A Scorpion was a drink with brandy, rum, and gin, with an orchid floating in it. After one Scorpion, you're gone. Dalí ordered himself a glass of hot water.

Shep and I took all this in. When his hot water arrived, the Dalí reached into his pocket and pulled out a jar of honey and poured a long, thick stream into his hot water. While he was doing that, he put his other hand into his pocket and pulled out a pair of scissors, and then he cut the ribbon of honey. I nudged Shep. "He's got scissors and he's cutting honey."

Tomorrow, the Dalí announced, we were going to start shooting the hologram. Only, I couldn't understand most of what he said. He spoke in Spanish, Portuguese, French, and English, so I understood about every fourth word.

The next day, we arrived and the press was there. It was a major production, filming in this big, white video production room. He had cameras arranged in a circle. I wore $2 million worth of Harry Winston diamonds, a necklace and a tiara. No shirt. I held a Venus de Milo microphone and bit its head off as I was shot in the round. Before the shoot, security men guarding the jewelry checked all the exits.

For the second day of shooting, the Dalí walked in with his hands behind his back. Then he revealed his surprise.

"This is the Alice Cooper brain." It was a ceramic sculpture of my brain with a chocolate éclair running down the back, with painted ants crawling on the brain that spelled out "Dalí and Alice."

"That's great! Can I have it?"

"Of course not," the Dalí sneered. "It's worth millions."

Nobody can tell me where my brain is now. It's not listed in any museum. I have a picture of him holding it, pointing to it as I nobly sit. If I could find the Alice Brain, I'd be willing to invest the money to buy it back, but to this day, it's never reappeared. The First Cylindric Chromo Hologram Portrait of Alice Cooper's Brain lives in the Museum of Dalí in Figueras, Spain.

At the press conference, one of the reporters asked, "What is it like working with Dalí?"

"Well," I confessed, "I gotta be honest with you. I can't understand a word he says."

Dalí jumped up and blurted out, "Perfect! The best form of communication is confusion."

As it turned out, Dalí understood everything. He was well aware of what was happening around him. He spoke perfect English. He was an amazing artist—consider, Dalí's Last Supper oil painting is the size of two large walls. It looks like a photograph, it's so perfectly done. And that's just one painting. I was at an art gallery in Rome where there must have been two hundred to three hundred of his sketches, and that represented only a tiny percentage of his prolific output—paintings, sculptures, sketches. He was *always* working.

After the hologram exhibit, every once in a while we would get a call. I'd pick up the phone in Shep's office.

"Mr. Blemmings!"

"Hello, Salvador. It's Alice." He'd go on and on and on with his multilingual gibberish. "Mr. Blemmings is right here." Then I'd hand over the phone to Shep and shrug.

On another night when we went out to dinner with the Dalí, the bill came to a couple thousand dollars. Dalí took the bill and signed his name. I guess he figured his signature was worth the price of the dinner. I asked, "Should I leave the tip?" So I signed, "Alice Cooper."

♀   ♀   ♀

I first met Groucho Marx when Erin Fleming, his controversial guardian, brought him to our show. Eventually, Groucho, Shep, and I became close buddies.

"Groucho," Shep asked him, "between you and me . . . would you let me do something for you?"

"What's that?"

"Would you let me go through your books? I want to see if I can help you with your expenses and stuff."

As Shep went through he books, he found peculiar expenses. For instance, somebody was being paid to get Groucho invited to parties.

"Groucho, do you ever have any problems getting invited to parties?"

Of course, the answer was no. Groucho could show up to any party, anytime, anywhere. He was an immediate guest. As Shep went through the books, he found many people getting paid for doing nothing, and eliminated them while Groucho and I watched TV. Groucho would yell out to Shep in the next room, "Hey, Shep! It's been ten minutes. Sue somebody!"

We once played together at a cancer benefit that Sinatra had put on.

Groucho had Marvin Hamlisch playing piano. Groucho and I sang a great old song, "Lydia the Tattooed Lady" from *At the Circus*. I loved it.

When you went to dinner at Groucho Marx's house, you had to perform. It was one of those old Hollywood traditions. After dinner, the guests would adjourn into the living room and Groucho would get up and do a couple of songs. Then he picked somebody out—say it was me—so I would tell a joke and do a song. Sheryl might dance. Everybody had to perform. It didn't matter if you were any good; if Groucho pointed to you, you were on. Maybe you had a great story to share, so while you were telling your story, Marvin Hamlisch would play sweet backup chords behind you.

One day I was over at Groucho's house when he said, "C'mere, Alice."

I followed him into his room, and he showed me a giant round bed taken from some movie he had made during the 1930s.

"Alice, would you like this bed?"

"Sure. If it's your bed. Yeah, I want it."

"Take it. I never had much luck with it."

Groucho wore these silly Mickey Mouse ears and smoked his cigar as he supervised the removal of the round bed.

"Move to the left just a little bit. No, your left, not my left." It took four guys to get Groucho's huge round bed out of his house. We knocked paintings off the wall. It was a scene right out of a Marx Brothers movie. Finally, I took the bed and I put it in my house.

Later, Sheryl and I were in England and Paul and Linda McCartney invited us to their place in Mull of Kintyre in Scotland. Paul wanted to show me his farmhouse, where they had this big round room, a conservatory.

"What's this room going to be?" I asked Paul.

"This will be my meditation room."

"Have I got a house gift for you!"

I shipped him Groucho's round bed. Paul read the card: "I hope this bed is luckier for you than it was for us. Signed, Groucho Marx and Alice Cooper."

The round bed now lives in McCartney's house, in the round room. He said that after he put Groucho's bed in, suddenly it no longer felt like a meditation room anymore. He turned the room into something different.

We told Paul, "If you ever get tired of the bed, send it to somebody else. It has a history now."

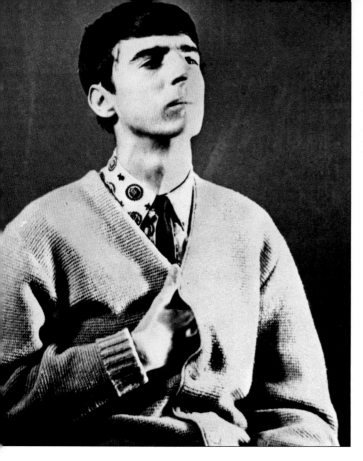

Alice as Cortez High School newspaper columnist "Muscles McNasal."

The high school talent show where Alice and his track buddies did a Beatles send-up.

Although it's a little blurry, Alice on stage in 1969 during "the chicken incident" in Toronto, right before he threw the bird into the audience (thinking it could fly).

Opposite: Playing for 158,000 fans in São Paulo, Brazil—the largest indoor concert ever staged. Check out the chaos at the front of the stage. Alice is on stage in the upper left and on the lower right-hand corner is a gun pointed next to an empty holster.

School's out forever. Alice on stage in white top hat and tails. *(Ken Ballard)*

Salvador Dalí holding the ceramic sculpture of Alice's brain celebrating the First Cylindric Chromo-Hologram Portrait of Alice Cooper's Brain, produced in 1973. Alice wears a tiara and is draped in Harry Winston diamonds, worth millions. *(Bob Gruen)*

Alice appears on the *Tonight Show with Johnny Carson* in 1977.

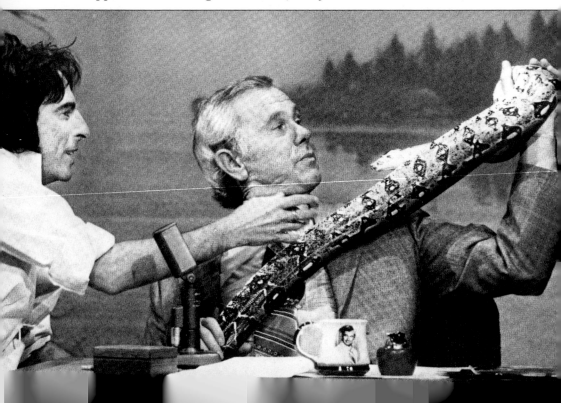

Alice hanging out with Fred Astaire.

Ringo Starr, Alice Cooper, Mae West, and Keith Moon star in the 1978 film *Sextette*.

Vincent Price and Alice exchange gibes during the Welcome to My Nightmare tour.

Alice performing "Only Women Bleed" with his dancer wife, Sheryl, in 1977. *(Ken Ballard)*

Alice (wearing an English soccer jersey) sits with Sheryl backstage at a London after-show party following a 1975 sold-out Wembley Arena concert.

Sometimes you can't run from the truth. Alice on stage during the 1979 Madhouse Rock tour.

Alice and the dancing booze bottles he had onstage during the 1978 From the Inside tour to represent the demons he was battling. *(Brad Elterman)*

Alice in chains and leather during a 1988 concert. *(Ken Ballard)*

Alice gives some putting tips to tennis great Venus Williams. *(Courtesy of Erik Luftglass and the VH1 Fairway to Heaven Tournament.)*

Alice with Arnold Palmer at the 1998 Bob Hope Chrysler Classic. *(Photo by Bob Hope Chrysler Classic photographer Scott Avra.)*

Alice golfs with Darius Rucker and Justin Timberlake at the 2006 Bob Hope Chrysler Classic. *(Photo by Bob Hope Chrysler Classic photographer Marc Glassman.)*

Groucho was a fabulous guy. Sometimes I would walk into his living room and Sheryl would be sitting on his lap. She'd look at me and shrug. "Alice, he's eighty-six. What's he going to do?"

I took him to the Polo Lounge at the Beverly Hills Hotel for his eighty-sixth birthday. I have a picture of us toasting. Groucho and I were checking out the menu when the waiter asked, "Mr. Marx, what would you like?"

"What kind of drugs do you have?" he yelled out.

Everybody looked over at our table. I slumped down.

Then Groucho said, "Excuse me, Alice, I gotta go insult the maître d'." He walked over to the maître d' and I watched the two talking. Pretty soon the maître d' started getting really angry. Groucho looked back at me and smiled. Apparently, he had accomplished his mission.

Groucho was also a hopeless insomniac. He'd call me up at two in the morning. "Alice, I can't sleep. Come over."

So I'd go over and sit next to Groucho with a six-pack of Budweiser while he sat up in bed with his beret and his cigar. The TV was always on—usually some classic Hollywood film.

"See that guy there?" This macho handsome cowboy actor in some old movie. "He's gay."

Another old movie would come on with a beautiful actress. "See her? Chico and Harpo both nailed her."

"See that guy there? I played poker with him one night. I won everything, so he had to take his pants off."

Groucho kept me in stitches. After a while, I'd look over and Groucho would be sound asleep. I'd put out his cigar, turn off the television, cover him up, turn out the lights, and quietly leave.

A couple nights later, the phone would ring. "It's Groucho. Come on over. I can't sleep."

I was the go-to guy when Groucho couldn't sleep. He was my good buddy. Maybe he saw a little of himself as a young man in me. I knew all his movies, all his great lines. And he trusted me. We connected. The fact that Shep and I were best friends—that we didn't even have a contract with each other, and that we trusted each other that much—maybe that was what Groucho wanted all his life: somebody he could trust. I was proud to have earned his trust and his friendship.

Alice (far right) with Michael Douglas (center) and Mark Wahlberg
at the Michael Douglas & Friends tournament.
(Courtesy of Michael Douglas & Friends Tournament)

The Seventh Step of Golf Addiction

Play with Those Who Inspire You

My Guinness Records trio. Swingin' with the stars. Rubbing elbows at the Friars Club. Play with a card-carrying pro. Frankenstein swings. Alice and Arnold.

Surround yourself with the most interesting and talented people you can—celebrities, pros. Whoever plays better than you. Whoever inspires you.

In the early days, CEOs, teachers, preachers, and politicians would have nothing to do with me. Now all kinds of folks want advice on their swing, they're curious what scores I've been hitting, they want to ask what kind of irons I use. The social barriers have come down. That's because we're talking about the same thing: We all have to hit a tiny ball into a tiny hole four hundred yards away, and we need any information we can get from each other. It's the common denominator between us all.

Golf is a social sport. You should play with friends *and* competitors. Playing with people you like tightens up relationships; playing with people you want to beat sharpens your game. I could go down a long list of the famous people I've played with. Some of my favorite celebs are the old-timers, like the old Borscht Belt comedians. Legends now dead.

I once played golf with Sammy Davis, Jr., in Acapulco. He was exactly the same guy on the fairway as he was on TV or on stage with the Rat Pack. He'd stand there and laugh and smack his knee. He wasn't a particularly good player, but he really enjoyed the game and his enthusiasm was infectious. Bob Hope was outstanding because he was really marvelous and poised, with a natural and athletic swing. Although he was certainly past his prime when we played, I could tell that at one point that swing had been really fine.

I've played with celebrities I grew up watching on TV as a kid, like Don Knotts (Barney Fife from *The Andy Griffith Show*) or Jay Silverheels, better known as Tonto on *The Lone Ranger*. Dean Martin was passionate about the game. I even played with Jackie Gleason, which was a rare thrill. Gleason played the clown at all times, even when he teed off. "And away we go!"

Johnny Mathis is a good player. He once took out a two-iron on the first tee and smacked it down the middle. He was a much better player than I was at the time, an incredibly great ball striker.

Sometimes I'll play with Glen Campbell, another Arizona resident. Glen is country, and I'm rock 'n' roll. So, of course, Glen will rail on me, and I'll hit back by calling him a hillbilly. Then we'll do a verse of Donny Osmond's "A Little Bit Country, A Little Bit Rock 'n' Roll," only I'll take the country part. The crowd loves it—it's a throwback to the golf showbiz tradition when Sinatra, Dean Martin, Jerry Lewis, and Bob Hope threw barbs back and forth at each other as they played to the crowd at Bing Crosby's Clambake. That kind of fairway banter was what begat the Rat Pack and what still makes playing celebrity tournament golf fun today.

One time I was staying at the Plaza Hotel in New York City, and I had a game scheduled the next morning up in Westchester County. Somebody told me, "You know, Alice, the Presidential Suite is right above you. Do you know who is staying right above you? President Gerald Ford." I suggested we call him and ask if he wanted to go out and play with us the next day. Why not? I called his room and some White House functionary answered the phone.

I said, "Hi, this is Alice Cooper. I'm staying right below you guys in the hotel. Three of us are playing in Westchester tomorrow, and I was wondering—if the President wasn't doing anything in the morning, would he like to come out and play nine or eighteen holes with us? It's very low key, a private game. Nobody knows that we're going."

I heard a pause on the phone. "Hey, Jerry, Alice Cooper wants to know if you can play golf tomorrow."

I heard him say, "I think I can. I'm supposed to do this thing with the Koreans, but I could postpone that. Tell Alice we'll call him right back."

I got a call back later. "We're sorry. Something's just come up. President Ford has to be somewhere, but he really wanted to play." I knew the White House people weren't BSing me, because I had heard it from his mouth. "Believe me, if it was up to the President, he would rather be golfing with you tomorrow."

I host a *Guinness Book of World Records* golfing trio that gets together every week in Arizona. All three of us hold Guinness world records. I'm in the Book for playing for the largest indoor audience, at the São Paulo, Brazil, gig in 1973. I also play with a guy named Scott Flansburg, who is dubbed the Human Calculator—he's in the *Guinness Book of Records* for speed counting and calculation. He can add up a column of numbers in his head faster than a computer could do it. Finally, there's Freeman Theriault, who has forty-four holes-in-one. We all play together, with similar handicaps. Competing with those guys always sharpens my game.

Playing with Arnold Palmer was like collaborating with my hero Salvador Dalí. Arnold is a legend. One time I was in Florida when Callaway had me there as a staff player, and I was out playing when a squadron of golf carts showed up. It was Arnold Palmer with another eight guys, and he was giving them a guided tour around the course. Since he also represented Callaway, he pulled out one of their new drivers and handed it over to me. I couldn't believe that it was happening.

"Alice," he said, "tee this up and show these people what this driver can do."

Do you realize what kind of pressure that is, being Arnold Palmer's Iron Byron?

I teed it up and I hit it 290 yards.

"We always let Alice hit it," Palmer told his guests, "because we know he's going to hit it straight."

As he drove away, I was speechless.

I critique rock bands the same way I do golfers. "Wow, that's a great guitar player! He's really good. But, you know, if you can get your drummer to simplify what he's playing, you'd sound much better. It looks like he's as busy on stage as the guitarist, so maybe you need to simplify the drum parts."

I'll suggest that the drummer listen to some Creedence Clearwater Revival or Ringo Starr or Charlie Watts. What do they do? They lay down the beat. You don't hear busy Keith Moon–type drum fills from most great drummers. Keith Moon did that because he was the greatest rock 'n' roll drummer ever, bar none, but most drummers should stick to laying down a solid beat.

The same thing applies on the golf course: Don't expect too much out of yourself by throwing in all the fills. Lay down a solid backbeat. Simplify your swing. All of a sudden, it feels so much better. Keep it basic! I'll often ask a guitar player, "Do you know what made George Harrison such a great guitar player? It's what he *didn't* play." Likewise, if you perfect your swing or putt into one easy, simple, continuous motion, it will make a difference.

Back when I started, very few rock 'n' rollers played golf. The game was associated with our parents. But golf was what got me in with a new group of friends who were established in showbiz. As I was first rising to the top, I was the scourge, the butt of the jokes you heard on Bob Hope and Dean Martin Christmas specials: "At least you don't look like Alice Cooper!"

I was the new Tiny Tim to those upper-echelon guys—but then they eventually made me a member of the Friars Club in Los Angeles. I was unexpectedly invited to Friars Club functions, and there were Jack Benny, George Burns, Frank Sinatra, Dean Martin, all the heavy hitters. Hanging out with Alice Cooper. At first I couldn't figure out how I got in and became accepted by guys like Bob Hope and Jerry Lewis. I didn't even ask to be one of them, but they gave me the thumbs-up: "This guy's one of us."

I used to drink with Don Rickles, Mel Brooks, and all those top comedians. I even got invited to Steve Allen's birthday party, and there were literally two hundred of the biggest comedians in the world wearing tuxedos, while I showed up in black leather.

Somebody said to me, "Hey, Bob wants to talk to you." So I went into the other room and there's Bob Hope, Jackie Gleason, and President Ford. Bob says, "You know, Alice, I'm pushing the ball right."

I say, "Well, relax your right hand. You're just not releasing. You're not letting it go properly." So now I will forever have a picture of me giving Bob Hope golf tips. I cherish my days with those guys.

Nobody ever questioned the fact that I was there. It was as though I was one of them. Still, to this day, I'm the only rocker ever admitted to the Friars Club. And I attribute that to the fact that at first they were asking, "What is Alice Cooper doing playing golf?" And later: "He's not just hacking, he can play really well." And finally: "If he can shoot 78, then I want him on my team. I don't care if he's wearing makeup." Milton Berle would say, "If Alice can shoot 78, then with him I can win money off Jack Benny. He's mine."

I remember attending a Friars roast for Muhammad Ali when Don Rickles grabbed me and walked me up to Sinatra. "Hey, Frank," he said to the Chairman of the Board, "tonight I'm sitting with *this* guy. You know why? Because he fills up baseball stadiums! You play bars." Frank laughed and waved him off, with me standing there silently.

Soon I felt totally at home with those guys. I sometimes think they saw the bigger picture of my music, more than a lot of my rock fans. Like Groucho Marx, they considered me as one of the last of the vaudevillians. I was the new face, the guy who did what *they* used to do. Entertain people. Make them laugh without taking myself too seriously.

Had I not been a golfer, I would never have been there in the first place. And that was the key. I got my introduction to those guys through the game. Plus, it helped that I didn't have any problems laughing at myself—because they were going to make merciless fun of me.

The Hillcrest Country Club, one of the most conservative clubs in the country, was full of those classic comedians. I played there when I had just started, while I was still drinking. The club didn't appreciate me being there at the time. I didn't even keep score then; golf was just one big party. One day I saw Don Knotts and Morey Amsterdam in the Hillcrest locker room. That was it. I was impressed.

Anytime you have a high-caliber entertainer and take him or her out of what they do best—like, for instance, Jerry Lewis directing and acting instead of wisecracking, or Bob Hope with a golf club instead of a microphone in his hands—suddenly everybody feels humble and equal. Golf! The great common denominator!

♀ ♀ ♀

Anytime you get the opportunity to play eighteen holes with a tournament player, a PGA pro, do it! Even though you may hit the ball well, or you have a low handicap, a PGA player can look at your swing and immediately determine numerous things that you do wrong, all at a glance. I once had the good fortune to play a foursome with Vijay Singh. He took one look at my swing and immediately noticed something wrong.

"Alice, you're falling back on your shot."

"What do you mean?"

"You're hitting the ball and falling back just a little bit. If you fall back, the face of your club opens a tiny bit, and your ball drifts to the right." I did notice I had been hitting the ball slightly to the right all day. "Don't forget to follow through when you hit the ball," Singh suggested further.

If an amateur told me that, I would have thought they were out of their mind. But if it's Vijay Singh telling me, then he must be right. If only I had known that at the beginning of the round . . .

When a pro is watching your swing, he may tell you something like "You're a great player, but relax that right hand and your ball will go straight all day."

A professional golfer has an eye for detail. It's like that with other sports, like when a boxer watches another fighter for a tell. Suppose every time he throws a left hook he drops his right hand—that's when he's most vulnerable to get hit or knocked out. Trainers and players constantly watch their opponents to analyze and size up the mechanics of their swings—whether it's in the boxing ring, at home plate, or teeing off at the golf course.

Johnny Miller may watch a guy line up at least two degrees too far to the right every time he drives. "If he were my partner," Johnny would say, "I'd go right over and tell him. But he's not my partner, so I'm going to let him hit it to the right all day."

A great swing is an amalgamation of the many different ones you pick up through your golf life. Like a music career, you're a work in progress. You incorporate a little piece of everybody's advice until it's your own. Pretty soon you've got a Frankenstein swing.

You may say, "Well, that's easy for you, Alice. You have the connections to play with these kinds of pros." My response: What's your golf game really worth to you? Are you willing to invest what it takes financially (and help a charitable cause) to improve your definitive Frankenstein swing?

Say you're a pretty good player with a decent handicap. There's a major tournament playing near you, and a PGA card carrier is playing. Let's say it's $10,000 to play the Pro-Am charity match. A golfer might play Pro-Ams maybe forty times a year, having different amateur partners each time, so maybe you could score that one chance to play with him. Okay, Tiger Woods is probably not for sale unless you're the Sultan of Brunei. Money talks in this game, but there are other great, legendary players whom you could play with.

What's it worth to you? How devoted are you to improving your game?

Perhaps you can amortize the cost by splitting the charity bid with three other players. I sell myself to play tournaments for charity all the time! People might bid maybe twelve grand, or $3,000 a head for a foursome, to play with me—and not only do they get to hear my crazy stories, but I'll also give out valuable tips. I'll make it worth your bid. We'll take a bunch of grip-and-grin pictures, but I can also show you how to fix your game, a little or a lot, if you'll listen to me. If I see a guy doing something out of the ordinary in the foursome, I'll try to give him well-meaning helpful advice.

One time I played with a guy at a Pro-Am and he was using a seven-degree driver with an extra-stiff shaft. In my opinion, for a guy with a 25-handicap, he was making the game way too hard for himself. He needed more loft on his driver, so I suggested my eleven-degree driver with a bigger head and a softer shaft. With a softer driver that was easier to hit, he smacked it down the middle and thanked me all day.

That's why Callaway is so easy for me to sell—they're the easiest drivers to hit. If I see a guy with a seven-degree driver with a stiff shaft, I'll give him mine to try. He'll improve his shots immediately, and then he's got to have one. It's not a hard sell; I'm giving him something that works. That's why Callaway hires me to endorse them. I'm a walking advertisement.

Another time I was playing with a guy who kept getting pissed off at himself because he wasn't hitting the ball straight. I told him, "The easy cure is not to change your swing. Relax your right hand, like you're holding on to a bird. Why? If you're squeezing too hard or gripping too tight, you can't release. If you're limp with your right hand and firm with your left hand, the head of the club can now do more. Relax your hand."

Next hit, revelation! A miracle.

So play with people who inspire you. Let the game open doors for you. We're all in the same boat. How bad are our mistakes really going to be? And who's going to remember after the eighteenth hole (besides you)? *Everybody* understands how hard the game really is. If you hit it great, amazing. If you don't hit it so good, it's okay, too—tomorrow's another day. Plus, as amateurs, we're not supposed to be great at this game. We're expected to be occasionally crummy, until we gain a reputation as a ringer. After that, you'll be amazed who reaches out to you.

Alice presents George Burns (right) with his Alice Cooper Living Legend Award at the Friars Club in 1973 with Jack Benny (left). (Bob Gruen)

Chapter 18

Hanging with the Legends in Hollywood

I BECAME IN HIGH DEMAND as the very first king of all media in a time when rock 'n' rollers, golfers, and television and movie icons didn't mix. By spending time with legends like Jack Benny and George Burns at Friars Club roasts and events, or with guys like Johnny Mathis on the golf course, and also making bizarre appearances on daytime and nighttime television talk shows, sitcoms, game shows, and award shows, I stayed in constant flux and kept my rock fans in a constant state of confusion.

In 1978, I was asked to do *The Muppet Show.* At the time, it was the most popular show in the world, I think because its pretext was international and nonracial. All over the world, kids watched a purple thing have fun with a red thing. Or a green thing dealing with an orange thing. So everybody got behind it.

In the weeks before I was scheduled, my friends Peter Sellers and Vincent Price both made appearances. I couldn't wait to do the show! It was the hippest thing on TV. So I did their Halloween show, a takeoff on *Faust,* where I tried to get Kermit the Frog to sell his soul to become a rock star. It was extremely well written and funny. What was great about the Muppets was that you could be as stupid as you wanted to be on that show and people would accept it.

It's hard to believe, but television talk shows in 1974 weren't standard fare for rock 'n' roll. Bands appeared, but they were usually ghettoized and kept at arm's length. Do your song and get off. There was very little interaction with the star host. I did *The Mike Douglas Show* a couple of times. Mike was a very cool guy and his show was one of the biggest daytime talk shows on television. John Lennon and Yoko Ono later guest-hosted with Mike for an entire week!

161

But nothing compared to appearing on *The Tonight Show with Johnny Carson*. Once they found out I could talk and make people laugh, I was in. During my appearance, I had Johnny laughing, and of course Ed McMahon and I had the Budweiser beer thing in common—Ed was Bud's spokesman and I was their biggest customer. I fit right in with *The Tonight Show*, which perplexed my audience even more. My crowd, who were perceived as anti-Johnny, didn't quite get it. They were even more confused when I appeared on *Hollywood Squares*.

♟ ♟ ♟

I was being "a square," but it all seemed logical to me. As a member of the Friars Club, I was accustomed to hanging out with a new stratum of stars. Sinatra. Dean Martin. Don Rickles. I was a "roaster" on a few occasions at their celebrity roasts. Also, over the years at the club, I presented my annual Alice Cooper Living Legend Award to Jack Benny, George Burns, and Groucho Marx. I'll never forget Jack Benny complaining, "Aaaaaaalice, everything I pick up has got your picture on it. It's ridiiiiiiculous."

The actual Friars roasts were so vile even I sometimes blushed. The Friars went for the throat during those roasts. It was a cutting contest, legendary comedians trying to burn other legendary comedians, no holds barred. You were allowed to bust a guy if he was with a girl the night before, even if his wife was sitting there. It could get rough. The tapes they sell with roasts of Dean Martin and Sinatra are milquetoast compared to what really went on behind closed doors at a Friars roast. The one guy who could walk into the Friars Club and everybody would back off and look at him in awe was Jonathan Winters. He was the king of crazy, and even spent time in a mental hospital.

♟ ♟ ♟

I have been a huge James Bond fan ever since I read Ian Fleming novels as a schoolkid. So when I got the opportunity to record the theme for the Bond film *The Man with the Golden Gun*, I jumped at it. Well, maybe I didn't jump fast enough. I set up sessions with an arsenal of background vocalists that included the Pointer Sisters, Ronnie Spector, and Liza Minnelli. Jack Richardson and Jack Douglas did a great job putting all the cloak-and-dagger James Bond musical hooks in the production. You could almost see the movie in the song. After we delivered the tapes, we found out that we were too late and they had signed a contract with Lulu, who submitted the wimpiest song in Bond history. They were sick after they heard our version. Since I wasn't about to throw it away, it appeared on the *Muscle of Love* album.

One time I took home the coveted grand prize at a major Hollywood charity event—I won one of the original Maltese Falcons, the famed statuette from one of my favorite films! The event was a Monte Carlo night. When you attended, you picked up your chips at the door, and the winner with the most chips at the end of the night won the Falcon.

By evening's end, it was down to actor David Janssen of *The Fugitive* and me. David and I each had a ton of chips. It was very close, so other attendees gave us their chips. I remember Carol Burnett giving me hers, and I beat David by two hundred chips. I had amassed $275,000 in chips, while he had $260,000. David tried to buy the Falcon from me at the end of the night. I told him thanks but no thanks.

Rather than stash it at home in Malibu, I kept it locked up on display at a Carlos 'n' Charlie's restaurant in Mexico that I was part owner of. I should have never put it there—I owned it for only a little while until it was stolen. Even though we insured it for some ridiculous amount of money, I was heartbroken to lose it. I often wonder where it lives today.

♀ ♀ ♀

I loved meeting Hollywood legends. I got an opportunity to work with Helen Hayes when I appeared on an episode of *The Snoop Sisters,* a television detective show, in one of my first dramatic TV roles. Helen Hayes and Alice Cooper! I played a character named Prince, an informant. It was a one-time deal. I think they would have liked to have me as a regular on the show, but it was 1974 and I was working my butt off on the road.

One of the high points of my "acting career" was working with Gene Wilder. I was a big fan of *The Producers, Young Frankenstein,* and *Blazing Saddles.* Gene is a funny guy and a supertalented actor. I played his noisy next-door neighbor on his television show *Something Wilder*, which ran for a year in 1994. As part of our episode, Gene came next door to tell us to quiet down. Of course, the party was going hot and heavy. Gene ends up with Alice Cooper makeup on, passes out, and wakes up the next morning and can't get the makeup off. I had about nine pages of dialogue with Gene, back and forth. When I arrived on the set, he asked me,

"Do you know your lines?"

Of course I did. I was terrified; I knew everybody's lines.

"Alice, all you have to do is say your lines and move anywhere on the set you want, and I'll follow you."

Gene's timing was impeccable. We did our scenes in one take, in front of a live audience. It was like a Broadway show. Do your line. Stop. Wait for the laugh. Move. Deliver. I'd watched so much television, acting was something I was able to mimic. I didn't want to blow it, so I forced myself to be good.

One of the most stylish legends I've ever met was Fred Astaire, gentleman of gentlemen. Classy and complimentary, he seemed like a regular guy . . . but I knew I was seated among royalty. His technique was beyond great. Nobody could touch him, not even Gene Kelly. He was the Beatles of dance. When he came to our show, he came backstage afterward and complimented our dancers on their tap and lyrical ballet. They freaked out.

I met Rock Hudson when I was invited to perform a *West Side Story* routine, a rock version of "Gutter Cats vs. The Jets" at the Hollywood Bowl as part of a benefit for Shakespeare in the Park. (*West Side Story* was considered Shakespeare because it was based on *Romeo and Juliet*.) Paul Newman and Joanne Woodward also performed. Rock Hudson did a scene from *Kiss Me Kate*. We met backstage after the performance. I have a priceless photo of me on a couch, shirtless, with Rock Hudson glaring down my pants. This was before he had officially "come out," and I guess I was the only guy in Hollywood who didn't know he was gay. I mean, didn't he make love to Doris Day and Elizabeth Taylor in the movies?

I've been lucky; I've met a lot of legends. I was excited to meet Jack Nicholson when he was working with the Monkees on their movie *Head*. But it was the day I met Frank Sinatra that was one of the highest points, if not *the* pinnacle, of my showbiz career.

I was playing on a celebrity softball team with the Carpenters, Steve Martin, Albert Brooks, Kenny Rogers, and some others. We would meet in Las Vegas and play for Steve Wynn's charity against other celebrity teams. Sometimes these games would draw around 10,000 people.

I was sitting on the bench and there was a kid, about twelve years old, who wanted to watch the game but couldn't get in. He wouldn't give up, though, and I finally went over and grabbed him and sat him on the bench next to me and Steve Martin. The kid was happy as a clam.

That night I was out on the town when this guy came over to me. "Hey, Alice, the boss wants to see you."

I asked myself, "Who's the boss?"

I follow this guy and it's Frank Sinatra. "Hey, Coop," he said.

I was totally flabbergasted. "How are you doing, Mr. Sinatra? This is really an honor."

"Hey, man, you did me a real solid today. I owe you."

Sinatra owes me? "What did I do?" I asked.

"You know that kid you let into the baseball game? That was Jilly's kid." Jilly Rizzo was Sinatra's closest confidant. "I owe you one."

I called my mom after that. "I just met Sinatra! And he owes me one!"

Some time later, I got the call that he was going to sing one of my songs at the Hollywood Bowl—that was how he was going to pay me back. He was also going to do "Your Song," one of Bernie Taupin and Elton John's songs. Bernie and I were all excited: We were actually going to hear Sinatra perform our songs.

At the show, again we got the nod. "The boss wants ta see ya's."

Of course, we went backstage. I had my picture taken with Sinatra. He had his tux on, cigarette and martini in hand, ready to go on stage.

"Hey, Coop, how you doin'? Who's this guy?"

"This is Bernie Taupin. He cowrote 'Your Song.' Listen, I can't tell you what a compliment it is," I said, "that you would do our songs."

"You keep writin' 'em, kid, and I'll keep singin' 'em."

I sent my mom the picture of Sinatra and me. She told me that it was then that she felt like "little Vince really has made it." My meeting Sinatra spoke loudly to her.

In New York, we would often run in to Ringo Starr—he hung out in the clubs there. Or we might go to Max's Kansas City and George Harrison would be there. But one day, Shep called me from his office on Thirteenth Street. We had just recorded the song "Elected."

"You gotta come down here right now."

"Why?"

"John Lennon is here."

"What's he doing there?"

"He's listening to 'Elected.' He heard about the song."

The very idea that one of the Beatles knew any of our songs was pretty amazing. It was the first time Lennon and I had met. At the time, he was very political, and he loved the test pressing of the song. Of course, I was being satirical. I was just coming in just as he was leaving.

"Great record, you know."

"Thank you," I said.

Then out of the corner of his mouth he said, "Paul would have done it better."

Later, we got to know each other. Every time he and Yoko would get into an argument or have a problem, he'd come to L.A. Harry Nilsson was his best friend, and also one of my best friends. So they would invariably end up at my house or Harry's house, or at the Rainbow Bar and Grill. It was John on one side, Harry on the other side, an Irish guy and an Englishman knocking back drinks and continuously arguing. If one said black, the other said white. It seemed that all they wanted to do was argue. I was the peacekeeper in the middle, and drink was the common denominator between all three of us.

♀   ♀   ♀

On the Rox was a private club on Sunset Boulevard in L.A. You had to be somebody to get into On the Rox. Sheryl and I were there a lot, and we would see John Belushi, my pal Bernie Taupin, Ringo, Harry Dean Stanton.

One night at the club, Bernie had just broken up with this girl and was really down in the dumps. It just so happened that Belushi, Dan Aykroyd, and Joe Pesci were there that night. Belushi was trying to cheer Bernie up.

"That girl from Chicago? We used to call her the Dragon Queen."

Belushi goes on and on, tearing her to pieces, trying to cheer him up—but Bernie was getting madder and madder. Finally, he just turned around and swung at Belushi. Belushi took a swing back. Nilsson was holding Belushi back and I was holding back Bernie, and then it just turned into a total melee—the funniest fight scene ever, because everybody was so drunk they couldn't hit straight.

I lived in a house in Horseshoe Canyon. Micky Dolenz lived next door, and Frank Zappa lived close by. Micky's and my places were almost connected, so we hung out a lot. He knew these comic geniuses I'd never heard of—yet. Steve Martin was a banjo player. Albert Brooks was a comedy writer. They ended up at my house, the party house.

I woke up one morning, went into the living room, and Albert Brooks was asleep under the coffee table. I poured him a cup of coffee and went back into my room. Then Albert spent six hours in the bathroom, emerging that afternoon.

"Okay, is this funny?" Albert did about twenty minutes of material he'd just written in the bathroom. He was hysterical, a conceptual humorist. I would be on the floor laughing at his stuff.

"Albert, that is so funny."

"Naw," he scowled, and then went back into the bathroom. Two hours later, another bit. I think Steve Martin may have been writing for *The Smothers Brothers Comedy Hour* and *The Sonny and Cher Show* at the time. I think Albert later wrote for *Saturday Night Live*.

When I lived in New York, I used to go to the comedy club Catch a Rising Star, to catch a rising star. I went there once a week with one of my road managers. We'd watch all these comedians, guys like Robin Williams, Jerry Seinfeld, David Brenner, Garry Shandling, all young pups doing their twenty minutes.

One night we were there, laughing and drinking as usual, until this strange comedian walked into the club. Someone at my table gave me a nudge. "Wait until you see this."

"What?"

"Just wait."

The comedian had a record player, put on a disk and lip-synched the theme from the *Mighty Mouse* cartoon. Then he sang operatically while he played conga drums.

Nobody knew if Andy Kaufman was serious or a put-on. But he sure was funny. No jokes, but a showstopper. When I met him, he was soft-spoken, but his eyes would drift off, looking over your shoulder, unable to focus on you.

$$\text{\raisebox{0pt}{\small ♟ \quad ♟ \quad ♟}}$$

I did Mae West's movie *Sextette*, which was based on a play she wrote—a play that was considered so dirty for 1927 that she was thrown in jail for ten days. (She did eight days with two days off for good behavior. I understand she was allowed to wear her silk panties inside the jail.) I worked with Miss West fifty years after that, playing an Italian waiter. We did a song together.

Mae was eighty-six years old. She wore an earpiece so that they could feed her lines. At one point, she invited me back to her trailer and asked if I wanted to fool around! She was dead serious, too. Tony Curtis, Ringo Starr, Timothy Dalton, George Hamilton, Keith Moon, and George Raft were all in *Sextette*, and I found out she came on to every one of those guys.

But the one night I got the ultimate lesson in Showbiz was from Diana Ross.

We were cohosting *The American Music Awards*. I felt a little uncomfortable, as it wasn't really Alice's scene being an emcee, while Diana Ross was Miss Showbiz. So we decided to use that—at one point Alice would crack in the middle of the show.

"I can't do this anymore. I really can't."

I knocked over the podium, ran out into the audience, grabbed a girl from the front row, pulled her on stage, and ripped her clothes off. Underneath she was wearing black leather. All of a sudden, this big production broke out—guys and girls with whips came out on stage and we performed "Go to Hell" together. It went great. Alice brought down the house.

After our wildly successful song, at the break, with another hour to go on the show, Diana Ross called a quick meeting with the producers and the director. The next thing I knew, I was presenting Diana Ross with the Entertainer of the Century Award. I later asked the producers, "Entertainer of the Century? When did this happen?"

"We just invented it."

Diana Ross wasn't going to let me steal the show. I could only look at

Shep with sheer admiration. "You know what? That's simply brilliant." We both laughed. "Entertainer of the Century."

Shep and I love that kind of power play! It's something we might have attempted to pull off: an award literally invented midshow and presented as the very last award of the night. Diana Ross, showbiz genius.

But our ultimate showbiz hangout occurred when Shep and I were in Las Vegas.

"You know," I told Shep, "I really want to see Liberace."

"Me too."

So we went to the show. Since he's so flamboyant, we just had to meet him. We got lucky and he invited us back after the show.

Liberace had *two* dressing rooms. He had his meet-and-greet dressing room and another private area for his closest friends. We went back to the meet-and-greet room, and he told us, "Look, if you guys could just wait in the other room, that would be great."

Inside the meet-and-greet room were all these little old ladies filing in and out. Liberace was showing off his jewels. He had a couple of little dogs yapping around him.

Now, this is the weird part.

As soon as everybody leaves, Liberace kicks the dogs away. "Get these freakin' mutts outta here. They're drivin' me nuts."

It was Liberace speaking in a voice I'd never heard him speak in before. It wasn't the lazy-tongued effeminate Liberace voice. It was a regular, straight-guy voice.

"Where's my beer?" he shouted.

No kidding. Then Liberace comes out wearing a pair of Levi's, a white T-shirt, and cowboy boots. "Hey, guys, let's go grab a beer someplace. Don't worry. Nobody'll recognize me."

Liberace looked as normal as anybody in his street clothes. Shep and I looked at each other. *What?!?!?* To this day, I don't know if Liberace was even gay. Shep and I still wonder. Was that just a macho put-on staged for us or was it the real deal? Did we actually see the *real* Liberace, sick of the whole gig? I don't know. If he was messing with us, he was *really* good at it.

Alice swilling on a bottle of Budweiser in Japan at a 1974 press conference.

Chapter 19

From the Inside

WELCOME TO MY NIGHTMARE was a very tough act to follow, and my next few albums became total concept albums, with my alter ego Alice fighting epic battles. The question became Where do we send Alice for the next album? Finally, we decided: Let's send Alice to hell. Let's see if he can outhustle the devil.

Writing ballads is the easiest thing in the world for me. (Oddly, writing a three- or four-chord hard-rock song is much more difficult because it's too easy to sound like everybody else.) For example, "Only Women Bleed" came to me as a simple phrase. It's a tribute to a woman's mental state—not an anthem for menstruation. I was working with Dick Wagner, a great guitarist and a melody writer. When we set out to write "Only Women Bleed," we needed a beautiful ballad to offset all the horrors of *Nightmare*. We wrote the song in ten minutes, but it was beautiful—so beautiful that people who heard it at first refused to believe it was Alice Cooper. After we recorded it, the guys from the label, Atlantic Records, sat down with all their new records and played it for their staff as a blindfold test. Who's singing this? Some guessed James Taylor and Bread.

"Only Women Bleed" was eventually covered by thirteen different female artists, from Tina Turner to Etta James to Lita Ford. A girl named Julie Covington had a number-one hit with it in England.

After "Only Women Bleed," I put a ballad on every album. I felt it was my duty to my female fans to break their hearts at least once with a sad one. I was still drinking heavily when I wrote "I Never Cry," the ballad off *Alice Cooper Goes to Hell*. It was partially an alcoholic confession about how I had drunk away most of my emotions, a realization I came to after I found that

171

I couldn't remember the last time I cried. The song basically said that even if you kill me and break my heart, I'll never cry.

"I Never Cry" became the biggest hit single we ever had, even bigger than "School's Out." After that, another ballad, "You and Me," appeared on the next album, *Lace and Whiskey*. (That was the song Frank Sinatra performed at the Hollywood Bowl.) I still get people telling me that "You and Me" was their wedding song. It's hard to imagine an official Alice Cooper wedding song. Who would have thought?

Now I had three hit ballads in a row, much to the annoyance of our rock fans, who were beginning to grumble. Little did I know that I would have much bigger problems than upsetting my rock fans.

Alice Cooper was on his way to his own personal hell.

♀　♀　♀

By October 1977, I was totally out of control with my drinking. I was a depressed drunk, and I had hit bottom by the time Shep and Sheryl staged an intervention by literally grabbing me and forcing me to check myself in. They took me to a sanitarium called the Cornell Medical Center in White Plains in Westchester County, New York. This was rehab before there was rehab, before celebrities fashionably spent weeks drying out in the desert— Betty Ford wouldn't open her world-famous clinic for another five years, in 1982.

Everybody knew I drank. The drinking had become a dominant part of my personality. Shep and I were both young when we started, so neither of us really knew where the road to fame was headed. We had no experience with alcoholism, its symptoms and its treatments. Drinking was an everyday part of life in the fast lane. It was a symptom of the times, the late 1970s when we all felt immortal and invincible.

After the habitual drinking reared its ugly head, when it wasn't fun anymore, I was hiding vomiting blood every morning. The phrase "What's it all about, Alfie?" kept popping up into our heads. What *was* life all about? Shep felt like my well-being and health rested on his shoulders—we respected and loved each other, and he had taken on the role of a father figure as well as my manager. He finally realized that he had to take the responsibility, to force me to take the action that I wouldn't.

Which he did.

I was in a cold and severe lockdown ward for drug addicts, alcoholics, and people with severe mental disorders. This was definitely not drying out in comfort and remote splendor—these were times when alcoholism was equated with mental illness. Alcoholics were winos, drunks, skid row bums. Cornell was *Cuckoo's Nest* and beyond. Unfortunately, at the time the best sanitariums were more broad-based, and there weren't a lot of places that specialized in alcoholism. I was truly on the inside—but I handled my "commitment" better than anyone expected.

It was a sad and traumatic time not only for me, but also for Shep and Sheryl. Shep had a house about an hour away from Cornell, which enabled him to stay close by. During the two months I was on the inside, he visited me just about every day. Sometimes *he'd* have to get drunk just to show up. It was a rough place to go.

The Cornell Medical Center was a mysterious, ivy-covered place. To this day, I still don't totally understand what this place was really all about. It seemed like some kind of spooky, weird, country-club insane asylum with tennis courts. They also had a quiet room, which some might call a padded cell—if anybody went off their rocker or totally berserk, they'd get a hit of Thorazine or something stronger and get placed in the quiet room. But otherwise it was all beautiful Westchester scenery. I could stroll the grounds. I could even escape if I chose to. But I didn't.

They had a golf course.

After barely being able to sign my name to check in, somehow I made it through the first day. It only took a few hours for my last alcohol binge to wear off. Now I was on my own. Frazzled. They put me on Valium, enough to put down a horse, in order to soften the inevitable crash landing. I even slept on and off that night. Next morning I woke up a little hungry, so I had a little something to eat. I was still fragile, but not nearly as breakable as I was the day before. I looked around. This place had all kinds of psychosis growing under one roof. One guy would eat his dinner so fast it was dangerous—they had to stand over him and force him to eat slowly.

Some of the patients didn't seem that crazy to me. Some, I suspected, were hiding out from hard time, doing their stretch here as opposed to a jail or prison. The one thing I had in common with the inmates was that we all seemed wealthy.

After about a week in this place, I began to feel pretty good. Now that I could leave, I said no. I would stick out my treatment. I hadn't had a drink in a week! I regained my appetite—my stomach was coming around. I became alert. I slept through the entire night. One morning I even got up and ran a little. Eventually, I started my days at 7:30 with a little golf. Pretty soon I'd go to sleep dreaming about teeing up the next morning. I'd forgotten what it felt like to go to bed tired and wake up feeling good.

Two weeks into my treatment, I began to realize that some of the inmates were criminally insane. One girl murdered her brother, or maybe it was her boyfriend, and chopped him up into bits. To me, she seemed like the sweetest girl in the world.

Another girl saw CIA agents hiding and creeping behind the trees. Every once in a while, she'd run to the window. "Can't you see them? Can't you see them?" Eventually, she freaked out, ran toward the radio, picked it up, and smashed it into a million little pieces. I guess she didn't realize she was living in a community. We had only one radio, and now it was gone. I watched TV every day. That became my only link to the outside world.

One night, she made a run for the television. She must have weighed about ninety pounds, so I clotheslined her on her way toward it. She hit my outstretched arm and spun around, flipping over like a cartoon character. Then I laid down the law.

"Don't. Touch. The. Television," I said. "The only reason I'm still sane right now is because of that television. If you break it, I break you."

And I was dead serious. I would have.

After that, every time she even got close to the TV, she'd look over at me. I'd wag a finger at her, as if to say, "Remember. Break the television, I break you."

One lady looked like Lily Tomlin's comedy character Ernestine. She carried a handbag and a jewelry box. She drank dozens of cups of coffee and Coca-Cola every day. She'd tell me, "My lawyer's coming in today." At first

I didn't believe her, but sure enough, her lawyer would pull up in a long black limousine. They would meet and talk for hours and then he'd leave. I later found out that "Ernestine" owned a Fortune 500 corporation.

I spent time with this one guy, an Irish guy. I suspected he wasn't sick at all. He was obviously faking it. Every time the doctor came around, he'd act real psychotic. As soon as the doctor left, he was back to normal. I got a feeling this guy was hiding out. Finally, as I was about to leave, I asked him outright: "You know who I am. I'm a singer. I'm not with the press. I'm not a reporter or a cop. What are you doing here?"

"I'm hiding. I had a lot of money that I was supposed to use to buy arms for the IRA. I lost the money and they're out looking for me. I figure they'll never find me here." Good story. Whether or not it was true, I don't know.

While I was in the hospital, I called Bernie Taupin. I still wanted to work with him on an album project, which would later become *From the Inside*. I ended the call with "Bernie, I'll catch you later, but first I have to fix myself here."

The weirdest part about being inside was that I wasn't treated as special. I was Alice Cooper, but nobody seemed to care—they were far too involved in their own problems, fantasies, insanity. They didn't care about a rock star. They didn't have time for me.

♀   ♀   ♀

The most productive time I spent inside was in therapy. My psychiatrist was great—a cool guy with an Ivy League education. (He sort of looked like Burt Bacharach, which helped considerably.) He knew my story. The responsibility and pressures of my success and my obligations to Alice were tied with my need to drink myself onto the stage each night. He asked all the right questions, starting with a key one.

"How much do you drink on stage?"

"You mean Alice?"

"Yes, how much does Alice drink on stage?"

It suddenly dawned on me. "Alice never drinks on stage."

"Wait a minute. You drink all day. You do a two-hour show. How much do you drink when you're on stage?"

"Alice never drinks!"

"You're telling me that Alice, the character you play, your alter ego, doesn't drink?"

"I guess so." It never occurred to me. Alice never touched a drop of alcohol on stage. I drank water to keep myself hydrated when he performed, but Alice didn't *need* alcohol.

"So," Dr. Bacharach concluded, "there's you, Dr. Frankenstein, and there's Alice, the monster. You're blaming the monster for your drinking. But Alice doesn't even drink! Whose problem is this? The monster's or yours?"

I thought about it, and the doctor was absolutely right. While I was working, Alice never drank. As the creator of what I thought was the monster, I was the real monster, the one with the problem. When I was performing, I was doing what I loved. I was totally in my own world.

I'd heard stories about Dean Martin from guys like George Burns and Don Rickles. Dean never drank while he performed. Off stage, according to some of his friends, he drank quite a bit. On stage, he probably drank grapefruit juice or something. I think it's the same with a lot of performers who wrestle with drugs and alcohol. When we're doing what we do best, and we're in front of an audience working (or golfing, for that matter), we don't need whatever it is that the alcohol gives us.

"So," my doctor asked, "do you know the difference between a schmuck and a nice guy?"

"What's a schmuck?" I'd heard the word before. Lots of showbiz comedians used it.

"It's a Yiddish word for a fool and a gullible dolt. While a nice guy is someone who does nice things and you respect him for it. You may think you're a nice guy, but you are a schmuck."

"How's that?"

"You keep right on working while you're dying. Everyone else looks at you and thinks, 'Schmuck. Why doesn't he just quit drinking?' But you want to be the nice guy. Well, you're not a nice guy, you're a schmuck."

Confrontational, but correct. I couldn't argue with him.

"Alice is fine. You're the problem. After you're done performing, Alice is going to be fine, but you're not. You're the one who needs to get his act together. Alice is the professional. You're the schmuck."

Aha! Breakthrough!

I left the hospital straight. I saw being straight as my only chance to keep going.

☙ ☙ ☙

After Alice's trip to hell, I hooked up with Bernie to write lyrics with me. I wanted to write *From the Inside,* which would take place inside a mental institution, based on my time inside the Cornell Medical Center. If you listen to the songs on *From the Inside,* you can see that everybody on that album is a composite of the characters who were inside the ward.

I also saw *From the Inside* as an opportunity for Bernie and me to finally work together. I had so many stories to tell him, so many characters to flesh out. So we played a version of musical Ping-Pong—I'd throw him a line and he'd feed me one right back. We'd challenge each other.

Bernie and I eventually wrote a song called "Quiet Room." Maurice White, the leader of Earth, Wind & Fire, performed it as a duet with me. It was a revealing and transparent song about the real Quiet Room at Cornell.

"Quiet Room" contained many real chilling images: the sterilized white room that resembled a tomb; the place where they could keep me from hurting myself; its haunting atmosphere with just a mattress on the floor. I called it "my twilight zone, my strangest dream."

Bernie sent me a great phrase based on a real guy who was on the inside: "Jackknife Johnny, you're a bad jungle monkey, tool of a dagger's drawn world, them old vets gotta hate you, for bringing home that VC girl." He was painting a picture of a shell-shocked vet coming home with a Vietnamese wife. Then we needed a melody—musicians like Dick Wagner, David Foster, Davey Johnstone, and the guys from Toto would supply the music. The song became "Jackknife Johnny." The creative process was great.

After the songs were written and recorded, Shep and I put together a road show idea for the album. Sheryl choreographed it. She'd take a song like "From the Inside" and figure out where the tequila bottle wearing the sombrero would come dancing on stage. Or a whiskey bottle dressed as a cowboy. It was an alcoholic nightmare of bottles dancing inside Alice's head—*my* nightmare after having just gotten out of a mental hospital. We had to make funny out of scary.

There was one crucial scene where we re-created the Quiet Room on stage. I sang the song in a straitjacket. I used movie blood packs on my wrists and breakable beer bottles made out of sugar. As I sang the song in the Quiet Room, I would break a beer bottle and cut myself on my wrists . . . and then suddenly the white gauze bandages around my wrists gradually turned crimson and began dripping blood. It was powerful stuff and great rock theater. The audience was moved. It really told my story of my stay at Cornell, and it represented how I had been killing myself with alcohol.

But there was one song in particular on which we worked extra hard, which became my next big hit. Yikes, another ballad!

Bernie started it with "Dear darlin', surprised to hear from me? Bet you're sitting drinking coffee, yawning sleepily."

I sent him back a reply: "Just to let you know, I'm gonna be home soon. Kinda tired and afraid the time has changed your point of view. How are you going to see me now? Please don't see me ugly, babe. Because I let you down in oh so many ways."

The song became "How You Gonna See Me Now." When Bernie and I scored the song (with Dick Wagner), we were crying. It was a song about reuniting with Sheryl after my stint at the hospital. That was my deepest fear: I was in the hospital constantly thinking, *My wife has never known me totally sober. She married another guy, different from the man I now was. What if she doesn't like the new sober version?*

As soon as I got home, I felt immediately vulnerable—I no longer had my alcoholic armor to protect me. No ammunition to shoot back with. Before, I couldn't make mistakes; I was anesthetized. I would shrug off my shortcomings because I was Alice Cooper. Now I was just this guy who was going to make mistakes in life, who had to actually feel what it was like to be wrong. I was terrified that she would look at me and say, "You know what? It's just not the same. I don't love you anymore."

Maybe I was also a little worried that, in my current state of sobriety, I wouldn't love Sheryl the same way, either. How would we know? I was always in a bit of a fog before.

My wife stuck with me, and I was relieved. I really appreciated her loyalty, but now I had to get to know her all over again. And she had to get to know this stranger who was coming home from the inside. "And your name is?"

Alice all wrapped up in real snakeskin during a 1988 road show. (Ken Ballard)

Chapter 20

More Fog! More Blood!

A S THE 1980s KICKED IN, so did the hard-rock hair bands, and I was a relevant influence to that scene. I was busy again, and everything was going great. I stayed sober for a couple of years—didn't touch even a drop. I wish I could tell you I rode the entire eighties decade on a wave of sobriety.

Unfortunately, I can't.

Sheryl and I were on our way to Lake Tahoe when we stopped at a restaurant for lunch. She ordered a nice Dover sole and a little glass of chardonnay. When her food arrived, I innocently reached over and took a sip of her wine. Why I did that, I have no idea. I *hated* every type of wine imaginable—red, white, rosé, whatever. In fact, if wine had been the only kind of alcohol on earth, I never would have become an alcoholic. I couldn't stand the sight of it.

Yet that one sip of white wine pulled the trigger.

Next thing I knew, once I got back home, I was hiding bottles all over the house. At this point, everybody trusted me because I had gone so long without the slightest taste of alcohol. Nobody gave it a second thought when I said I was going out to grab some Cokes. Instead I was buying a pint here, a pint there, and stashing them. I was back to being a full-blown alcoholic.

My relapse put me back in the fog. As a result, I made four albums I hardly remember writing, recording, or touring on: *Flush the Fashion* in 1980, *Special Forces* in 1981, *Zipper Catches Skin* in 1982, and *Dada* in 1983. You've heard of lost weekends—well, those were my lost *years*. I ambled through those albums and tours in a foggy haze. By the summer of 1983, I was drinking hard, rail thin, malnourished, and knocking on death's door. Again.

It was more than Sheryl could stand—she could no longer watch me kill myself. She told me we had to divorce. The papers were filed. Terms were agreed to. She had already moved to Chicago with our first daughter, Calico, while I was in Los Angeles still trying to drink myself to death. Finally, Sheryl, her lawyer, my lawyer, and I were on our way to court. Then something jumped into my head. That's when I said, Stop! When we arrived, I grabbed Sheryl. We went into a conference room. Alone.

"This is all wrong," I told her. "I know this is my fault, but this marriage cannot end like this."

"I know," she agreed.

We sent the lawyers and the parents home. I committed to stop drinking.

Calico was two years old when her father crawled back into rehab in September of 1983. I stayed at the Camelback treatment hospital for about a month. My stay was uneventful, filled with twelve-step meetings and more full-blown therapy sessions. It was upon my leaving that something extraordinary happened.

When I left Camelback, I felt strange, like I had never been an alcoholic, and more important, like I would never be one again. Something had happened inside me. It wasn't as if I'd just quit drinking; it ran much deeper than that. In the past, I had left rehab full of fear and cravings—this time it was a much different story. After I checked out of Camelback, I never went to a meeting. I didn't feel one single craving for alcohol. It was as if the alcoholic demons were gone. Expelled! I know it sounds preposterous and that people will tell you it's impossible, but it was as if I had finally proclaimed, "That's it. I'm done. The boy's had enough."

I know there's a difference between being cured and healed, and I was healed. It was as if I had lung cancer and one day my X-ray showed my lungs were full of deadly cancer cells, and the next day no cancer, no trace. Where had my cravings for alcohol gone? Why was it this time, on my way out the door, that I told myself with such certainty, "I'm never coming back to a place like this again"?

The craving for alcohol wasn't the only thing that left my body. Before I married Sheryl, I was with a lot of women. So many women, it was stupid. Though I've never cheated on Sheryl once since our marriage in March of '76, I now felt an ever-stronger bond with my wife. Had you known me before my married days, you wouldn't believe it—I was as bad with women as I was with drink. Girls were available, and I took full advantage of them. Now, the only two things that could possibly ruin my life, the temptations of alcohol and infidelity, were both taken away. Permanently. By September 28, 1983, I had beaten my demons.

♀   ♀   ♀

By that time, I'd had enough of the grind. I stopped recording music and stayed off the road to spend some badly needed time with my family. I needed a new addiction, a new fix on life. That's when I immersed myself in golf. I had a strong desire to really study the game and take it much more seriously. I started spending every day on the golf course playing thirty-six holes. My son Dashiell was born in June of 1985, and between my family and golf, I had fresh diversions. I wouldn't return to the record-and-tour/record-and-tour treadmill until late 1986.

When I made my decision to return to music, I recorded a heavy-metal hard-rock album called *Constrictor,* with guitarist Kane Roberts. It was a comeback album of sorts, released on my new label, MCA—I had left Warner Bros. after twenty-five years. *Constrictor* was monster rock 'n' roll. So I put the makeup and the black leather back on to tour again.

I had my first official return show on October 20, 1986, in Santa Barbara. Before going on, I walked around in a vicious circle in my hotel room for about five hours. One of my biggest fears leaving Camelback Hospital after gaining sobriety was no longer the drinking—rather, if I were healed, would Alice leave me and disappear?

My head was exploding with "what if"s. What if I went out there and Alice didn't show up? What if I'm dressed in all this black leather and I'm

Don Knotts instead of Bela Lugosi? What if it's over? I mean, *really* over? I honestly had no idea what was going to happen. I wouldn't dare show my fear and weakness to the audience or the opening bands. (An unknown and unsigned new young band called Guns N' Roses was opening for us.) But backstage, I was physically sick, worrying about getting through the first song.

Finally, moment of truth: I stepped on stage. I looked up. My chin jutted out. My spine straightened up.

I knew immediately—Alice was reborn. The crouched-over, worrying Alice was still backstage, and the arrogant villain Alice was back and in charge. I literally attacked the audience. I blistered them. I was strutting and goose-stepping, twirling my cane, spitting mad at the audience. It was me against them.

And it felt great!

I knew every lyric. I was healthy again, feeling sober and clear. I wasn't even tired as I walked off the stage triumphantly. I couldn't wait to get back on stage the next night. It was a brand-new Alice.

You can't believe what a relief it was.

It felt incredible being productive again. For the next three years, I made a series of hard-rock albums that put me back in the swing of things—especially *Trash*, which went multiplatinum and yielded my first hit single in almost ten years, "Poison." It was an extremely commercial album, geared toward the legions of fans flocking to see Mötley Crüe and Guns N' Roses on stage and *Friday the 13th* and *The Evil Dead* on movie screens. I toured the world with a vengeance, with an arsenal of new hard-rock songs, buckets of blood, and girls fainting from the sheer shock and violence of it all. I was *Nightmare on Elm Street* put to music. The nightmare returns! More blood! More fog! That became my battle cry. We were even banned in Britain again, back to fighting the censors who found the new Alice way too bloody, violent, and much too hard-core. I was back with a continuous slate of live shows, back on the charts, and riding a winning streak of sobriety.

After I lost my father in 1988, I found comfort in the fact that my sobriety had been a good sign to him that I would eventually get back on the path. You see, my dad had a lot of faith, and looking back, he might have been the only person on earth who knew what else was waiting around the corner for me—that I was yet to make the most controversial, rebellious move of my entire career. It would be a move that would shock Alice fans all over the world like they'd never been shocked before.

Alice tees off at the Kraft Nabisco Championship.
(Courtesy of the Kraft Nabisco Championship. Photo by Scott Avra)

The Eighth Step of Golf Addiction

Replace the Bad Addiction with the Good Addiction

Killing and filling time. Chasing the high.
One great shot. Feeding the Golf Monster.

An alcoholic's worst nightmare is too much free time—dead air, as they say in radio. A rock singer by night has all day to kill.

I used to kill my time on tour drinking and watching TV. I'd check into a Holiday Inn in Wichita at nine in the morning, sit on the plastic turquoise couch that every Holiday Inn had at the time, turn on the TV, and drink. There were times when I'd catch myself watching heaven knows what! My assistant would come into the room and ask me, "Coop, why are you watching a Chinese cooking show in Spanish?"

"Was I? Change the channel." I wasn't really watching; I was a million miles away. I thought I was watching TV, but it was my mental tranquilizer. I was relying on my best friend, the television—and booze—to kill time.

Once I quit drinking, I had a huge dilemma. "What am I going to do with my time? How am I gonna fill the dead air?" Drinking is still a habit with me. All I did was replace what was in the cup. In the old days, it was whiskey and Coke. Now it's Diet Coke.

But I was in a fragile state. I needed to make some serious changes in my everyday life, especially since I was either at home with nothing to do, or else headlining a fifty-city tour playing in

187

front of thousands of screaming fans every night. Both scenarios left me with hours of free time on my hands.

"I gotta get out of this hotel room! I gotta get up and do something."

How about golf? If I needed to kill time, one golf match could easily devour five hours of my life. That's a pretty healthy chunk of time.

So I put on my shoes, grabbed some clubs. Found a decent course. Got out there and hit some balls. Played eighteen holes. Had lunch. Wait a minute—I've got seven more hours to kill. Okay, another round of golf. It was infinitely better than another round of drinks, and pretty soon I found I could fill ten hours of the day golfing.

It was my first (and most important) step toward maintaining sobriety—and my first step toward becoming a golf addict! Thirty-six holes a day, every day for a year. I knew I was headed for a pretty serious golf habit. But I was cool with exchanging the bad addiction with a much healthier one.

Initially, golf was one of those things I did out of boredom when I first went out with my road producer, Joe Gannon, in 1973. He and Shep were both low-handicap players—Shep's father was a teaching pro. In the beginning, I didn't take golf too seriously—I would hit a few balls, drink a few beers, then hit a few more balls. It was just something to do—not so much golfing as hitting the ball. I was usually drunk on the fairway. In the beginning, I had no business wasting other people's time out on a course or country club. Looking back, I should have spent my first two years at the driving range, but instead, I just played blindly . . . and I played just well enough to get invited to play along.

But all that changed after I finished my second round of rehab at Camelback Hospital in Phoenix. It was the day after I got out in 1983. Although I was "healed," I wanted something to fill my time, to avoid any chance of thinking about drinking. I needed a new addiction to replace the old, so I picked up some golf clubs, found a local country club, and threw myself onto the mercy of the course. That began my total immersion and addiction to golf.

I met two guys, Jim Mooney and Craig Yahiro, the assistant pros at the Pima Golf Resort in Scottsdale. I told them I wanted to become a golf addict. "I want to learn how to play golf for real," I pleaded. "I can hit the ball, I have a natural swing, but I need to master this game. I need to learn about the different clubs and irons—when do I use an eight-iron or a five-iron? I want to become a borderline pro." My personal stakes were so high that I really needed to succeed.

Jim and Craig were proactive about my situation. As Alice Cooper fans, they were only too glad to play golf with me—at that time, not too many rock 'n' rollers darkened the doorway of a country club. (In fact, none.) But they told me that if I wanted to become a golf addict, I needed to get serious. Like thirty-six holes a day serious. Each day turned into an eight- or ten-hour golf lesson.

Jim and Craig stuck with me. After my daily thirty-six holes, they would drop hundreds of balls and we would practice chip and sand shots. I was literally playing golf as if it were my full-time job, each and every day. It became my occupation away from rock 'n' roll. I'd get up in the morning and Sheryl would point to the front door: "There's your clubs. You know what you have to do. I don't want to see you until dinnertime."

What was the difference between me playing with Craig and Jim and me in the old days at the Hillcrest Country Club in L.A., playing in cutoffs with my beer bazooka? Simple. I became totally serious and committed to golf . . . because I didn't have alcohol in my way anymore.

Fortunately, I was better than average to start with, just a lucky natural. It was like running cross-country when I was in high school—I had a natural inclination for golf that I never knew I had. And I learned fast. While sometimes I'd fall back on a shot, pretty soon I was playing well. By the end of the year, I was an 8-handicap. I know it usually takes most people twenty years to to go from total beginner to 8-handicap, but I reached that goal in fifty-two weeks. I was that strung out on the game.

I've met lots of people who have confessed to me that golf was their ticket out of a world of addiction—pills, drugs, alcohol.

Talk to any addict: It's all about chasing the initial buzz. There's no high like that first high, and you want that next high to be as good as the first high. And when it isn't, you chase.

The very same principle applies to golf. Whoever takes up golf quickly finds out that the first time you hit the ball really well and watch it disappear down the middle of the fairway, you get the most addictive jolt in the world. Look out, crack and heroin! There are few things in life greater than standing and watching a ball soar 260 yards. You want that feeling back, again and again.

Next, you're wondering, *If I can hit one great shot, then why not more?* Now you're getting addicted. You're chasing the high. You want to hit two great shots . . . then four . . . then eight. And so on until all you're thinking about is playing the game and getting better at it.

Next round, you take the driver back and hit it—you catch the ball perfectly and it drives down the middle of the fairway again. You've hit the ball so solidly, there's virtually no reverberation in your hands—like hitting a home run on the sweet spot of the bat. So good. But then you miss the next shot. Then the next one. Then you chip it to the hole. Okay, you've gained back a little piece of the original ecstasy—which is just enough to keep you coming back for more.

Let's say, for example, starting out, you hit a 130. But you hit four good shots—those are the ones you're going to remember, not the other 126. As you improve, you'll hit six good shots out of 120. Then ten good shots out of 110. Once you break 100, there are more and more good shots to savor. And the more good shots you make, the more addicted you become. Just like drugs and alcohol, the golf addiction evolves as it feeds on itself.

After about a year, once you begin hitting, say, 30 good shots a game, you're seriously considering quitting your job to be out on the green. You look around—you are not alone. You see people at the airport surreptitiously leafing through golf magazines. All you're thinking about is the last time you played and how you hit a five-iron dead center. The more you evolve as a player, the greater the compulsion. Congratulations. If you had a bad addiction before, it's been replaced—only now, instead of endangering your health by drinking or taking drugs, you're outside getting physical exercise. Now you're a golf addict.

Growing older was something none of my rock 'n' roll peers saw coming. We were kids when we first got into this game, and nobody expected to live to see the light of middle age. In fact, with the drink, drugs, wine, women, and song, none of us even saw middle age coming.

Now all of a sudden we're married. We have kids and families. We're still on the road, only now we're sitting in our hotel rooms and, instead of chasing groupies or buying drugs, we're looking to score a tee time.

I've been golfing now for twenty-five years, an average of eighteen holes nearly every day. I will never tire of the addiction. Today, I hit 70 great shots, and now I find the addiction process has reversed itself—I now think about the four shots I *missed* instead of the 70 great ones. I'm obsessed with that horrible chip shot I made on the twelfth hole, which is ordinarily my best shot. Sometimes I even lie awake at night, wondering about the motion of my swing or where I put my hands.

The sad reality behind being a golf addict is that the better I get, the smaller the number of shots I get to take during a round of golf. I can no longer treat myself to 115 jolts of joy. I'm down to 75 or 80. I'm still as addicted now as I was after my first great shot— every time I stand over the ball, I can't wait to hit it and see where it goes—only now, with fewer shots per round, the paybacks are far less. That's why I might play thirty-six holes a day now.

I definitely have an addictive personality. I warn you now, if you're the same way, and by chance you don't *want* to play this game a lot, and you don't *want* to dedicate a large portion of your life to it—just hope you're not any good at it. If you're at all proficient, prepare to sacrifice a large amount of your business, time, and career feeding the Golf Monster.

Golf is a game fraught with the power and potential of pure addiction. Fortunately, it's a good kind of addiction—and in my case, the addiction that filled my time and saved my life.

Alice looking extremely "Heavy Metal" during his 1989 *Trash* hit record days.

Chapter 21

I Am Not Worthy

WITH MY ADDICTIVE PERSONALITY, as an "all-in" guy, I've been addicted to a whole host of things.

Alice's Addiction List

1. **Alcohol** Goes without saying.
2. **Golf** Complete and utter victim of the Golf Monster.
3. **Horror movies** It was never one or two. I had to own all of them.
4. **Televisions** Once I stopped drinking, at one time, I had twenty-seven televisions in the house. And no stereo. If somebody wanted to play me a tape, I don't even have a machine, but if you want to watch TV, you have your pick of twenty-seven. When you're on the road, television becomes your best friend, the only constant thing in an ever-changing world of hotel rooms and rock venues. When I walk into a hotel room, the first thing I do is turn on the TV. Doesn't matter what's on; I leave it on at all times. It's a tranquilizer, and it keeps me from being lonely. It's still an old habit.
5. **TV shows and trivia** Between Glen Buxton, Flo & Eddie, and me, we were TV trivia addicts. Who played Floyd "the Barber" Lawson on *The Andy Griffith Show*? Howard McNear, of course. Who played Frenchie, the secretary on *77 Sunset Strip*? Jacqueline Beer, who was Miss France 1954 and was married to Thor Heyerdahl, who wrote *Kon-Tiki*. What was Gilligan's first name? Willy.
6. **Watches** I never owned a watch until my mother gave me a 1935 Gruen in the mid-1990s. I wound it up and put it on, and within two days, five people asked me about that watch. The next thing I knew, I

was visiting pawnshops while on tour to find more watches. I ended that tour with two hundred of them. My suitcases looked like I robbed a jewelry store. I never got into the high-end stuff like a Patek Philippe or Rolex—I cared more about older deco watches.

7. **Shopping** I'll shop continuously with my daughter Calico. Shopping is the heaviest addiction I have besides golf. I'll come home with suitcases full of stuff that there's not even room for in my house. For me, the worst thing in the world is being on tour and sitting in my hotel room. So when we travel to Amsterdam, Copenhagen, Stuttgart, the minute we check in, Calico and I will hit the shopping streets. We know where the great stores are. We left with four suitcases to tour Europe for three months, and came back with fourteen, mostly impulse buying. Presently, I have between five hundred and six hundred pairs of pants. On my radio show, I'll give away pairs to people who answer trivia questions. If they get it right, I'll sign the pants and send it off to them—that's how I get rid of pants.

8. **Really bad kung fu movies** I used to sit and drink before a show, anxiously walking around to get ready. After I stopped drinking, I needed to kill an hour and a half. I never eat before a show, which goes back to my cross-country running days—you always want to be hungry. So instead, I began watching Chinese kung fu movies from the sixties, seventies, and eighties. They're like bad westerns—there are thousands of these films with guys who were every bit as good as Bruce Lee. They all have terrible story lines. I'm so addicted to them that watching them before a show has now become a ritual. Different musicians have different rituals they go through before going on stage. Peter Frampton irons. He has an ironing board in his dressing room. So does Robert Plant. Roger Daltrey practices fly-fishing into a bucket.

⚲   ⚲   ⚲

I performed "Feed My Frankenstein" in the movie *Wayne's World*. They were looking for someone of mythic proportions for Wayne and Garth (Mike Myers and Dana Carvey) to deliver their big catch line: "We're not worthy!" It had to be somebody everybody knew and somebody who could act.

I fell right into it. What they didn't tell me when I showed up for shooting was that I had lines. No problem—I could handle lines; dialogue is something I had done before. But when I got there, Mike Myers handed me about five pages of detailed script.

"We added a little dialogue."

"No problem." I looked at the dialogue. It was fairly complicated. "When are we going to shoot this?"

"In about half an hour."

The script had me pontificating silly, minute details of the history of Milwaukee. When I walked out on camera to do the scene, I honestly couldn't remember the details in the lines, so I started winging it. I ad-libbed about half of it. Every time we did another take, I did something totally different. But we got through it, and it seemed to work—many said it was the funniest part of the movie.

♀ ♀ ♀

All through my career my father saw the image I was portraying. He understood what I was trying to do artistically. He always said, "Okay, be the villain on the stage, but I can't support the lifestyle off the stage. I love the music, but I can't condone sleeping with every chick in Hollywood. I can't say that drinking your brains out every night is a good idea."

While he couldn't back the whole Hollywood lifestyle, he loved me and was very supportive. But he took a lot of hits from the members of his church. He went through a lot of problems when articles would come out about the decadence that was going on with the Alice Cooper tours.

But a lot of my songs from the early days—for instance, songs like "The Second Coming" or "Hallowed Be My Name" off *Love It to Death*, are theological. I freely show my influences—heaven and hell, good and evil. If you look back over my entire body of work, you'll notice there was never one time when I condoned Satanic philosophies, rituals, or behavior. On the contrary—unlike some heavy-metal bands, I completely avoided blatantly Satanic material.

In my heart of hearts, I knew that at some point I was going to have to come to terms with spirituality and my music. I was going to have to get off the fence. Even when I'd reached the point where I had every car I could drive, all the money I could spend, and all the women I desired, I remained unsatisfied, like an empty vessel waiting to be filled.

What would satisfy me? Another car? Another house? Another hit record? More applause and awards? After all the drinking was over, I was still looking for something to fill the empty bottle in my soul. All this "stuff," the fame and the money, still hadn't quenched my inner thirst for contentment. But I needed to find out for myself what would ultimately satisfy me.

♀　♀　♀

Back in 1983, when Sheryl and I nearly broke up and I committed to stop drinking, one of the conditions of our reconciliation was that we would both see a Christian marriage counselor. He laid down the terms. First, he said, we had to go back to church together. Next, we were to sleep together and get to know each other all over again, since we had been living apart.

Sheryl was a Baptist, and her dad was a Baptist pastor. We didn't know the differences between denominations, so we went to the North Phoenix Baptist Church. The preacher was a hellfire orator, a good old Southern boy who could fry you and scare you to death. Through my upbringing, I knew most of the stories, books, and verses in the Bible that the minister was preaching from—and I knew that the hellfire the preacher was preaching was true. Still, I kept avoiding it. Pushing it back.

I was squirming the entire hour. I was being tried, convicted, and executed. The Truth was beating me over the head and I couldn't deny it, but I was still protective of my alter ego, Alice. I couldn't give him up.

But what's more important, said a voice in my head, your soul or another hit record?

The worst thing was, I had to agree with the voice inside me. My soul was much more important, and it was in deep trouble. Once church service was over, I felt relieved.

I was still clean and sober, and things were coming back into focus. Sheryl and I switched churches and started going to Camelback Bible Church. The minister, Tim Savage, was a different style of pastor, more contemporary and less fire-and-brimstone than the previous minister. He preached the same message, but he was a surfer. Plus, he listened to Led Zeppelin. He even owned a few Alice Cooper albums. He was just a little bit younger than me, educated at Cambridge, but when he preached, it spoke to me. I couldn't wait to go back.

Before I began writing my album *Last Temptation*, I met with Tim.

"I'm a Christian now," I told him, "and I can't really be Alice anymore."

"Vince," he said. (It's funny. He calls me Vince *and* Alice.) "Do you believe that God makes mistakes?"

I answered honestly. "I think God is incapable of making mistakes."

"Then look where he's put you—right in the Philistines' camp. He's given you all this knowledge. What speaks louder? You preaching the word? Or is it your lifestyle that communicates with people? You're in the world of rock 'n' roll, booze, and sex. Yet you're the guy who never cheats on his wife, who doesn't go to strip bars with the boys, and doesn't get high. Your band sees you reading the Bible at night on the bus. What speaks louder than that? I don't see any reason why you should quit being Alice Cooper."

I was surprised. It was definitely not the answer I expected. Then I asked myself, Is rock 'n' roll really the Devil's music?

♀   ♀   ♀

Heavy metal doesn't automatically have to be Satan's music—only if the lyrics go that way. Does a chord progression necessarily constitute music that's evil? I don't think so. People talk about diminished-fifth chords supposedly being the devil's music, but I think that it all depends on the lyrics you put in there. If you're saying, "Worship Satan!" then sure, that's Satanic—though most rock and heavy-metal musicians don't believe in that anyway, not even most of the guys playing so-called black metal.

Of course, there are real Satanists. I met the late Satanist Anton LaVey many years ago in San Francisco. Coming from a Christian home, I was both interested in it and repelled by it. I knew it was wrong, but I didn't know how much of it was a joke.

When you go to Norway and you see all these Norwegian black metal bands, it's very pagan, back to the Norse, a godless sort of Viking paganism.

I meet these guys face-to-face and some of it is just a show—but there are guys who burn churches and play black metal.

If you think that hell is going to be someplace to hang out and get high with Jim Morrison, you have another thing coming. Biblically, we're told that hell is an unquenchable thirst—like having a toothache in all of your teeth forever, with absolutely no relief in sight. It's certainly not where we want to go for eternity. People might say, "No, God is too good for that. He would never let that happen to me." Well, biblically, God is very wrathful. I tell people, Don't be afraid of Satan. Satan can only do so much. Be very afraid of an angry God.

People who play around with Satanic music are juggling with nitroglycerin, and most don't even know it. I almost feel it's my duty to ask, "Guys, do you have any idea what you're doing?" I don't know anything about witchcraft. I know nothing about spells. But I know about this stuff.

If somebody came around and plunged an Alice Cooper doll with voodoo pins, I'd just sit and laugh at him. Play that crap on someone who doesn't know what I know. Me, I'm protected—my God is so much more powerful than yours, it's laughable.

♀   ♀   ♀

When I finally wrote *Last Temptation,* I saw a way of doing something clever, making a rock record that was as good as any rock record I'd ever made, with songs that rock like on *Love It to Death* and *Killer,* but with Alice talking about morality. For people who aren't paying close attention to the lyrics, they'll give the album a thumbs-up when normally they might not be into religious music. It's one of the best records I've ever made. Sure, I was walking on thin ice using Alice as the medium, but I felt like I was being guided through the process. I feel to this day that whenever I go on stage, I can have a dark and satirical sense of humor about what's going on in my world.

♀   ♀   ♀

My commitment to Christianity hit the newswires. I was now officially off the fence, intellectually, spiritually, and publicly. I immediately lost sales and bookings. So I sat Shep down in my living room. He thought I was quitting music and that I could no longer be Alice. But I told him that I could definitely still be Alice, I just had new guidelines. He didn't think it would ever work. The fans were going to hate it—Alice Cooper, a Christian? They would rebel and soon I'd lose my base.

I knew I'd lose some fans for a while, but I put it to Shep like this: "When have you and I *ever* avoided controversy? What made us? Controversy! What could be more controversial than this?"

Ultimately, becoming a Christian became the most rebellious and risky thing I've ever done. I was now rebelling against the very business that had invented me, and that's true rebellion. Who's the biggest rebel to ever live? Jesus Christ.

Part of my transformation involved a lot of study. I now study the Bible a few verses or chapters a night with books that explain and help light the path I'm walking as I'm reading. Since my conversion, I've gone through the Bible seven or eight times, and I'm just barely scratching the surface.

When I see preachers on television healing people, that stuff scares me. In fact, most Christians I know are repelled by that kind of behavior. And I believe that if Jesus were here, he'd wonder just what's being done in his name. But still, we live in the world. We turn on the TV, and there's a naked girl. Are we attracted to it? Yes. How long do we sit and look at it before we change the channel? That's the battle we fight each day.

As a Christian, I don't declare myself a "Christian rock star." I'm merely a rock star who's a Christian. To me, a Christian rock star is somebody who gets up on stage and sings praise music, preaching the gospel. Alice Cooper is still a guy who entertains the audience—he just happens to be a Christian.

Left to right: Alice at the VH1 Fairway to Heaven tournament
with Brett Scallions (lead singer for Fuel), *Melrose Place* actor Grant Show,
Bret Michaels (lead singer of Poison), and Bobby Dall (Poison bassist).
(Photo courtesy of VH1 and Erik Luftglass)

The Ninth Step of Golf Addiction

Construct a Spiritual Support System

That Works for You

John Daly and Alice. Giving alcohol too much credit.

John Daly is the most loved guy in golf, because he'll take a 17 on a hole, then birdie the next five holes. But when he had his problems with alcohol and betting, who was the only one who would take him in? Ely Callaway did, and at a time when many people in the golf world gave up on Daly and did not want to be associated with him. Ely offered Daly to come on staff with Callaway Golf if he promised to control his drinking and gambling. Then, if Daly played with Callaway clubs, Ely would take care of the Las Vegas gambling debt.

Back in 1993, Callaway had gone out of his way to give another alcoholic another chance: me. Alice Cooper and John Daly: two misfits, two guys who both upset the applecart. The great unwashed public these days loves to give the equally great unwashed famous people who screw up a second chance. Maybe that's one of the advantages of being a celebrity who has experienced ups and downs. Becoming a celebrity simply does not come with a book of instructions. Fame and money distorts one's sense of reality. You're in the intense public spotlight, and eventually you have to get it right because everybody and their dog knows about your personal problems. The whole concept of rehab is so heavily in the public consciousness now, in fact, I think it's become almost a rite of passage. You read about it every day. When you go to rehab, you go to quit or you go just to cool out. I went to quit. I was serious about quitting. Some people just go to cool out, and these will be the ones in the rehab revolving door.

I remember when I was first with John Daly on the road for a Callaway promotion. I had fifteen years of sobriety, and John had fifteen days. I said to him, "Okay, John, let's look at it this way. It's just me and you out there, and you know I drank way more than you did. I made five platinum albums and two number ones under the influence. Then, after they took the alcohol away, I immediately thought, *You can't take my formula away! I'm never going to make another good album again if you take this away from me!* I know that you won two majors drinking. So now, John, they're taking your alcohol away and you're probably thinking that it's like taking your driver away." He nodded.

But what we got wrong in our post-alcohol logic was this: I would have made *ten* platinum albums if I didn't drink alcohol, and John Daly would have won four or five majors! The alcohol did nothing but hold us back, and we kept giving it the recognition instead of giving the credit to our own abilities!

I had to help John get that thought in his head: *Don't give alcohol false credit for your ability. We were lucky we could even function with the alcohol.*

When I think of all the time I wasted drunk, it makes me cringe. There are *four albums* that I don't even remember writing or recording! I look back at those albums and there were some good songs on them. I would love to rerecord some of those tunes now that I'm sober and make them into really great songs. They may have turned out okay, but I know they could have been so much better.

Think about how many shots you missed on the fairway because you weren't on your game or you were buzzed. Sure, you won, but you could have won five times more than that. You might have been hungover that morning and lost by a putt.

Maybe you lost that tournament because your hands were shaking a little bit.

John Daly and I got to be pretty good friends. When we'd play golf together, he'd bring along a case of Diet Cokes. He would drink one after another and then say to me, "Man, I'd kill for a beer right now."

"Yeah, yeah . . . so here's another Diet Coke." And look out for the Golf Monster.

Alice on the spooky bed during the Nightmare tour in 1975. (Ken Ballard)

Chapter 22

The Importance of Being Alice

THE IDEA THAT I'M PLAYING SOCIETY'S VILLAIN is not inconsistent with my spiritual views. In fact, both Alice and I maintain that what the world needs now is a gigantic hypodermic shot of morality and common sense, and satirizing the villainy in the world might just help.

Alice started out as the villain, and he remains one. But think about it—there's a villain and a hero in every Shakespearean play, in every movie you see. I don't see Alice as any more dangerous a villain than, say, Captain Hook. What does he really do? He takes the stage, face snarling and smeared with makeup, ready to kill. We stop him and put him in a straitjacket. He breaks out. We put him on a guillotine—off goes his head. He comes back in white tails and top hat. Balloons spill from above as the audience is covered in confetti and stage blood. Everybody laughs. How evil is that? To me, it just sounds like a fun party.

But satirizing villainy isn't a unique concept. For example, take Marilyn Manson. He has a woman's name and wears makeup—how original. It was the same guy—tall, gaunt, made up . . . outrageous theatrics . . . frightened parents. Of course, Alice was never a devil worshiper or a drug addict—but basically, all Marilyn Manson did was systematically reinvent Alice.

When I first saw it, I laughed. Yet I defended Marilyn Manson's right to free speech when he tore up a Bible after the Columbine shootings, even though, theologically, we had nothing in common. Because while tearing up a Bible on stage initially angered me, it also made me stop and think—that's what I did in the 1970s. What Marilyn Manson has done is up the ante in a much more outrageous and vicious way gearing himself to the new industrial high-tech generation. He uses MTV, whereas I didn't have an

MTV early in my career, but he also uses the straight press and word of mouth just like we did.

Of course, what ultimately separates me from Marilyn Manson are the hit songs, and that's what made Alice so dangerous in the first place. I've lasted over forty years because of my fourteen Top Forty hits.

Mind you, I can no longer go on stage and represent something I don't believe in. There a few songs, like "Trash" and "Spark in the Dark," that I won't do anymore. But there aren't many of those—from the beginning, I didn't allow swearing or nudity on my stage. Whereas most bands use the F-word as much as they can, I didn't go for anything so obviously outrageous.

I still see the world as a place in sore need of a massive shot of not only morality, but also satire, and as long as Alice is willing and able, I will continue to take shots at the absurdity of the world through my music.

Touring is in my blood. I love the art of it. My show is fun for everybody—it's never dirty or cheap. The songs are great and all very tongue-in-cheek. It's been like that for years—but today is the best of times to be Alice. I'm having the best time of my life now, because I'm Alice on my terms, having found my faith and mixed that with being Alice.

At first Shep was a doubting Thomas, but I urged him to stay with me—I always thought it would work out. Eventually, when we made it out of the storm, even Shep shook his head in disbelief. He doesn't understand it—I confess to the world I'm Christian, I'm no longer singing about sex, and we're still making money. In fact, we're working harder than ever.

I walk a very thin line with my musical reputation balanced with my beliefs. Many people look at me and see a hypocrite—how can I be Alice and proclaim myself a Christian? I've had this very debate with not only other people, but with myself as well. So I'll ask, "How am I a hypocrite? What does Alice Cooper do that I can't live with as a Christian? Please tell me. If it's bothering you, then maybe it's something I should be thinking about. I want to live my life with a clear conscience."

Is it the songs? The big hits? "I'm Eighteen"? I have no problem with that song. Since we wrote it, it hasn't gotten any easier to be eighteen. In fact, it's gotten much harder. "School's Out"? Are you kidding? That's not an evil song. Kids will always be happy to get out of school. It's just Alice—he is rock 'n' roll.

We are now at the heart of the debate. Rock 'n' roll. So I ask, "What's the difference between rock 'n' roll and Shakespeare? They're both art, both showbiz." I look at what I do on stage as art and theater—entertainment. There's nothing morally wrong with what I do up there. If there were, I'm confident I would feel it and rectify it. A lot of Alice's show is satirical and cynical. Alice is a distorted and exaggerated reflection of society taken to extremes—I'm holding a mirror up to evil itself and making people think about it. By making fun of society from the fringes, I never have to worry about being mistaken for a sugarcoated praise performer.

♀　♀　♀

I'm often asked what goes into becoming Alice for the night.

Before I assume the role of Alice, I have to be totally immersed in the character. Everything about becoming Alice is based on ritual. I don't know how other performers do it, but when I play Alice, I have a routine. I know I need an hour-and-a-half nap. Even when I was younger, I always felt rest was really important, because there's so much that goes on during the day that I need downtime. Even if I don't sleep, all the lights are out for an hour and a half. Curtains closed. No phones.

My assistant wakes me up a half hour before I have to leave for the venue. I get up and have a chocolate-chip cookie, to get a little sugar in my system. Then a Diet Coke. I watch fifteen minutes of whatever's on TV. Then we'll go to the gig exactly an hour and a half before showtime.

The first hour, I'll watch kung fu movies. Really bad ones. I have a collection of more than two thousand really bad kung fu movies—I go out of my way to find them. Not Bruce Lee movies; that would be too good. These are movies that are beyond bad, horrific films like *Real Kung Fu vs. The Nine Vampires*. I'm addicted to them. If someone says we don't have a playback system for me to watch my kung fu movies, I'll at least try to watch them on a computer.

Sometimes my assistant will moan, "Is this the one with the flying guillotine? Alice, you've seen this one five times." I can't help it. It's like a tranquilizer for me. Sometimes Shep comes in, going, "How can you watch this crap?" Well, because it's great!

At half an hour before showtime, I leave the movie on but start putting on the pants, the boots, and the rest. I dress in layers. Then I put the makeup on. Ten minutes before I go on, off goes the kung fu movie—I need those ten minutes to become Alice. That's when *nobody* comes in.

So what happens in those ten minutes that no one has ever seen? There's pacing. I practice different moves with my canes, spinning and catching. The canes are Alice's fighting sticks, and I can now spin two of them. I come out on stage spinning these canes, and sometimes kung fu guys in the audience assume I've studied Thai stick fighting. No, it's just the mimic in me—I picked it up from the movies. The stick twirling kind of goes back to Fred Astaire—the cane, the top hat, the (twisted) tuxedo—except my cane is a little more dangerous than Fred's.

The makeup is a quick thing. I use a regular base, then grease paint. I slash Alice's raccoon eyes on with a brush. Next, I'll decide whether I'm going to do the pointed lines, the two clown lines (if I'm feeling severe), or the Bette Davis spider eyes. It varies from night to night. To be honest, I don't know what makes the final determination; it's just whatever my hand does that night. As soon as the makeup and the hair are in place, then it's gloves on. Usually, I've still got five minutes to spin the sticks.

And then I pray. Alone in the room. I stop everything to pray.

That's when I fully realize that now, on stage, I have boundaries. And that's what makes it really fun, the fact that I can be this villain without ever crossing those boundaries, without compromising my morals. It wasn't always that way, of course. In the beginning, I was bad on stage. I would do terrible things—putting a hatchet to mannequin parts and pulling a baby out. I'd go out of my way to be vile, anything I could do to be shocking.

One thing I used to do was hang over the breast half of the mannequin and spit. The spit would dribble slowly down the breast of the mannequin, and when it got to the bottom, I'd get underneath and catch the spit in my mouth. Then I'd spit it back into the audience. That always got thunderous applause. When I was the old drunk Alice, I used to think that the audience was going to love anything I did on stage, the grosser the better. I now realize the less you do, the more subtle you are, the scarier it is. I think of Alice as this arrogant mastermind, strutting around with his chin up and out. He's Hannibal Lecter; he might kill you. I will never let him become a clown. He looks at the audience like they're his plaything, and his attitude is "You're here for me. You are not in control of me, I am in control of you!"

As far as stage chatter, Alice *never* says thank you. If the audience goes crazy, he'll go into the next song. He'll never acknowledge the crowd's affection. Adoration is something he expects. Which is funny, because I am so much the opposite. If I were on that stage as myself, I would be humbly spewing my thanks. But the audience loves and expects Alice to be his usual arrogant and condescending self; it's part of his image. Alice is a great character to play. I think he has a lot to say.

♀ ♀ ♀

At the end of the show, the very last thing I do is wipe off the makeup and come out for the encore. That's the only time I step out of character and talk to the audience. The makeup is what separates me from Alice–without it, I can laugh with the audience, introduce the band, be funny, and tell my daughter to get off the stage and go put some clothes on. "Kids these days . . . geesh!"

We still overload our audience with spectacle–there are so many visuals and so much music, their imaginations sometimes play tricks on them and we hear accounts of things that never happened. I can't tell you how many times I've heard people distinctly recalling me on stage killing a chicken, ripping its head off, and spitting the guts and blood back into the audience. The truth is I've never, ever hurt an animal on stage–the closest I got was that chicken, and I felt terrible about what happened to it. Nevertheless, there are people who would have bet their house they saw me kill something, and honestly believe it to this day.

Some of my recent material–for instance, the albums *Brutal Planet* and *Dragontown*–puts Alice into a new situation and gauges his reactions. Let's see Alice in the future, or in hell. In *The Last Temptation,* Alice has his own diabolical circus that parallels the one in Ray Bradbury's *Something Wicked This Way Comes.* I use the adventures of Alice wherever he is–whether he's in the past, present, or future, whether we put him in a time machine or a mental hospital. He's my durable character. I don't need champagne, prostitutes, and cocaine–give me a stupid kung fu movie, some Diet Coke, and a concept that people can relate to, and I'll give you a great show.

Left to right: Former NFL quarterback Jim Plunkett, actress Kassie DePaiva
from *One Life to Live*, Alice, and Dandy Don Meredith of Dallas Cowboys
and *Monday Night Football*. At the 2005 Toyota/Kraft Nabisco
$1 Million Hole-in-One Contest finals.
(Courtesy of the Kraft Nabisco Championship. Photo by Scott Avra)

The Tenth Step of Golf Addiction

Learn How to Play Through

The Curse of Playing Through. Hitting into someone.
If you're an amateur, relax. Be a pressure player.
Play to the crowd.

Let's say I'm on the fairway with three of my low-handicap friends. We play pretty fast. We hit the ball down the middle, keep it on the green. We can play the course in three and a half hours. Now let's say the people in front of us are borderline hackers— playing really slow, in no hurry. To them, it's a social thing.

We're stuck—it's golf gridlock. We can't go anywhere until they finish each hole, so we just have to wait. It's annoying, and it's screwing up the momentum of our game. Wouldn't it be better to just wave us past?

The problem with playing through is that afterward, *you* start hitting your worst shots. I call it the Curse of Playing Through. Say a slower group waves you on and you play through—on the next par three, some kind of voodoo sets in. You're in a hurry after having played through, worrying that now the group behind you will have to wait on you—so you don't get the great shots you need.

Beware of the Curse of Playing Through. It's one of those weird things when your whole rhythm gets thrown off and your concentration is rushed. Concentration, momentum, and rhythm are the necessary ingredients for any good game. I've been with some really great foursomes, and with them, after the people ahead of us let us play through, none of us hits anywhere near the green! The ball ends up:

- in the water
- in the sand
- in the rough

. . . everywhere but where it should be going. Yes, it's the Curse of Playing Through.

Maybe we've rung up a great score and we only have five holes left to play. Should we play through? My rule is: No! Because I know I'll blow that next hole if I play through. I'll ruin my score.

So how do you get around the Golf Monster here? How do you solve the problem, short of pulling an Uzi out of your golf bag and gunning down the entire party ahead of you? Get up early with the farmers and the milkmen. When I hit the green at 7:00 in the morning, there's almost never anyone in front of me. So my group can finish the eighteen holes at our own quick pace.

♀   ♀   ♀

Besides playing through, there are those awkward times when you hit into somebody. When this happens, you're likely to see something like road rage. Ever notice how brave we are in our cars when all the doors are locked? That's the funniest part of human nature. And, of course, a golf course is a microcosm of society. People are generally civilized, but you never know when belligerence and hostility may rear its ugly head.

Hitting into somebody, or getting hit into yourself, can be as precarious as playing through. Say I'm two hundred yards out, waiting to hit my second shot. Theoretically, the people behind me are supposed to wait until I'm out of the way, on to the next hole. But sometimes golfers get overanxious—usually dim-witted amateurs with 52-handicaps. So you're standing there and here comes a flying Titleist, careening past your ear.

You shake your fist. "Wait a minute, fella. Who the heck do

you think you are invading my space? You could have hit me." People have gotten killed on golf courses by getting plunked on the head—a speeding golf ball can resemble a speeding bullet.

Getting "hit into" is like a slap in the face—no respect. It doesn't matter who it is behind you—it could be the Church Lady or Hulk Hogan, but you turn around and give them hell.

Just remember—it happens all the time, and more often than not, it's accidental. So relax. I've accidentally hit into people when they were around the corner and out of my sight lines. We all have.

One time I thought the party in front of me had finished, so I drove a ball that turned the corner and hit square into them. They came running back, all ticked off, armed with the fattest driver in their bag. I admitted my mistake immediately, of course. "Oops! My apologies. I thought you guys already hit." Usually, after that, they'll back off. But if you hit into them again, then it's Let's Get Ready to Rumble Time! I've seen full-on fights break out after being hit into twice. Sometimes the golf marshal who patrols the course steps in and expels the offending players.

So keep your head.

Of course, that said, there are also the obnoxious types, drunks, who hit into you to try to speed you up. That's when it's time to drop the gloves. Remember that scene in the movie *Sideways* where Miles and Jack suddenly go berserk and charge after the four guys hitting into them? I could see that happening to me. Golf is a gentlemen's game, but if a fight does break out, the worst thing about being on a golf course is that every player has his own arsenal of titanium weaponry. If you have two drunken groups going after each other . . . look out! There's a riot going on!

I've had incidents where I've accidentally hit into somebody— maybe I didn't see them, or I whacked the ball too hard with the wind behind me—and they're so pissed off they hit my ball back. Now, that's an insult. So I'll drive up and confront them.

Of course, by that time, they'll recognize me and they're totally cool about it. "Can I have your autograph? Will you sign the ball? Could you hit into us again so I can I tell my friends? Maybe sing a few bars of 'Workin' Up a Sweat'?"

It's surprising more people don't get bonked at Pro-Am tournaments. Those events can be real mob scenes. I've played a ton of Pro-Ams, especially the big celebrity ones, like the Dinah Shore and the Bob Hope—they're my chance to play with the big guys. Normally, tournaments draw a few thousand people in the gallery, but if there are tens of thousands—at the Phoenix Open, there can be as many as 100,000 spectators—that's when I usually play my best. It's just like being on stage. Having a large crowd watching me flips the switch in my head—I can sink more long putts, score six birdies, and maybe shoot one under par.

But sometimes all the spectators can be a bad thing. At a recent Bob Hope tournament, I teed off a beautiful shot on a par-five hole, then I drove a blind shot right down into this little valley—it was a beautiful line-drive bullet. It nearly broke the sound barrier. So I pulled out my seven-iron and whaled on the ball again. When I got to the top of the hill, I saw people standing around someone on the ground. It was a spectator, a woman, who was lying there bleeding. It turned out that my ball hit her, and she fell like a wounded deer and hit her head on the cement.

I ran up to her, feeling horrible. She was dazed. They had a towel wrapped around her head. "I am so sorry."

"Was that your ball?" she asked me.

"Yes," I admitted in front of thousands of eyewitnesses.

"Alice, I'm a big fan of your music," she said.

I signed the ball. What else could I do? It had blood all over it, which, when you think about it, is par for my course: "Alice Cooper Autographs Bloody Golf Ball."

"It's okay," she told me, as she made her way to the shuttle that would take her to the hospital for a few stitches.

That night, I still felt bad. I decided to send her some kind of present to cheer her up. I had a gift basket made up, except it wasn't your average assortment of fruit and candy. Instead, I had the basket filled with Advil, Excedrin, Aleve, Tylenol, and a bicycle helmet. I later interviewed her on my radio show—she thought it was the coolest thing. She was a real good sport.

♀ ♀ ♀

Direct hits aside, I consider myself to be a pretty good pressure player. At Pro-Ams, most players are pretty nervous at the first tee. I see CEOs from the country's largest companies literally shaking in their spikes. I say to them, "Relax. Nobody is expecting you to hit it great. They expect Sergio and Tiger to do that. We're the amateurs, not the pros."

Remember, in a big tournament you only have to look good twice: the first tee and the last shot on eighteen. That's where most of the VIP spectators hang out. If you get your first tee shot off down the middle and, instead of polite golf claps, you get the "ooooh" and the grand applause—that's great.

So if you're gonna do something, don't be "kind of" good at it. Be *really* good at it, or be *unique* at it. You have the choice of turning it on or turning it off. When I see a crowd, I take it up a notch, whereas some amateurs shut down and turn it off. They might get so anxious, they can't hit the ball at all. Because of the nerves, they forget the fundamentals.

Not the case with me. When everybody gets quiet, I usually tell the crowd, "Make all the noise you want. I'm used to 60,000 people screaming at me." The audience turns me on. I don't think you can learn that, but just remember to look at yourself and think: *You know how well you can hit this ball. This is the time when all of those elements have to come together. Your head's got to stay down. Your rhythm has to be great. You have to look like a pro right here. Otherwise, why do you play golf?*

Teeing off at a Pro-Am is like walking out on stage. Being a rock 'n' roll golfer, if I'm gonna make a spectacle of myself, I can handle the applause, the laughs, and the abuse. I'm saying to the crowd: "Look at me." If I'm wearing electric green pants and a hot pink zebra shirt, I had better play well. If I shoot a 105, I'm a clown. If I shoot a 73, I'm a genius—a Billion Dollar Baby.

The late, great Ely Callaway, hero and mentor.

Chapter 23

Ely and Alice

MY ASSOCIATION WITH CALLAWAY GOLF began when I played at a VH1 function called Fairway to Heaven. (Finally, a music cable channel had gotten around to covering rockers who play golf!) I was invited each year and became their A player; my team won the competition five years in a row.

I was at that game, and the actor Robert "Arli$$" Wohl introduced me to Ely Callaway and his sales VP, Bruce Parker, suggesting that it would be great if I did a commercial for Callaway. He thought it would be a funny thing.

Being a Callaway guy myself, I jokingly said to Ely and Bruce, "Hit the ball, Alice? Well, I *am* Alice and I always hit the ball with your equipment." ("Hit the ball, Alice" is a popular golfing term, telling someone to put some muscle into their shot.)

That started them thinking, but Bruce initially wrote the idea off. "I don't think it would work," he said. "Your rock image is so different, and it just doesn't represent what Callaway is about."

Ely took another view, though. Ely Callaway was a Southern gentleman from Georgia who resembled an everyday laid-back senior citizen—but in reality he was as sharp as a razor blade. He listened up when I told him, "Well, you know the reason why I play golf? Golf saved me from drinking." He was surprised. "I quit drinking and took up golf, which became my new addiction. So I had started playing *seriously*, and I no longer wanted to play with average clubs—I wanted to play Callaway, because that's the best club."

We spoke about their upcoming product line. At the time, Callaway clubs were the most expensive clubs on the market. The company wanted to reach the next level of consumers, the everyman and -woman. They wanted everyday people to feel comfortable playing Callaway. They were coming out with two product lines: One would be very high-end and the other would be a medium-priced line that would appeal to the average weekend player.

Ely had already made his mark in the business world in the 1960s as president and director of the textile giant Burlington Industries, which he made into a billion dollar company. Then after leaving Burlington and creating a successful winery, Callaway Vineyard and Winery in Temecula, California, he retired briefly and played a lot of golf. He bought half interest in a pitching wedge he spotted in a Palm Springs–area pro shop called the Hickory Stick. Soon Callaway Hickory Stick USA was renamed Callaway Golf, and the sport has never been the same since.

There was no obvious reason for Ely Callaway to hire the most notorious shock rocker of all time to represent the most conservative golf club company in America, unless it was time for a drastic change at Callaway. I think I did eight TV commercials with Callaway, which was, by the way, when they were selling the most clubs. There was obviously a method to Ely's "madness."

Back when the company was founded in 1982, the average guy *would not* play Callaway. Instead, he might go down to the local discount sporting goods store and pick up a set of Wilson clubs for $400–woods, bags, irons, everything–whereas a Callaway driver alone would cost $400. Callaway was originally equated with Mercedes and Rolex–a very posh product that the average guy felt uncomfortable buying. In other words, if you were going to play golf with the guy in the cubicle next to you, and you went out to the golf course and he had Callaway equipment, it was almost pretentious. It was like you were living beyond your means. Only the boss played Callaway.

I told Ely and Bruce that I thought humor was the best way to lure the typical weekend golfer into feeling comfortable with their brand. Make them laugh–if you can't make light of your product, then the everyman won't relate to it.

So they hired an ad agency to produce a set of commercials that featured me, Kenny G, Sugar Ray Leonard, Smokey Robinson, and Mac Davis–all entertainers who loved to play golf and used Callaway. Everybody knows John Daly, Gary Player, Johnny Miller, and Arnold Palmer can hit Callaway. But what about Alice Cooper and Sugar Ray? Hey, we play Callaway too.

So we became the celebrity endorsers who could reach the masses.

I showed up for my first Callaway commercial shoot with Johnny Miller. I had my hair all tied back and a visor on, kind of like a disguise—I figured I should be very conservative. But soon Ely took me aside on the set and asked, "Alice, where's your hair? I want to see the rock 'n' roll Alice Cooper."

There was a giant python sprawled out on the putting green. I said to Ely, "Isn't one of the big no-no's in advertising—never use a snake because it bothers people, especially women? They'll switch off the commercial."

"Don't worry," Ely said, "we'll deal with women later." So I did my hair and we put the big snake on the course. The commercial showed me putting the ball, which bounced off the snake and went into the hole. Then Johnny Miller said, "Nice putt, Alice." It all connected: Alice, the snake, and the golf phrase "I'm going to snake this one in." I didn't realize until later, but Ely was also killing two birds with one stone. Cobra was Callaway's biggest competitor at the time, and the snake was their symbol. With me as their spokesman, as heavily associated with snake imagery as I was, now the snake became a subliminal Callaway image. He essentially hijacked Cobra's symbol.

Ely was breaking all the rules—taking a very conservative company and changing it right in front of our eyes with one commercial spot—and I liked that about him.

Next Johnny and I played off the popular golf saying "Hit the ball, Alice." Suppose you make a putt and it's right on line, but you hit it too soft and it comes up short. Everybody says, "Hit the ball, Alice." It's like saying, "Hit the ball, you little girl."

The commercials became a big hit and I ended up doing many more spots. There was one ad with me and a couple other celebs as blue-collar guys working in the Callaway factory, making clubs, then driving golf balls off the shipping dock on our break, with the foreman yelling at us, "Get back to work!"

One of my favorite ones hit particularly close to home. I was shown at a twelve-step group meeting. There was an empty microphone, and I walked up and started my rap: "Hi. My name is Alice Cooper."

"Hi, Alice."

But I wasn't a real alcoholic—I was a bona fide golf-aholic. "Since I hit the new Big Bertha driver, I now play twice a day now. I can't help it, and I understand I have a problem."

"One round at a time, Alice."

I suspect that for some reason, maybe something in the Callaway lineage, Ely had compassion for people with past addictions. Think about it: Ely hired me to represent them, and I was a known cured alcoholic who had traded booze for golf. Ely loved the fact that the game was a positive force in my life. He also hired John Daly, who had addiction problems too. He never openly stated it to me, but Ely seemed supportive to guys like us. He definitely gave us a second chance.

♀ ♀ ♀

I remember a conversation Ely and I had, when I told him about the time I got banned in England based on hearsay and rumors that weren't true. After that, I said, our record went to number one and we sold out every ticket. I reminded him of the old business adage: People want what they can't have.

Ely responded, "Say I built a driver that could go ten yards longer and it cost $600, which is 50 percent more than our other driver on the market. Suppose it was made illegal. What would happen?"

"You wouldn't be able to build enough of them," I replied. "If people think they can buy ten more yards, they'll spend the extra $200."

So in 2000, the ERC driver was born. Callaway looked at the specifications on the club face of a typical driver and determined that it had to be a certain thickness so it couldn't act with a trampoline effect and *spring* the ball outward—a driver isn't allowed to do that. Then he reduced the club face on his driver one one-thousandth of an inch under the specs, in order to make it only infinitesimally under—but technically illegal. You needed a microscope to see how small the difference was, but of course, if a driver is not approved by the United States Golf Association, then pros can't use them in American tournaments—the driver was essentially banned. Illegal. The Callaway controversy hit page one of all the golf trades.

Sound familiar?

It was a huge story in the sport. People called me from all over the world. I was laughing, because I knew exactly what the selling plan for the ERC was—Ely was totally behind all of it. He took a page out of my rock career and he made it work for golf.

The ERC sold like gangbusters.

What we've learned from the steroid situation in other sports is that anytime an athlete can pick up even a slight advantage, even if it's illegal, they're usually going to do it. So financially, even though it was originally banned, the ERC was a success. ERC drivers could fetch as much as $2,500 on the black market.

The interesting part of the whole fracas was that you could still use the club in competition outside the United States, where the USGA had no jurisdiction. And all over the world, golfers embraced the driver. The Japanese and the Europeans went crazy for them and sold them for more than $900. When the Americans were competing outside of the United States—like playing the British Open at St. Andrews—some were hitting the ERC driver. I have pictures of golfers who had their own golf-equipment lines hitting the Callaway ERC driver! Why? Because using it, they were able to gain fifteen extra yards on Tiger's woods.

By 2003, the storm had finally passed. Then Callaway introduced the ERC Fusion Driver, which fused titanium and carbon. With its new modifications, the driver was now legal to use on American USGA-sanctioned golf courses. But for a while there, Ely and Callaway were just a little bit rock 'n' roll.

♀   ♀   ♀

Ely was the first guy to use titanium in his drivers. They were actually using the same titanium used in the Russian ICBM missiles that had been aimed at America—after the Cold War ended, the Russians were stuck with all this titanium, so they sold it to golf companies who made clubs out of it. A weapon of mass destruction turned into a golf club. How ironic. I like that!

Ely always tried to find new materials, something unique that was going to make golf easier for the common person. He felt the game was difficult enough, so what's wrong with making a big head driver that older players could hit? A lot of older men in their sixties and seventies quit playing golf because they couldn't hit a wooden driver far enough. When Big Bertha came out, his new titanium driver with the oversized club head that was light and easy to swing, older guys could hit the ball farther and keep up. Ely Callaway was responsible for bringing hundreds of thousands of golfers back into the game.

I still love my Big Bertha driver. I've done the commercials for all of them—I would never endorse a product I don't support. If I were going to play a golf game where my life depended on it, I would be playing with the Great Big Bertha or the Biggest Big Bertha driver—I just think they have the best driver head ever made. Even to this day, with all the new high-tech Callaway stuff available—and it's all great stuff—I would still go with the simple Biggest Big Bertha driver head. I've gotten some memorable shots from it, and it's the driver I will hit for the rest of my life.

Ely changed golf because his products made the game easier to play—and anytime a game gets easier and more accessible, it gets more popular. When Callaway was going full stride with Ely at the helm, you saw a tremendous boom of interest in golf—many more courses were being built, and golf greats like Tiger Woods rose to fame. Callaway and their equipment helped fuel the boom.

My relationship with Callaway has always been top of the line. I call them before all my annual celebrity charity tournaments. Normally, a company will donate a putter for everybody, which is nice—a $150 putter is a pretty good tee prize. I remember one time I called Ely and asked if he had some old travel bags to give away at a tournament I was going to host. No way: Ely gave me a slew of brand-new ERC drivers for every celebrity who played in the tournament. "When I give something away," he said, "I want it to be the best product I have, not something I can't sell. If your tournament has fifty celebrities, and it cost $3,000 to register, then they should get our $600 driver! In the end, maybe they'll convert exclusively to Callaway."

And many of them have.

I admired Ely greatly. Before he died in 2001 from pancreatic cancer at the age of eighty-two, he didn't make a big deal out of the fact that he was ill. He simply went into the hospital and never came back out. His death was a bit of a shock to me. When the light of your company goes out and you lose a guy who made everything work, it's difficult.

In the beginning, my public image was centered on rock 'n' roll. But now, thanks to my affiliation with Callaway, when people recognize me at the airport, half the public knows me for my music while the other half knows me as that rock 'n' roll golfer. When my fans see me at a tournament, they'll go to my bag and make sure everything is indeed made by Callaway. I'm proud to be a spokesman for a company who, like me, stepped out and did something completely different.

Alice with LPGA pro Grace Park.
(Courtesy of the Kraft Nabisco Championship. Photo by Scott Avra)

The Eleventh Step of Golf Addiction

Pay Attention to Innovation and Technology

Wood vs. Titanium. The ERC Driver Controversy.
Lost Without GPS.

"Aw, it looks so good.
Aw, she's made out of wood."
—The Velvet Underground

Golf can be too traditional a lot of times. In the modern world of technology, being unable to break from tradition can cause problems. Like for example, the case of persimmon wood clubs versus metal ones. Back in the old days, everybody played using a wood driver. Jack Nicklaus. Arnold Palmer. Gary Player. Sam Snead. Once they found a persimmon driver to their liking, it would stay in their bag for decades.

Ely started Callaway Golf in 1982 with the goal of selling high-end equipment—the most technologically advanced clubs, balls, and assorted gear. He didn't mind spending tens of millions of dollars on research and development, just as long as their products became the standard. Ely hired Richard Helmstetter from a pool-cue firm in Japan to be his head designer, and Helmstetter experimented with a driver made of steel with a wider club head, which was truly unique for the 1980s. He designed a driver that didn't have a hosel—instead, the shaft bored straight into the club head, which shocked players. Helmstetter was the genius behind new technology, an expert on graphite who experimented with different types of compounds, metal and steel instead of the traditional woods. He was the mad scientist of Callaway.

The Big Bertha, the first wide-body driver in stainless steel, came out in 1991. Then the Great Big Bertha doubled the size of the club face. At first, people looked at it and feared it was impossible to maneuver. But the metal-head revolution started when the pros found that they could hit the ball twenty or thirty yards farther with metal or graphite. Even the most traditional and conservative pros soon turned to oversized and titanium heads. That revolution was spearheaded by Callaway.

If you take a Callaway driver alongside a wooden one, the Callaway driver will improve your score a ton. It's better designed and can make the ball travel noticeably farther with its extra carry and roll. The large-club-face drivers give you a much bigger sweet spot—with wooden drivers the sweet spot is the size of a quarter, and with the Biggest Big Bertha driver it's eight times that big! Also, with the club heads made of light space-age metal, the ball could propel off the club face much faster than with conventional wooden drivers. Callaway designers also redistributed some of that driver's weight away from the club face and into other areas, which expanded the gravity of the center of the face. For the average player, even when you don't hit the ball exactly the way you want, you can still hit it pretty well with the Callaway—if you miss a shot with a wood driver, the results can be catastrophic. But with the ERC driver, guys who could hit a ball 220 yards were now hitting it 235 without changing their swing one little iota. Some pro golfers on the circuit claimed it increased their distance by thirty yards! And that had *everything* to do with the equipment.

But a heavy-metal driver?

Technology invades the ancient game of golf. Because the titanium driver weighs less than your wood driver, you're going to get more speed on it. They perform really well. There was a time when if you said that Jack Nicklaus was going to convert to a metal driver, golfers would have told you no way! But over the past twenty-five years, we've seen so many people switching over to titanium—even traditional die-hard pros—that now nobody hits wood anymore.

I think that any future golf technology will be limited unless they can come up with brand-new metal alloys that can make a ball go farther or straighter. Of course, such innovation would still have to be approved by the USGA—and perhaps the USGA doesn't want the ball to go farther. Chances are, they would be as initially conservative and cautious about future innovations as they were about accepting the first ERC driver.

Technology has affected the putter for more than a century. Now we have those silly-looking long putters that you place against your body so they act like a pendulum. They do look ridiculous, but apparently they work better. Once again, the USGA balked at the new technology—they stated that according to the rules, you're not allowed to anchor the club against your body and use it as a fulcrum. But they haven't outlawed these putters yet, because guys who use them claim they are not putting it against their body—they put their thumb in between their body and the club. There's another putter called the belly putter that fits in your belly as a pendulum, and that one is illegal. But for now you can still use the long putter at any tournament where USGA rules apply.

A few sportswriters have fantasized that the PGA should go all wood, like major league baseball. One *Sports Illustrated* writer even said that if he were commissioner for a day he would bring back wooden clubs and set a four-year time limit on the use of metal or hybrid models. He cited that major league baseball "has it right" by using only wooden bats.

That sounds incredibly naive and idiotic to me. It's two entirely different scenarios! Wood versus aluminum bats in major league baseball is mainly a matter of safety. If Albert Pujols from the St. Louis Cardinals used an aluminum bat to slug a line drive, with all his power, down the third-base line, he would probably kill the third baseman! In golf, you don't have that safety issue. You still have to put the club in your hands, take it back, and swing it, utilizing timing and balance and good lateral motion to make that ball soar with a decent hang time.

High-tech clubs are geared toward a player who is an 18-handicap, giving him or her more yardage and a little more control, thus making the game a little more fun, because they're now hitting longer and straighter shots. I'm no purist—I agree with Ely Callaway's viewpoint. I don't see anything wrong with giving 95 percent of golfers a greater means to enjoy the game more.

Another piece of technology that I think is a great idea are the GPS navigation systems they've added at some of the better courses—they speed up and improve the game. If you play the Biltmore in Phoenix, you'll have a little computer that will say, for example, that you are 431 yards to the green. You hit your ball knowing precisely where you are and how far you are from the cup.

Without that technology, you have guys trying to figure out distance—walking around looking for yardage markers, then looking at the pin, then looking at the pin sheet. A whole golf course full of people tabulating shots and club selection instead of playing golf. With that GPS system, the average once-a-month player with a 22-handicap can look at the computer and automatically get out an eight-iron or seven-iron without doing all the calculations and math. That saves a whole lot of time for everyone.

In some ways I'm considered old school, because in my home life I don't constantly use computers and e-mail and I don't surf the Internet. But I do love GPS computer technology. When I'm out on tour, I make sure my rental car has GPS navigation—otherwise, my daughter Calico and I end up getting lost searching for some out-of-the-way shopping outlet. (Believe me, technology does mix well with shopping or golf addictions.)

So you have to pay attention to these new steps forward that the golf industry is always making. But regardless, it all comes down to one thing: You still have to swing the club. I've seen people use thousand-dollar hybrid drivers and swing them like hockey sticks. If you're hopeless, not even technology will help you out!

Alice on stage with his Errol Flynn dueling sword.

Chapter 24

Prodigal Son

F OR A TIME AFTER WORD GOT OUT that Alice Cooper was a Christian, I would hear a deafening hush when walking into a room filled with some of my buddies, longtime acquaintances, and musician friends.

"All of a sudden you can't swear around me because I'm a Christian? Guys, I've heard the words before, okay? I'm not a nun. I'm not the Pope. I'm still the same guy. I'm just a guy who's a Christian."

My life has improved in so many ways. My kids are great, a reflection of how my family is now grounded. My youngest, Sonora, was born in 1993. My relationship with Sheryl is beyond great. I couldn't ask for a more beautiful family.

For me, Christianity is an ongoing, every-single-day kind of existence. The first thing I do each morning is thank the Lord for yet another day aboveground. I look at where I am. I count my blessings—he gave me a place to live, a great wife, cool kids, a great manager and friend.

One way I've put my golf addiction to good use is by hosting my own Alice Celebrity Golf Tournament—it's been running since 1997. I bring in fifty celebrities for fifty five-person teams competing in a two-day tournament. Each team bids on a celebrity they want to play with—say, Leslie Nielsen or Elke Sommer. I don't necessarily gun for the biggest celebrity names—although we do attract big ones like Dennis Hopper and Cheech Marin—but instead I try to get unique people . . . a character actor from the movie *Blazing Saddles,* or the guy who played the trumpet in *F Troop.* Or somebody from a classic TV sitcom, like David Cassidy from the *Partridge Family,* Donnie Most from *Happy Days, Hill Street Blues*'s Ed Marinaro, Lee Majors of the *Bionic Man* . . . or a game-show host like Chuck Woolery, a movie star like Richard Roundtree from *Shaft*, or a rocker like Meat Loaf, Dave Mustaine, Dweezil Zappa, Jack Blades, or Don Felder. Those are the celebrities who are fun and memorable to play with. They also have extremely appealing personalities, with a million stories to swap on the green.

All proceeds from my tournament go to the Solid Rock Foundation, which I founded in 1995. Solid Rock is a nonprofit goodwill foundation that helps address the physical and social needs of teenagers and children. All the money that goes into Solid Rock is distributed to various other teen organizations that we believe in and research heavily, or for college scholarships. For example, recently we gave money to one center that specializes in eating disorders for girls. We gave money, a sizable sum per year for ten years, to another organization in Arizona called Neighborhood Ministries—they *really* take on the hard cases of disadvantaged kids.

When you first start a foundation, before you're established, nobody really believes in you. So we started by putting on our golf tournament and an annual Christmas variety show, Christmas Pudding, for which I get every kind of artist imaginable to sign up to do two or three songs. Country, pop, rock, metal, even magicians and dancers—it's a true vaudeville type of Christmas show. Now we hold money-raising events around the calendar, staging marathon events like "100 Holes of Golf."

Solid Rock has finally become so established that we have a bold new project lined up: We're preparing to build our own teen center. Grand Canyon College, who gave me an honorary doctorate degree, offered us access to five acres of prime real estate for us to build what we're calling The Rock.

I want The Rock to be a place for kids who have no place to go, especially kids whose worlds are mired in the drug scene or youth gangs. Instead of walking home from school and having to deal with street gangs and the temptations of drug dealers, kids can go to The Rock and do their homework or play basketball. Although it's a Christian-based charity, we don't beat them over the head with a Bible. We're just trying to do something good for a bunch of kids. Should they reach out, spiritual counselors would be available, but it's not about evangelism—it's about keeping our kids safe.

Such an undertaking is endless. It takes millions of dollars to take care of everything. There are so many things you don't plan for—insurance, security, parking, the list is endless. Grand Canyon College will help eliminate those expenses; all I have to do is come up with the money to build the building. So I'm tirelessly out there raising money to carry out the plans we've had drawn up. We need companies to donate building materials, for instance. I have a lot of rich friends who know they're in my Rolodex, who now fear me. But I'll stay on them—I know I'm going to make this happen.

The Rock is one of the biggest projects I've ever attempted in my life. Considering the funding and the permits, it may take years to get it together. The nice thing is, nobody's rushing us or giving us a hard deadline. We're going to do it right, and it'll be done when it's done.

♀   ♀   ♀

I am the prodigal son of rock 'n' roll. I was active in the church as a child. Then, during my musical career, my life took an alternate course. Now I'm back in the good graces of my faith. I get e-mails from people who admire what I stand for and for what I'm not afraid to say. I also get praised for not beating people over the head with my views. I've changed a few lives out there. My shows are still dramatic, tough. I don't come off wimpy. Alice still means business.

And I'm not kidding when I tell people what I believe in. There is so much left to know, and even more to learn. Sometimes I can't articulate my religious feelings exactly as I feel them, but if you listen, you know in your heart when something's absolutely true. You can't deny it when it comes from a still, small voice. Not a giant roar, but a still, small voice that says,

"This is true."

Alice and the serpent. (Ken Ballard)

Chapter 25

Snakes, Stars, and Swords

I OFFICIALLY CHANGED MY NAME to Alice in 1974 when Shep told me we needed to legally own the name. "That is, if you don't mind being called Alice Cooper for the rest of your life."

At the time, I didn't care—everything we were doing was day-to-day anyway. I was riding a wave I had never imagined, and I didn't know if my career was going to last. Somebody could have popped the bubble anytime and I would never have been heard of again: the next Totie Fields.

We got great press out of the name change because we were proponents of the old-fashioned Hollywood press stunt. I figured if it worked then, with stories planted in the press and PR agents planting stories in the gossip columns, why wouldn't it work for rock 'n' roll? So we pulled a Hollywood publicity stunt and changed my name.

What People Call Me

1. **Coop** The first guy to call me Coop was Groucho. He was a friend of Gary Cooper's, whom he called Coop. So when we hung out, Groucho started calling me Coop—I guess it was easier. It stuck. Real friends of mine call me Coop, like the guys in my band and road crew.
2. **Vince** My mother and my sister call me Vince. My dad and my uncles called me Vince. They're the only ones I'd respond to that name for. If I'm walking down the street and somebody calls out, "Hey, Vince," I won't respond. If you saw Elton John, would you yell out "Reggie"? Or if you saw Ringo, would you call him Richard? Why call me Vince?
3. **Vinnie or Boss** During the Nightmare tour, my Italian road crew called me Vinnie or Boss. They were tough guys from Brooklyn, so they could call me anything they wanted. Whenever we'd go through

customs, they'd assure me that if I was holding anything, they'd take the hit. (I always told them I never carried anything illegal.) They were good guys, very protective.

4. **Alice** Sheryl calls me Alice. (And Honey, and Sweetheart. All those endearing names. I tell her Your Majesty is fine.)

♀   ♀   ♀

On December 2, 2003, I was awarded a star on Hollywood Boulevard, across from Grauman's Chinese Theatre. It's an award, but at the same time, it's a rite of passage. Once I got down there, it sunk in—I'm right next to Gene Autry, Angie Dickinson, and Errol Flynn. You don't really feel like you belong there—I figured as soon as we walked away, some wino was going to fall down and puke all over it. Since my daughter now lives in L.A., once a month she can come down with a toothbrush and clean me up.

I'm still making music, touring, and golfing all over the planet. The shenanigans haven't stopped me. I still see the world from the stage.

I still have a crack four-piece band: two guitarists, drums, and bass. Some things never change. Originally, we patterned our lineup after the Stones: one lead player, one rhythm. Glen was our first lead player and Mike was rhythm. Now I play with guys who can both play rhythm or lead interchangeably. Damon Johnson is my lead guitar player, and Keri Kelli is on guitar, Chuck Garric on bass, and Eric Singer on drums. When I had Dick Wagner and Steve Hunter, they were both solid lead players. I tell my guys a great guitar player isn't what he plays, it's what he doesn't play. It's when he lays out. Guys like Yngwie Malmsteen, who plays through everything, to me that's not a great guitar player. A good guitar player is George Harrison, Jeff Beck, or Keith Richards. They play when it's time to play.

We still make the newspapers, and usually, just like the old days, it's for the most peculiar things. I'll give you a for instance: the time when Alice's sword was accidentally flung into the audience. I've used the sword on stage for a long time—it once belonged to Errol Flynn. We got it from the guy who gave him dueling lessons. One night we were brandishing a whip when the whip caught around the sword and propelled it into the audience. Luckily, nobody got skewered—but it was gone. So I offered a reward. The story made the newswire. I didn't say why the sword was so important to me. I just said I used it for fifteen tours and that it was my favorite sword. The family of the girl who caught it brought it back.

Another item that made the media had to do with my snake. During a recent tour, we put a heating pad into the cage of our snake, Popcorn. And he swallowed it. He had eaten a rat for dinner, and a little bit of blood got on the corner of the heating pad. Since snakes are virtually blind and there was blood scent on the pad, Popcorn began swallowing the heating pad for dessert. We opened up the snake cage the next day and, to our horror, Popcorn had swallowed the entire heating pad. The power cord was coming out of her mouth, still plugged in. We freaked out. What do we do? We called up the vet—do we cut the cord and pull out the pad? Not if we wanted to pull her stomach out. We were advised to let her digest it and see what happens.

The story made the papers. What? Jay Leno made an aging-rock-star joke about it on *The Tonight Show*.

Finally, when Popcorn couldn't digest the pad, we had the vet operate. We retired her immediately from the tour. We use a different snake for every tour. Once they're retired, we give them away to petting zoos. People think I have nineteen snakes in my house as pets, but they're not pets.

To my list of job descriptions (lead singer, fund-raiser, dad, amateur golfer), I recently added another—deejay. One day Dick Clark asked me, "What if you had a late-night radio show, seven to midnight, the time when radio's dead?" I jumped at the chance. Give me the seven-to-midnight spot, sure—but I demand total control of the playlist. So with *Nights with Alice Cooper*, on five nights a week in five countries, I can play music my way—Procol Harum, the Yardbirds, Them, Paul Butterfield, more obscure AC/DC, Led Zeppelin, the Beatles, and the Stones. Not the same old songs. If I want to play "Fortune Teller" or "Around and Around" by the early Stones, I will.

I guess the stations had nothing to lose, because I started out on five stations and they pretty soon turned into a hundred stations. While the other station across town will play only "TNT" by AC/DC for the fourteen millionth time, or "Stairway to Heaven" again and again, followed by "Freebird," I'll make fun of Rush, play a dozen songs you haven't heard in twenty years, and share some great rock 'n' roll tales. It's a lot of fun.

Alice with actors Chris O'Donnell and Samuel L. Jackson
at the Bob Hope Chrysler Classic in 1998.
(Photo by Bob Hope Chrysler Classic photographer Marc Glassman)

The Twelfth Step of Golf Addiction

Keep on Rockin'!

Golf 'til you drop. Music Biz 101.
The last of the rock royalty. Decades and decades of hits.
An "all in" guy. Holes-in-one and double eagles.

I look forward to playing golf 'til I drop dead on the back nine—I figure I have another thirty years left in me until then. I've golfed with a lot of guys in their eighties who can still whack the ball. Maybe they used to drive it 260 yards and now they'll hit it something like 160. But if they can still golf and score in the 90s, then it's a great day to be alive and they'll be back tomorrow.

Speaking of the nineties, I once played with a guy at my country club who was ninety years old. Once he got up on that first tee, it was as if he had a Lust for Life—and he hit the ball 210 yards! If I make it to his age, I should be so lucky to hit it that far.

Golf isn't like tennis, where once you get older and you lose several steps you can't hit the ball anymore. Golf you can play all your life. And that means a lot to me—coming from rock 'n' roll, an occupation that usually has a young retirement age.

I come from that unique first generation of arena rockers who are still playing the same music we played when we were eighteen or nineteen—and it still works, which is weird. That won't happen again, and I'll tell you why: Twenty-year-olds in rock bands are finding their careers cut short by the time they reach their thirties. Either the band breaks up or their short-attention-spanned audience loses interest.

These days the record business isn't the same as it used to be. Music—radio airplay and record sales (and even satellite radio)—is all about pleasing a niche and specialized demographics of fans. As a result, it's much more difficult to break through on a wider scale and develop a huge core of loyal, mass-appeal fans who will stick with you year in and year out, throughout your entire career. Forty years from now, I don't believe we're going to see any more guys like David Bowie or Elton John, artists who have stayed on top of the business for that long. It's not going to happen. The present music-business structure won't allow an artist to venture out past a certain age—before they get to middle age, they're declared "done." Major labels are impatient and have few marketing strategies other than throwing big money behind the newest thing, and are seemingly uninterested in developing artists who can't break after their initial first or second albums. That's sad when you consider the Alice Cooper band didn't break through until our third album.

When we were with Warner Bros., they'd spend a fortune on promotion because they knew they had a hit and they knew they were going to sell a certain amount of records. I can still go into any store and see an Alice Cooper section. But when you become a classic artist, and you've watched the music business become dissipated and diluted, you no longer know what category your music is in. Am I Classic Rock? Progressive Rock? Heavy Metal? I don't know.

The music business now chases strict and predetermined demographics, leaving no room for happy accidents, which is the worst thing in the world. That's stupid. That's the main reason why radio is so bland. Different stations appeal to different age groups. Their playlists are so tight, it seems like they play the same tunes every hour. Who wants to listen to that kind of play-it-safe, over-researched radio?

And the irony is that it was harder to snag a hit record then than it is today. If a record like "Eighteen" was a Top Forty hit in 1971, that meant you were in competition with the Supremes, the Beatles, Led Zeppelin, the Rolling Stones, Simon & Garfunkel—whoever was on the charts at that point, a huge range of good music. Take the guys in the Knack, a great band with a big hit like "My Sharona." After a one-album run, they were duly replaced by the Cars, who had a much longer string of hits. Despite an excellent first album, the Knack couldn't achieve a lasting pedigree. They weren't able to earn the credentials of a Bowie, Alice, Elton, or Rod. It all comes down to outdistancing the fads and trends while continuing to produce quality material.

The era of having *several* dominant multiplatinum rock bands operating at one given time—like having the Beatles, the Stones, Led Zeppelin, Alice Cooper, the Moody Blues, the Eagles, the Who, and Jethro Tull all making music at the same time—seems to be over with. Nobody's ever going to run that race again. We are the last of the rock royalty.

I feel sorry for the young bands of today. When people come to see Alice Cooper, do they come to see the guillotine and the snakes? Possibly, but nine times out of ten, they come to hear *The Songs*. "No More Mr. Nice Guy." "Eighteen." "School's Out." "Elected." Hits that were the soundtrack to people's lives—forty years of songs they can't let go of.

I don't think the bands of today write enough songs that are built to last. Think of each decade in terms of great songs. When I say the fifties, I can probably rattle off the names of a thousand hits.

The sixties. I think of the early crooners, the British Invasion, Motown, Psychedelic, and hard rock—all within one ten-year span! And I can probably name seven hundred songs right off the top of my hat, from Sinatra to the Supremes to the Beatles.

The seventies. You have Bowie, Alice, Queen, Fleetwood Mac, Springsteen, Boston, Pink Floyd, the Bee Gees, disco, and even punk rock. I can still name at least five or six hundred hits that we'll remember forever.

The eighties. Now it starts getting thinner. Prince. Duran Duran. The Cars. Hall & Oates. The nineties. We're starting to scrape bottom. Guns N' Roses. Nirvana. Sheryl Crow.

The 2000s. Destiny's Child? Coldplay? Britney Spears? I'm at a loss. The list of timeless melodies seems to be shrinking dramatically.

When I think of gourmet music, I tend to think backward, not forward. I could even make a convincing case that there were more timeless songs written in the twentieth century *before* 1950 than after 1950. Go back to Cole Porter, George Gershwin, Rodgers & Hart, and Johnny Mercer—those are the songwriters who gave us a rich twentieth-century songbook of timeless classics and standards. As a culture, we've gone from musical gourmet to fast food.

For better or for worse, bands today aren't forced to have the annual album-and-tour cycle—maybe that's why they're not grinding it out and becoming *huge* rock stars like we used to be. Hits on the radio seem more disposable now; we're back to a strict singles-format mentality thanks to the current download iPod technology. Music doesn't cross over between America and the UK as dramatically as it did before. Name *five classic songs* from the twenty-first century. I would know them if I heard them, and not much comes to mind.

♀ ♀ ♀

I'll admit it. I'm what you call an "all in" guy. I have that addictive personality. All or nothing. I still tour every year. I'm "all in" on my stage show—I invented a brand of theatrical rock that has never died and that I refuse to radically alter. Like the ninety-year-old golfer, I'll keep touring, recording, and writing songs until I can't do it anymore.

Today, Alice Cooper is woven into the American fabric. If I were doing tonight's show back in the 1970s, it would be just as shocking, but nowadays, I don't even try to shock my audience—because I don't think you can. Rather, I try to give them something that is flashy, hard, and overwhelming, so overbearing they can't look away. Plus, if I continue giving them the hit songs and theatrical visuals I'm known for, they'll keep coming back.

I believe in giving the audience more than their money's worth. Rock 'n' roll, horror, comedy, and romance all bunched together, kinetic and fast paced. If we didn't cut Alice's head off with the guillotine at the end of the show, it would be like putting on the Barnum & Bailey Circus without the tigers and the clowns.

It's the same with golf. I like to shock people. I now play many celebrity Pro-Am tournaments, but the first time I played in public, I was out there with the pros—Phil Mickelson and Davis Love, names I was in awe of—and there I was, on the same golf course! I was a little rock guy nobody expected to play very well, but every once in a while, I shocked people when I'd shoot a 74.

I've said it before, but it bears repeating: Playing golf is like being a rocker on stage. You have the choice of retreating into your shell and gazing at your shoes, or becoming a power performer in front of your crowd. I much prefer the latter. Like everything else I do in life, once I'm able to back it up with ability and skill, I play to win with as much flash and panache as possible.

Back when it was still the early days, when parent groups used to hate my act, I used to tell my fans, "If you really want to hit your dad below the belt, tell him that Alice Cooper, that drunken freak with the makeup, could play him this Saturday on the golf course and take him apart on the green."

It was the lowest punch you could have thrown.

♀   ♀   ♀

A hole-in-one and a number-one record are very much in the same league—the odds against a person doing either are astronomical.

I'll never forget my first hole-in-one.

I was playing with Shep in Hawaii when I hit a two-iron and sh*nked it horribly. That's how bad a shot it was. I didn't even know where it went.

We looked everywhere. Just as I was getting ready to tee up another, Shep walked over to the cup.

"Alice, you're not going to believe this," Shep said.

"What?"

"It's in the hole."

"No, really, where did it go?"

"Alice, it took a horrible bounce, and then it rebounded off the rocks back toward the green."

"And?"

"Then it rolled down two tiers, hit the pin, and went right into the hole, 210 yards away."

I picked up my ball. It had a big nasty black gash on it from the impact of the lava rocks. Sure enough, my ball came down, hit a lava bed, bounced up in the air, hit the green, rolled down two tiers, and beelined it into the hole. It was like that Donald Duck hole-in-one you'd see in a cartoon.

"Yes! *That's* how good I am!" I yelled victoriously.

I barely broke 100 that day. But I savored the moment! My ball is now mounted prominently on my wall—my first hole-in-one! Of course, out of tradition, I bought everybody in the clubhouse a round. For me, on a Saturday in Maui at the Wailea Golf Course, where beers cost $8 apiece, my tab ran up to about $1,500. But it felt fine.

I've had three holes-in-one so far in my life. The other two were your more typical holes-in-one—balls that hit the green, spun back, and sailed into the cup. The difference was, I tried to hit those shots into the hole. But my first was a spontaneous, Rube Goldberg–like, unplanned work of art.

Even more amazing than scoring a hole-in-one is the fact that I have *two* double eagles—two strokes on par fives. One, I hit at the Pima Country Club. The other, I hit at Oakbrook in Chicago. It's said that a double eagle is even rarer than a hole-in-one. Five hundred and fifty yards in five strokes? Par for the course is a drive, a second shot for distance, a third shot to the green, followed by two putts. Par five. Boom, you're in. Good players regularly score sixes and sevens on a par five.

In order to hit my double eagle, I hit with my driver, followed by a three-wood shot, which got up in the air and onto the green . . . and then rolled down and plunked in the hole. A total of two shots. I think it's the best feeling you can achieve on a golf course. With every double eagle you shoot, the course sends you a special pin with an eagle with two heads. Only a few players wear them. Me, I wear two of them.

Double eagles, holes-in-one, and number-one hits. They're all reasons to keep on swinging. I'm never gonna shake this golf-junkie jones in my soul, and neither should you. Keep on rockin'.

Alice Cooper receives his star on Hollywood Boulevard on December 2, 2003.
(Matt Coddington)

Appendix

Alice's Golf Clinic

15 Tips for Achieving Your Best Game

I COULDN'T RESIST THE CHANCE to leave you dear readers with a round of my personal golf tips. Good luck on the green and steer clear of the Golf Monster! Oh yeah, and don't forget to hit the ball, Alice!

1. Hybrids Rock!

The coolest thing in golf is hybrid clubs. You are absolutely cheating yourself if you don't have hybrids in your bag. Irons range in length—L wedge, sand wedge, pitching wedge, 9, 8, 7, 6, 5, 4, 3, up to 2. The longer irons, the 2 through the 5, are going to go farther, but they're much harder to hit. Take them out of your bag and replace them with hybrid 5, 4, and 3s, and your life becomes a hundred times easier—hybrids are much easier to swing and hit with. The basic rule-of-thumb distances are 210–215 yards for a hybrid 3 driver, 200 yards for a hybrid 4, and 185–195 yards for a hybrid 5. You don't even have to change your swing—just change your club and you're immediately a better golfer.

2. Straight Shot vs. Distance

The hardest shot in golf is right down the middle, dead straight. That's my specialty shot. I can compete with a guy who hits much farther than me—I just hit straight. It doesn't matter if he hits the ball thirty yards past me, we'll be looking for his next shot while mine's comfortably on the green.

3. Successful Chipping

How many strokes you save on the green depends on how good a short game you play when you're about thirty, forty feet from the pin. The trick is hand position. Don't be behind the ball. Don't put your hands behind the ball. If I position my hands and set it up like a putter, by pressing my hands forward, that creates a leading edge that's just like a putter, only I've got loft. It's going to get me over the high grass and onto the green.

4. Alice's High Cut Shot

Let's say I have a sand trap in front of me—that means I have to hit the ball high and let it come down soft on the green so it won't roll too far. If I hit it too far, I can't get it near the hole. Instead, I want the ball to go nice and high. So I take a full swing, but I keep it open and give it a soft landing. This is my normal shot. This is my high cut shot.

5. Alice's Elbow Chip Shot

Maybe I'm the only one who does this, but I find it makes my shots much more accurate. I anchor my right elbow into my side during my chip shots. Normally, my right elbow is away from my body, but lots can go wrong with that. So I've simplified my shot by touching my elbow to my body, and now my chips are more accurate. Remember, the better you chip, the more money you're going to make.

6. High Hands!

You'll never see a picture of Tiger Woods (or almost any other pro) finishing a drive without their hands high and up over their head. Finish high after the swing! Since your swing is an arc, finishing high gives you a bigger arc and more force. Amateurs always finish their swings low, swinging the club more like a baseball bat. Take advantage of more arc.

7. Straight Up and Down Putter

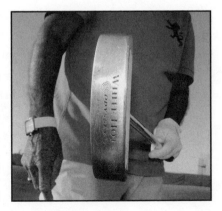

Putting is a very individual thing. The nice thing about golf is that everybody can putt—it's something you can do without having to adhere to a uniform technique. And there are so many different kinds of putters for different styles. I personally like to use a putter that's uncomplicated. I use a center-shaft, weight-balanced putter, a straight up and down design. Nothing complicated. That way I can look at the hole and line the club up with the hole without having to worry about curvature and angle.

8. Keep Your Head Down! No Peeking!

People wonder why, if they're perfectly set up, they still miss putts—it's mainly because they're not keeping their head down while putting! Once you're set, stay down and *stay set*. Keep your head in position and don't move it until after the ball is halfway to the hole. Too many guys want to peek to see where the ball is going, but your head is part of your body mechanics—if you move your head after setting up square, the face of the club moves too.

9. Point Your Finger Down on the Putter

While everyone has their own putting style, it might not be a bad idea to extend your finger down the club so that your finger is pointing right down at the ball. That way, when you swing, you make sure to end up with your finger pointing at the target. It's kind of an amateur move—later on, you can take your finger out of it. But it might help ground your swing to try it.

10. The Big "Don't"

Here is the big "don't" in putting: No hands behind the ball! Don't ever get your hands behind the ball. Your hands go straight up and down—if you want to, you might even want to press them forward one or two degrees.

11. Right Eye or Left Eye Dominant?

Very few people have perfect vision—almost everybody is either right eye or left eye dominant. Find out which one you are, then compensate your feet, arms, and hands. Your brain may be getting corrupted information from your right eye that says you're set up straight when you're really not. Compensate and make sure your aim is true; otherwise, you're never going to hit your target properly. And then believe that you're straight, even if you can't quite convince your brain that you are.

12. Don't Sweat the Stance

It doesn't matter what your putting stance looks like—do what works for you. I've seen guys with the worst putting stances in the world who are the best putters. Billy Mayfair, the best putter in the business, cuts his putt. But he does it exactly right every time, so why change?

13. Get Rhythm!

If you're over fifty, you might consider stretching—even though, truth be told, I seldom do. I'll take four or five swings, and I'm ready to hit the ball. But I play every day. Luckily, I'm built wiry and I don't get sore. But if you're someone who's a little overweight, or who sits at a desk all day and only plays golf once every couple of weeks, then take a lot of warm-up swings to get the blood going in your arms and *to get some rhythm*. The whole game of golf is based on rhythm, so get into yours before you start playing. Golf is not a game of strength. It's all about timing and weight balance.

14. Do Your Homework!

Learn all the Seven Basic Swings (according to Johnny Miller).

1. A high fade
2. A high draw
3. A low fade
4. A low draw
5. A hook
6. A slice
7. A straight shot

Take the time to research and learn them. They're basically a matter of different hand positions. If you can get the Seven Basic Swings down, you'll save yourself a ton of strokes and have more shot weapons in your arsenal.

15. Momentum Counts in Golf!

Unlike in other sports, momentum is key in golf. A good shot or three *will* propagate more good shots. If you have a bad shot, don't lose your temper—golf is a game of confidence, concentration, and momentum. If you hit that one bad shot and allow the anger to get the best of you, your adrenaline will go to all the wrong places and you'll be hitting the ball too far or holding your hands wrong. Stay cool and relaxed. I play my best when I don't have a thought in my head.

Acknowledgments

Special thanks to Sheryl Cooper, Ely Callaway, John Daly, Michael Douglas & Catherine Zeta-Jones, Roger Dunn, Shep Gordon, David Ledbetter, Toby Mamis, Keith Maxwell, Gary McCord, Rocco Mediate, Johnny Miller, Jim Mooney, Graham Nash, Brian Nelson, Bruce Parker, Mike Smith from Acapulco, Scott Waxman, Craig Yahiro, Danny Zelisko, Kent & Keith Zimmerman, and all the Callaway reps all around the world who still owe me money.

And thanks for the photos: Ken Ballard, Ward Boult, Matt Coddington, Brad Elterman, Bob Gruen, Erik Luftglass, The Kraft Nabisco Championship, The Bob Hope Chrysler Classic, The Michael Douglas & Friends Tournament, and the VH1 Fairway to Heaven Tournament.

—Alice Cooper

Thanks to Alice, Shep Gordon, Toby Mamis, Brian Nelson, Scott Waxman, Farley Chase, Lindsey Moore, Kristin Kiser, Luke Dempsey, Richard Levy, Deborah Zimmerman, Gladys Zimmerman, and the guys in H-Unit.

—The Zimmermen

Index

Note: Page numbers in *italic* indicate photographs.

addiction, 191, 193–194. *See also* drinking and alcoholism
adrenaline, 87–91
albums and tours
  Alice Cooper Goes to Hell, 123, 171–172
  The Alice Cooper Show, 124
  Billion Dollar Babies, *98*, 99–103
  Brutal Planet, 209
  Constrictor, 183–184
  Dada, 181–182
  Dragontown, 209
  Easy Action, 77
  Flush the Fashion, 181–182
  From the Inside, 175, 177–178
  Killer, 95
  Lace and Whiskey, 123, 172
  The Last Temptation, 198, 209
  Love It to Death, 81–82, 94
  Madhouse Rock tour, *7*
  Muscle of Love, 116
  South America tour, *98*, 101–103
  Special Forces, 181–182
  Trash, 184, *192*
  United Kingdom tour, 78, 84–85, 99
  Welcome to My Nightmare (album and tour), 4, *118*, 120–123, 132–133, 171, *204*
  Zipper Catches Skin, 181–182
alcoholism. *See* drinking and alcoholism
Alice Celebrity Golf Tournament, 231–232
Alice Cooper band (original)
  Billion Dollar Babies, *98*, 99–103
  breakup, 116–117, 119–120
  chicken incident, 79–80
  in Detroit, *74*, 75–77
  Easy Action, 77
  fame and influence of, 99–100, 115–116
  first record contract, 61, 64–65
  in Japan, *62*
  Killer, 95
  in Los Angeles, *38*, 42–43, *52*, 53–67, 77
  Love It to Death, 81–82, 94
  money and finances, 111–113, 119–120
  Muscle of Love, 116

  playing poker on the road, *110*
  Pretties for You, 60, 66
  School's Out, *92*, 96–97, 99, *114*
  signature sound, 81–82
  snakes, 83–84, *114*
  songs and songwriting, 82, 93–97, 95, 116, 117
  sword accident, 88
  United Kingdom tour, *78*, 84–85, 99
  Warner Bros. Records contract, 82
  Whisky a Go Go, 115
Alice Cooper Goes to Hell (album), 123, 171–172
Alice Cooper Living Legend Award, *160*, 162
The Alice Cooper Show (album), 124
Alice's Golf Clinic, 247–252
Amboy Dukes, 76
The American Music Awards, 168
Amsterdam, Morey, 156
Arizona
  Alice's childhood in, 19–21
  Biltmore Golf Course, *126*
  Camelback Bible Church, 196
  Camelback Country Club, 47
  Camelback Hospital, 182–183, 188
  charities, 231–233
  Cortez High School, *28*, 30–31, 32, 33–36
  Squaw Peak Junior High School, 29–30
  VIP Club, 35
Arnold, Tom, *104*
Astaire, Fred, 139, 164
Atlantic Records, 120, 171
Avedon, Richard, 84
Aykroyd, Dan, 166

ballads, 171–172
Bangkok, golfing in, 108
Barbarella, 55
Barrett, Syd, 59
baseball, 11–13, 23
Beatles, 31, 165–166
Beck, Jeff, 236
Belushi, John, 136, 137, 166–167
"Be My Lover" (song), 95

Benny, Jack, 154, *160*, 161, 162
Berle, Milton, 155
Beverly Hill Hotel Polo Lounge (California), 149
Big Bertha driver, 219, 221–222, 226
Billion Dollar Babies (album and tour), *98*, 99–103
Biltmore Golf Course (Arizona), *126*
Blue Cheer, 57
Bob Hope Chrysler Classic, *238*
Bogart, Neil, 119
Bond, James, 30, 162
Brandon, Jerry, 30
Brazil, 101–102
Brooks, Albert, 165, 167
Brooks, Mel, 155
Bruce, Michael, 36, 41, 95, 98, 117. *See also* Alice Cooper band
Brutal Planet (album), 209
Burns, George, 154, *160*, 161, 162
Buxton, Glen, 33–34, 39, 40

Cafuoco, Hot Ralphie, 124
California
  Alice Cooper band in, 42–43, *52*, 53–67
  Alice's childhood in, 17–19
  Beverly Hill Hotel Polo Lounge, 149
  Cheetah club (Los Angeles), 54, 58–59, 61
  Earl Warren Fairgrounds, 57
  Landmark Motor Hotel (Los Angeles), 61, 63, 64, 67
  Pebble Beach golf course, 105–106
  Rainbow Bar and Grill and "Lair of the Vampires" (Sunset Boulevard), 135–136
  On the Rox (Sunset Boulevard), 166
  Spiders, 37, 39–43
  star on Hollywood Boulevard, 236, *246*
  Troubadour (Los Angeles), *130*
  TTG, 100–101
  Valencia Country Club, 111–112
  Whisky a Go Go (Hollywood), 115
Callaway, Ely, 1, 201, *216*, 217–222, 225–226
Callaway Golf, 129, 153–154, 158, 201, 217–223, 225–226
Camelback Bible Church, 196
Camelback Country Club, 47
Camelback Hospital, 182–183, 188
Campbell, Glen, 129, 152
canes, 208
Carson, Johnny, 162
Carvey, Dana, 194–195
Catch a Rising Star (New York), 167

Chambers Brothers, 61, 63, 64
Checker, Chubby, 140
Cheetah club (Los Angeles), 54, 58–59, 61
chicken incident, 79–80
chipping, 248–249
Christianity, 9, 19, 35, 195–199, 206–207, 231–233
Church of Jesus Christ, 9, 19
Clark, Dick, 237
Clouseau, Jacques, 143–144
Cohen, Herb, 64–65
Constrictor (album and tour), 183–184
Cooper, Alice (Vincent Damon Furnier)
  addictive personality, 191, 193–194
  asthma, 14–15
  childhood, *8*, 16
    in Arizona, 19–21
    in California, 17–19
    in Detroit, 10–14
    Detroit-to-California trips, 17
    peritonitis (ruptured appendix), 20–21, 29
  children, 182, 183, 194, 231
  Cortez High School, 28, 30–31, *32*, 33–36
  father. *See* Furnier, Ether Maroni "Mick"
  golf. *See* golf
  mother. *See* Furnier, Ella McCartt
  music career. *See* music career
  name change, 117, 235–236
  religion, 9, 19, 35, 195–199, 206–207, 231–233
  sister, 10, 19, 33
  Squaw Peak Junior High School, 29–30
  star on Hollywood Boulevard, 236, *246*
  wife. *See* Cooper, Sheryl Goddard (wife)
Cooper, Calico (daughter), 182
Cooper, Dashiell (son), 183
Cooper, Sheryl Goddard (wife), 231
  Alice's alcoholism, 5, 172, 173, 178–179, 181–183
  choreography, 177–178
  and Groucho Marx, 148, 149
  meets Alice, 132
  and Peter Sellers, 143–144
  and Raquel Welch, 139, 140
  religion, 196
  at On the Rox, 166
Cooper, Sonora, 231
Cornell Medical Center sanitarium, 4–6, 172–177
Cortez High School, *28*, 30–31, *32*, 33–36
Cottle, Sherry, 58, 59
Creedence Clearwater, 61

Dada (album and tour), 181–182
Dalí, Gala, 145
Dalí, Salvador, 30, 139, 145–147
Dall, Bobby, *200*
Daltrey, Roger, 194
Daly, John, 25–26, 90, 201–203, 220
Davis, Bette, 55
Davis, Mac, 218
Davis, Sammy, Jr., 151
DePaiva, Kassie, *210*
Detroit (Michigan), 10–14, *74, 75–77*
Detroit Tigers, 11, 12–13
Dolenz, Micky, *130,* 167
Donovan, 100
"Don't Blow Your Mind" (song), 36
The Doors, 59, 100–101
double eagles, 244–245
Douglas, Michael, *104,* 150
Douglas, Mike, *44,* 161
Dr. No, 30
Dragontown (album), 209
drinking and alcoholism, 101, 131–137, *170*
    Camelback Hospital, 182–183, 188
    Cornell Medical Center sanitarium, 4–6,
        172–177
    golf and, 183, 187–191
    high school, 36
Dunaway, Dennis, 30–31, 33, 37, 39, 95, 97,
    117. *See also* Alice Cooper band
Dylan, Bob, 61, 73, 93

Earl Warren Fairgrounds (California), 57
Earwigs, 33–34
Easy Action (album), 77
"Elected" (song), 166
ERC driver, 220–221, 226
eye dominance, 251
Ezrin, Bob, 81, 82, 94, 96, 100, 119, 120,
    134–135

face-forward wedges, 128–129
Faces, 134
Falk, Peter, *44*
Febre, Ralphie, 124
Finland, golfing in, 107–108
First Cylindric Chromo Hologram of Alice
    Cooper's Brain, 145, 146–147
Flansburg, Scott, 153
Fleming, Ian, 30, 162
Flush the Fashion (album and tour), 181–182
Flynn, Errol, 230, 237
Forbes, 111

Ford, Gerald, 152–153, 155
Frampton, Peter, 115–116, 194
Friars Club, 154–155, 161, 162
From the Inside (album), 175, 177–178
Furnier, Ella McCartt (mother), 9–10, 17, 18,
    19, 20, 21, 53, 65, 94, 165
Furnier, Ether Maroni "Mick" (father), 10, 14,
    17–21, 23, 35, 53, 65, 94, 184–185, 195
Furnier, Lonson Thurman "Lefty" (uncle), 11,
    17, 18
Furnier, Nickie (sister), 10, 19, 33
Furnier, Thurman Sylvester (grandfather), 9
Furnier, Vincent Collier "Jocko" (uncle),
    10–11
Furnier, Vincent Damon. *See* Cooper, Alice

Gannon, Joe, 124, 188
Garcia, Andy, *104*
Garric, Chuck, 236
Gateway Tour, 50
Gleason, Jackie, 152, 155
Goddard, Sheryl. *See* Cooper, Sheryl Goddard
golf, *xii, 22, 68, 86. See also* golf clubs; golf
    courses
    adrenaline and, 88–91
    Alice Celebrity Golf Tournament, 231–232
    Alice's Golf Clinic, 247–252
    Alice's introduction to, 111–112
    Bob Hope Chrysler Classic, *238*
    chipping, 248–249
    double eagles, 244–245
    eye dominance, 251
    gambling and, 70–72
    GPS navigation systems, 228
    head games, 47–48
    hitting into someone, 212–214
    hitting someone, 214–215
    holes-in-one, 243–244
    imitation and, 23–27
    Kraft Nabisco Championship, *86, 186, 210,*
        224
    as lifetime sport, 239
    Michael Douglas & Friends Golf
        Tournament, *104, 150*
    Mike Douglas Show, 44
    momentum, 252
    morning tee times, 90–91
    playing through, 211–212
    playing to the crowd, 215, 243
    playing with friends and competitors,
        151–156
    playing with pros, 156–159

Pro-Am tournaments, 157–159, 214–215, 243
pros *vs.* amateurs, 49–51
putting, 27, 249–251
reasons to play, 69–71, 73
rhythm, 251
seven basic swings, 252
shanks, 127–129
simplifying the swing, 45–47, 154
straight *vs.* distance, 248
as substitute addiction, 183, 187–191
Toyota/Kraft Nabisco $1 Million Hole-in-One Contest, *210*
VH1 Fairway to Heaven tournament, *200*
women players, 48–49
golf clubs
  Big Bertha driver, 219, 221–222, 226
  ERC driver, 220–221, 226
  face-forward wedges, 128–129
  hybrids, 247
  putters, 227, 249–250
  spokesmen for Callaway Golf, 153–154, 158, 217–222
  titanium, 221, 226–227
  vs. golf swing, 49
  wood *vs.* metal, 225–227
golf courses, 1–4, 105–109, *126*
golf hustling, 71–72
Gordon, Shep, *62*
  Alice's alcoholism, 4, 5, 172–173
  and Alice's Christian beliefs, 198–199, 206–207
  and Diana Ross, 168
  golf, 188, 243–244
  and Groucho Marx, 147
  and Liberace, 169
  as manager, 63–67, 75–76, 79, 80–81, 82, 84, 112–113
  and Raquel Welch, 139
  and Salvador Dalí, 145–146
  Welcome to My Nightmare tour, 120, 122–123
GPS navigation systems, 228
Grand Canyon College, 232
Grande Ballroom (Detroit), 76
GTOs, 57, 60, 61, 67
Guess Who, 79
The Guinness Book of World Records, 103, 153
Gulbis, Natalie, 48–49

"Halo of Flies" (song), 94
Hamlisch, Marvin, 147, 148

Harrison, George, 166, 236
Hayes, Helen, 163
"Hello, Hooray" (song), 100
Helmstetter, Richard, 225
Hendrix, Jimi, 61, 63–64
Hillcrest Country Club, 156
holes-in-one, 243–244
holograms, 145, 146–147
Hope, Bob, 152, 154, 155
"How You Gonna See Me Now" (song), 178–179
Hudson, Rock, 164
Hunter, Steve, 120, 236
Huntington, Doke, 41
hybrid golf clubs, 247

Iceland, golfing in, 107
"I'm Eighteen" (song), 81–82, 95–96
imitation, 23–27
"I Never Cry" (song), 171–172

"Jackknife Johnny" (song), 177
Jackson, Samuel L., *238*
Jagger, Mick, 24
Janssen, David, 163
Johnson, Damon, 236
Jones, Bobby, 48
Joplin, Janis, 61, 63

Kaufman, Andy, 168
Kelli, Keri, 236
Kempf, Rolf, 100
Kenny G, *104,* 218
Killer (album), 95
Kiss, 119
Knotts, Don, 152, 156
Kraft Nabisco Championship, *86, 186, 210, 224*
Krieger, Robbie, 59
kung fu movies, 194, 207–208

Lace and Whiskey (album), 123, 172
Lafayette, Marquis de, 9
Lair of the Vampires, 135–136
Landmark Motor Hotel (Los Angeles), 61, 63, 64, 67
The Last Temptation (album), 198, 209
Lattanzio, Space, 124
LaVey, Anton, 197
Led Zeppelin, 115, 134
Lennon, John, 79, 80, 93, *130,* 161, 166
Leonard, Sugar Ray, 218

Lewis, Jerry, 152, 155
Liberace, 169
Locklear, Heather, *104*
Love, Davis, 26, 243
Love It to Death (album), 81–82, 94
Lovelace, Linda, 140, 143
Lydon, John (Johnny Rotten), 99
Lynne, Shelby, *104*

MacLachlan, Kyle, *104*
macumba, 102–103
Madhouse Rock tour, *7*
makeup, 208, 209
Malmsteen, Yngwie, 236
Maltese Falcons, 163
Manson, Marilyn, 205–206
marijuana brownies, 59
Martin, Dean, 152, 154, 162
Martin, Steve, 165, 167
Marx, Groucho, 73, *138*, 139, 147–149, 162
Mayfair, Billy, 251
MC5, 76, 77
MCA, 183
McCartney, Linda, 148
McCartney, Paul, 148
McMahon, Ed, 162
Meredith, Dandy Don, *210*
Michael Douglas & Friends Golf Tournament,
  104, 150
Michaels, Bret, *200*
Michigan, 10–14, *74*, 75–77
Mickelson, Phil, 49, 243
The Mike Douglas Show, 44, 161
Miller, Johnny, 24, 26, 46, 157, 218–219, 252
Minnelli, Liza, 140, 143
momentum, 252
Moon, Keith, 135, 136
Mooney, Jim, 189
Morrison, Jim, 59, 61, 64, 101
Moscow City Golf Club, 106–107
Mothers of Invention, 60, 66, 101
The Muppet Show, 161
Murray, Anne, *130*
Muscle of Love (album), 116
music
  gourmet *vs.* fast food, 242
  songwriting through the decades, 241–242
music business, 239–242
music career, *52, 56*
  addiction and, 132–133, 171–172, 181–182,
    201–203
  adrenaline and performance, 87–88, 89

Alice as villain, 205–207
Alice Cooper band (original)
  Billion Dollar Babies (album and tour), *98*,
    99–103
  birth of Alice, 54–55, *56*, 57–58
  breakup, 116–117, 119–120
  chicken and chicken feathers, 79–80
  in Detroit, *74*, 75–77
  Easy Action (album), 77
  fame and influence of, 99–100, 115–116
  first record contract, 61, 64–65
  in Japan, *62*
  Killer (album), 95
  in Los Angeles, *38*, 42–43, *52*, 53–67, 77
  Love It to Death (album), 81–82, 94
  money and finances, 111–113, 119–120
  Muscle of Love (album), 116
  playing poker on the road, *110*
  Pretties for You (album), 60, 66
  rumors, 85
  School's Out (song, album, and tour), *92*,
    96–97, 99, *114*
  snakes, 83–84, *114*
  songs and songwriting, 82, 93–97, *95*,
    116, 117
  sword accident, 88
  United Kingdom tour, *78*, 84–85, 99
  Warner Bros. Records contract, 82
  Whisky a Go Go (Hollywood), 115
The Alice Cooper Show (album), 124
ballads, 171–172
Beatles and, 31
canes, 208
Christianity and, 198–199, 206–207, 231, 233
Constrictor (album and tour), 183–184
current band members, 236
Earwigs, 33–34
Errol Flynn sword, *230*, 236–237
imitation and, 23, 24
Last Temptation (album), 198, 210
Madhouse Rock tour, *7*
makeup, 55, 208, 209
manager. *See* Gordon, Shep
The Nazz, 53
performance night routine (assuming the
  role of Alice), 207–210
"Poison" (song), 184
snakes, 83–84, *114, 180*, 219, *234*, 237
sobriety and, 183–184
songwriting, 171–172
Spiders, 34–37, *37*, 39–43, 53
swords, 88, *230*, 236–237

theatrical rock, 242–243
traffic accident, 53–54
Trash (album and tour), 184, *192*
trash talk, 89–90
use of video, 121–122
Welcome to My Nightmare (album and tour),
   4, *118*, 120–123, 132–133, 171, *204*
Myers, Mike, 194–195

Native Americans, 19
Neuwirth, Bobby, 61
Newman, Paul, 164
Nicholson, Jack, 136, 137, 164
Nicklaus, Jack, 48, 225
Nielsen, Leslie, *104*
Nightmare. See Welcome to My Nightmare
   (album and tour)
Nights with Alice Cooper (radio show), 237
Nilsson, Harry, *130*, 135, 136, 137, 166, 167
Nitty Gritty Dirt Band, 57

O'Donnell, Chris, 238
"Only Women Bleed" (song), 121, 171
Ono, Yoko, 79, 80, 161, 166
On the Rox (Sunset Boulevard), 166
Osment, Haley Joel, *104*

Page, Jimmy, 115
Palmer, Arnold, 153–154, 225
paper panties, *92*, 97
Park, Grace, *224*
Parker, Bruce, 217, 218
Pebble Beach golf course, 105–106
Pesci, Joe, *104*, 166
Petersen, William, *104*
PGA, 49–51
Pima Golf Resort (Scottsdale), 189
Pine Valley Golf Course, 1–4
Pink Floyd, 58–59
The Pink Panther, 143–144
Plant, Robert, 115, 194
playing through, 211–212
Plunkett, Jim, *210*
"Poison" (song), 184
Presley, Elvis, 23, 140–143
Pretties for You (album), 60, 66
Price, Vincent, 123
Pro-Am tournaments, 157–159, 214–215, 243
putters, 227, 249–250
putting, 27, 249–251

"Quiet Room" (song), 177

radio show, 237
Rainbow Bar and Grill (Sunset Boulevard),
   135–136
Reed, Lou, 1–2
religion, 9, 19, 35, 195–199, 206–207,
   231–233
reward, golf as, 70
Richards, Keith, 236
Richardson, Jack, 79, 80–81
Rickles, Don, 155, 162
Rizzo, Jilly, 165
Roberts, Kane, 183
Robinson, Smokey, 218
The Rock, 232–233
The Rocky Horror Picture Show, 99
Rogers, Kenny, 165
Rolling Stone, 93
Ross, Diana, 168–169
Rothchild, Paul, 59

San Carlos Indian reservation, 19
Satanism, 195, 197–198
Savage, Tim, 196–197
Scallions, Brett, *200*
School's Out (album and tour), *92*, 97, 99, *114*
"School's Out" (song), 96
Schottzie (waitress), 136
Scinlaro, Fat Frankie, 124
Scotland, golfing in, 108–109
Sellers, Peter, 143–144
Sex Pistols' Johnny Rotten, 99
Sextette, 168
shanks, 127–129
Sheen, Martin, *104*
shopping, 194
Show, Grant, *200*
Sideways (film), 213
Silverheels, Jay, 152
Sinatra, Frank, 152, 154, 155, 162, 165
Singer, Eric, 236
Singh, Vijay, 25, 49, 156
Sirico, Junior, 124
Smith, Neal, 40, 41, 117. *See also* Alice Cooper
   band
snakes, 83–84, *114, 180*, 219, *234*, 237
The Snoop Sisters, 163
Solid Rock Foundation, 232
Something Wilder, 164
songs and songwriting, 95, 241–242
   "Be My Lover" (Bruce), 95
   "Don't Blow Your Mind," 36
   "Elected," 166

songs and songwriting *(continued)*
  "Halo of Flies," 94
  "Hello, Hooray," 100
  "How You Gonna See Me Now," 178–179
  "I'm Eighteen," 81–82, 95–96
  "I Never Cry," 171–172
  "Jackknife Johnny," 177
  "Only Women Bleed," 121, 171
  "Poison," 184
  "Quiet Room," 177
  "School's Out," 96
  "You and Me," 172
Sorenstam, Annika, 48–49
South America tour, *98,* 101–103
Special Forces (album and tour), 181–182
Speer, John, 31, 33, 97
Spiders, 34–37, 39–43, 53
Spirit, 54
Sports Illustrated, 227
Springsteen, Bruce, 136
Squaw Peak Junior High School (Arizona), 29–30
Stanton, Harry Dean, 166
star on Hollywood Boulevard, 236, *246*
Starr, Ringo, 165–166, *166*
Stooges, 76–77
Straight Records, 64, 66, 77, 82
stress, 69–71, 73
swords, 88, *230,* 236–237

Tatum, John, 36
Taupin, Bernie, 136, 137, 166–167, 175
television collection, 193
television shows and trivia, addiction to, 193
theatrical rock, *38,* 242–243
Theriault, Freeman, 153
Thompson, Titanic, 71
titanium golf clubs, 221, 226–227
The Tonight Show, 131–132, 162
Toronto Rock 'n' Roll Revival Show, 79–80
Toronto Symphony, 121
tours. *See* albums and tours
Toyota/Kraft Nabisco $1 Million Hole-in-One Contest, *210*
track and field, *28,* 31
Trash (album and tour), 184, *192*
trash talk, 89–90
Trombley, Rosalie, 82
Troubadour (Los Angeles), *130*
Troyer, Verne "Mini-Me," *68*
TTG, 100–101

United Kingdom tour, *78,* 84–85, 99
United States Golf Association (USGA), 220, 221, 226, 227

Valencia Country Club, 111–112
VH1 Fairway to Heaven tournament, *200,* 217
Vicious, Sid, 99
video, 121–120
Vietnam War draft, 37, 39–41
villain, Alice as, 205–207
VIP Club (Arizona), 35
Volman, Mark, *110*

Wagner, Dick, 120, 178, 236
Wagner, Robert, *104*
Wahlberg, Mark, *104, 150*
Warhol, Andy, 139
Warner Bros. Records, 82, 97, 120, 124, 183, 240
watch collection, 193–194
Waters, Roger, 59
Wayne's World, 194–195
Weeds of Idleness, 40
Welch, Raquel, 139–140
Welcome to My Nightmare (album and tour), 4, *118,* 120–123, 132–133, 171, *204*
West, Mae, 168
West Side Story, 164
What Ever Happened to Baby Jane, 55
Whisky a Go Go (Hollywood), 115
Whistling Straits golf course (Wisconsin), 106
White, Maurice, 177
Who, 134
Wie, Michelle, 48
Wilder, Gene, 163–164
Wilson, Luke, *104*
windsor knots, 20
Winters, Jonathan, 162
women golfers, 48–49
wooden clubs, 225–227
Woods, Tiger, 26–27, 48, 49, 72, 73, 128
Woodward, Joanne, 164
worries, golf and, 70
Wynn, Steve, 165

Yahiro, Craig, 189
"You and Me" (song), 172

Zappa, Frank, 60–61, 64–65, 66, 80, 82, 101
Zipper Catches Skin (album and tour), 181–182